The Great Chicken Cookbook

More than 400 Chicken Recipes for Every Day

BY

VIRGINIA AND ROBERT HOFFMAN

THE CROSSING PRESS
FREEDOM, CALIFORNIA

We wish to express our appreciation for the help we have received in writing this book to the following . . .

- Dr. Francine Bradley, Ph.D., Extension Poultry Specialist of the Avian Sciences Department, The University of California at Davis, and Mr. Louis Arrington, Extension Poultry Specialist at the University of Wisconsin, for their generous contributions of time and effort in helping us learn about the development of the poultry industry in the United States and abroad.
- The National Broiler Council, which supplied us with recipes and informational material on chicken production, and the California Poultry Industry Federation for their support of our efforts in this project.
- The chefs, winemakers, and winery owners in the California Wine Country, where we live, for their recipes and support.
- Foster Farms, the leading poultry producer in California, which provided us with "uniquely California" recipes.
- Ms. Anne Salisbury of R.C. Auletta Company, our source of recipes from The Perdue Farms, Inc., one of America's largest poultry producers.
- David Thiel of Pilgrim's Pride Corporation, the foremost chicken producer in the Southwest, for his enthusiastic cooperation.
- The Canandaigua Wine Company, for permission to use some of their "cooking with wine" recipes.
- Jeanette Richardson of Tyson Food Service, who provided recipes and insight into food service uses of chicken.
- Pinpoint Publishing of Santa Rosa, California, our good neighbor, which provided us with the nutritional analysis program Micro Cookbook 5.
- Nancy LaMothe, who not only structures the recipes with us but also is a great "devil's advocate." This is her fifth book with us, and we are still on speaking terms.
- The executives and staff of The Crossing Press, who have worked so hard to make our books successful.

CONTENTS

INTRODUCTION

How to Use This Cookbook

Each recipe is identified on the upper corner of the page by type of food (soup, salad, etc.).

Just below that is the name of the chicken part or parts that are needed for the recipe. "Whole Chicken, Cut Up" is also "Whole Chicken" if you prefer to buy chickens whole and cut them up yourself. Precooked chicken includes leftovers.

While a recipe may call for chicken thighs, there is no reason you cannot use drumsticks instead, if that is what you have on hand.

Ingredients in all the recipes are available in most grocery stores and supermarkets throughout the United States. If we weren't sure, we suggested an equally satisfactory alternative.

Some recipes call for wine as an ingredient. If you prefer to cook without wine, we recommend you do not use those recipes. There is no substitute for wine in cooking.

Each recipe has a nutritional analysis based on the number of servings. Where a recipe states a range of servings (e.g., "6 to 8") the analysis is based on the larger number. The editors and publisher do not accept any responsibility for the accuracy of these analyses. Variations in ingredients can change these figures substantially.

For example, if you are on a low-sodium diet, and the analysis indicates a high sodium content, look at the ingredient list. How much salt does it call for? If prepared salsa is part of the recipe, remember that it is high in sodium, so you should eliminate salt as an ingredient or water the salsa down slightly. If you're calorie conscious, the analysis can show if you're within the limits of your diet. If cholesterol is a concern, look for the many low-cholesterol recipes. Nutritional analyses are provided as guideposts; please use them that way.

Chicken Is America's Favorite Meat

Chicken has become America's favorite meat in the past few years because of its taste, nutrition, convenience, and economy.

Most people buy chicken because they like it! There are so many ways to prepare chicken that you could serve it every day of the year and never get bored.

Chicken is low in calories and fat content, two of the most important considerations in a health-conscious diet. It is an excellent source of high-quality protein, iron, thiamin, riboflavin, and niacin.

A 3-ounce portion of skinless, broiled chicken has only 115 calories, as compared to 3 ounces of hamburger, which has 244, and roast pork, which has 310.

On a low-sodium diet? There are only 50 milligrams of sodium in 100 grams of white chicken meat and just 67 in the same amount of dark meat.

Seasoning with herbs and spices eliminates the need for rich sauces, making chicken ideal for those who watch their cholesterol and fat intake.

Today chicken is available in so many ready-to-use forms that it is quick and easy to prepare. It is perfect for both the novice cook and the experienced chef. Chicken is so versatile that it can be served as a casual snack food or as part of an elegant formal dinner.

Nothing compares with chicken when it comes to economy. Thanks to new methods of production, the cost of chicken today is less than one fourth its cost 50 years ago.

The Many Kinds of Chicken

All chickens are ready to cook when you buy them. If you are buying a whole chicken, it has been plucked and cleaned inside and out, and all inedible parts (head, feet, and interior organs) have been removed. The giblets (heart, liver, and gizzard) and neck have been washed, trimmed, wrapped, and placed inside the chicken. Then the chicken is weighed and priced.

Whole Chickens

Rock Cornish Hens (Cornish Game Hens): The smallest and tenderest of all chickens, they got their name from their parents: "Rock" from Plymouth Rock chickens, and "Cornish" from their origin in Cornwall, England. They are usually 4 to 5 weeks old and weigh from 1 to 2 pounds.

Whole Broiler-Fryer: All young chickens in America were originally called broilers, although they were also used for frying and roasting. They come about seven weeks old and weigh from 2 1/2 to 4 pounds.

Roasters: These are chickens that are about ten weeks old and weigh more than 5 pounds.

Capons: These are male chickens that have been surgically desexed, are about 16 weeks old, and weigh between 9 and 10 pounds.

Chicken in Parts

These are the most popular chicken parts sold today.

Chicken Halves: One half of the breast, one thigh, one drumstick, and one wing.

Chicken Quarters: Four quarter birds to a package includes breast, thigh, drumstick, and wing.

Drumsticks: Four, six, or eight pieces to a package and are great favorites for quick meals, particularly for children.

Thighs: Four, six, or eight to a package.

Drumettes: The meaty part of the wing, the drumette, is packed eight or more in a package. They are ideal finger food for large groups.

Breasts: Four, six, or eight to a package.

Wings: Eight or sixteen to a package.

Ground Chicken: Available as white meat, dark meat, or a blend of both.

Other selections: Breast tenders (also called fillets), breast strips and chunks, chicken livers, diced chicken, chicken patties, chicken nuggets, chicken sausage, and chicken bologna.

Chicken Nutritional Analysis by Parts

Part	Calories	Protein grams	Total fat grams	Saturated fat grams	Cholesterol milligrams	Sodium milligrams
Breast	116	24	2	0	72	63
Drumstick	132	23	3	1	79	81
Thigh	150	21	7	2	81	75
Wing	149	23	6	2	72	78

Serving: 3-ounce boneless, skinless portion
Source: United States Department of Agriculture

Buying and Handling Chicken

When buying chicken, there are a few things you should check. The most important is the freshness. Check the "Sell By" date on the package. This indicates the last day that the product should be sold. It will maintain its quality if properly refrigerated or cooked within a few days. And, of course, freezing the package as soon as you get it home greatly extends that time.

Skin color in chicken varies throughout the country. It can vary from a deep yellow to white. Color doesn't indicate a difference in nutritional value, flavor or fat content; it only indicates variations in the grain fed to the birds.

We firmly believe that the best chicken you can buy, whole or in parts, fresh or frozen, comes from a company whose brand name you know. These producers maintain the highest standards of quality. The birds' diets are carefully controlled, the feed is free of hormones, and the pens meet the most rigorous standards of space and sanitation.

Like all fresh meat, chicken is perishable and should be handled with care to maintain its quality. Refrigerate raw chicken promptly. Never leave it out at room temperature. Packaged raw chicken can be refrigerated in its original wrapping in the coldest part of the refrigerator, usually along the back wall. Freeze raw chicken if it is not to be cooked within two days.

Cooked, cut-up chicken is at its best when refrigerated no longer than two days. Cooked whole chickens will keep an additional day.

If the chicken is stuffed, remove the stuffing and place it in a separate container before refrigerating leftovers.

Thaw chicken in the refrigerator, not on the countertop. It takes about 24 hours to thaw a 4-pound chicken, and from 3 to 9 hours to thaw the same amount of cut-up parts. You can also thaw chicken in cold water in the sink.

Thawing chicken in a microwave is the fastest way. Thaw for two minutes on Defrost or Medium-Low, wait for two minutes, and repeat as necessary.

It Started at Plymouth Rock

When the Pilgrims landed at Plymouth Rock, they brought chickens with them on the ships from England. The settlers of Jamestown also brought chickens from England.

Some believe that Spanish and Portuguese explorers brought chickens to Brazil in the 1500s. Others believe that Christopher Columbus brought them to America in 1492. Still others say that they came to America much earlier, having been brought by Polynesian or Egyptian sailors before recorded history. We do know that before the Spaniards conquered Mexico, chickens were a staple of the native diet.

Originally a wild bird, "The Red Jungle Bird," chickens are now believed to have originated in 3000 B.C. in what is now known as Vietnam. They were not bred for food but for the arena—the Vietnamese used the roosters as fighters. (We can only assume that the practice of raising chickens for eggs and meat instead of entertainment originated with eating the losers.)

The pharaohs of Egypt incubated as many as 10,000 eggs at a time in large brick incubators to feed the slaves building the pyramids. The Chinese, too, incubated large numbers of eggs to feed the thousands of peasants who built the Great Wall of China.

Soon small flocks of chickens were to be found on farms large and small throughout the world. Chicken became the single largest source of food and supplementary income for farmers everywhere.

In time, particularly in England, farmers began concentrating on raising flocks of chickens for sale in the cities. Since refrigeration did not yet exist, the chickens were brought to the market live and sold that way. The purchaser was responsible for preparing the bird for the stove and table.

Commercial growing of chickens for eggs and meat truly began in the United States by mistake. In 1923 Mrs. Wilbur Steele of the Delmarva area (Delaware, Maryland, and Virginia) ordered 50 baby chicks and mistakenly received 500. Realizing that she soon would have enough hens laying eggs to feed the entire county, she resourcefully sold the extra 450 birds when they were still young and tender enough to eat. She got $1 a pound, a fantastic price for 1923! Greatly encouraged, she expanded her operation, as did her neighbors and friends, and 70 years later the Delmarva region now has the highest concentration of chicken production in the world.

In this same period, Railway Express (the predecessor of United Parcel Service), started a huge mail-order business, shipping baby chicks all over the United States, with Sears Roebuck as the principal supplier.

World War II provided a stimulus for the industry to greatly increase production to feed the armed forces. Many returning veterans—aided by easy-to-get, low-interest loans—went into the industry and thrived as demand continued to exceed production.

During these years, egg and meat production were combined, but in the decade after the war they were split, with chickens being raised specifically for meat or egg laying. Now, two entirely different birds fulfill each function.

Today, automation and technological improvements have made chicken one of the tenderest, tastiest, healthiest, and least expensive meats, selling for far less than Mrs. Steele's $1-a-pound chicken in 1923!

APPETIZERS

Dijon Chicken Drumettes Deluxe

1/2 cup fat-free, cholesterol-free
  mayonnaise
3 tablespoons Dijon mustard
1/2 teaspoon grated onion

20 chicken drumettes
2 cups cheese bread crumbs*
Pepper to taste

Preheat oven to 375 degrees. Cover 10 1/2 x 15 1/2 baking sheet with foil and spray lightly with vegetable cooking spray. In a small bowl, combine mayonnaise, mustard, and onion. Brush each drumette with mayonnaise mixture and then roll in cheese bread crumbs. Arrange chicken pieces in single layer on prepared pan and sprinkle with pepper. Bake for about 30 minutes or until chicken is brown and fork can be inserted with ease.   These are good served hot, warm, or cold.

Makes 20 drumettes.

*If cheese bread is unavailable for crumbs, cheese crackers may be substituted; however, the crumbs made from cheese bread form a lighter crust on the chicken.

Per Piece (approx):
Calories 146
Carbohydrate 8 gm

Protein 11 gm
Sodium 163 mg

Fat 8 gm
Cholesterol 31 mg

Asian Drumettes

5 1/2 pounds chicken drumettes
1/2 cup teriyaki sauce
1/4 cup peanut or vegetable oil
1/4 cup honey
1/2 cup white wine

1/4 tablespoon white vinegar
1 teaspoon ground ginger
2 cups lightly toasted, minced
  peanuts or pecans

In a large bowl, combine the teriyaki sauce, oil, honey, wine, vinegar, and ginger; mix well. Add the chicken pieces, stirring to coat well. Cover and marinate overnight in refrigerator. Drain the chicken and discard the marinade. Preheat oven to 375 degrees. Grease 2 large baking sheets; arrange chicken on baking sheets. Bake 35 minutes or until tender. Remove drumettes and roll in chopped nuts. Serve hot or at room temperature.

Makes about 48 drumettes.

Per Appetizer (approx):
Calories 162
Carbohydrate 3 gm

Protein 12 gm
Sodium 170 mg

Fat 11 gm
Cholesterol 31 mg

Mediterranean Drumettes

24 chicken drumettes
  (about 2 1/2 pounds)
4 cloves garlic, minced
1/2 teaspoon pepper
2 tablespoons olive oil
1/2 cup white wine
1/4 cup white wine vinegar

1/4 teaspoon dried thyme
1/4 teaspoon dried marjoram
1/4 teaspoon dried basil
1/2 teaspoon salt
10 cherry tomatoes
1 jar (12 ounces) marinated
  artichoke hearts, chilled

Rub drumettes with minced garlic and sprinkle with pepper. Place in shallow bowl in single layer. In small bowl, combine olive oil, white wine, and vinegar. Grind thyme, marjoram, and basil with a mortar and pestle; add to liquid and mix well. Pour half of marinade over drumettes and refrigerate remainder of the marinade. Cover chicken and place in refrigerator for at least 1 hour.

Preheat broiler or grill.

Remove chicken from marinade. Discard the used marinade. Arrange the chicken on a broiler pan or grill about 6 inches from the heat. Broil for about 20 minutes, turning and brushing with the reserved half of the marinade after 5 minutes. Continue to cook about 15 minutes more or until fork can be inserted in chicken with ease.

Remove the chicken to a clean, shallow bowl. Pierce each piece several times with a fork and sprinkle with salt. Pour reserved unused marinade over cooked chicken, cover and chill in refrigerator, turning at least once in marinade. To serve, arrange drumettes on a platter with cherry tomatoes and artichoke hearts. These are served cold. Makes 24 drumettes.

Per Serving (approx):
Calories 562
Carbohydrate 8 gm

Protein 42 gm
Sodium 515 mg

Fat 39 gm
Cholesterol 123 mg

Gingery Chicken Bites
with Dipping Sauce

2 tablespoons dry white wine
1 tablespoon minced ginger or
    2 tablespoons ground ginger
1/2 teaspoon salt, divided
2 whole skinless, boneless
    chicken breasts, cut in
    1-inch cubes

1 cup flour
1/4 cup cornstarch
1/2 teaspoon baking powder
3/4 cup cold water
Vegetable oil for deep frying
Cranberry Orange Dipping
    Sauce

In a medium bowl, mix together wine, ginger, and 1/4 teaspoon of the salt. Add chicken and toss to coat. Cover and marinate in refrigerator 2 hours or overnight.

Drain the chicken and discard the marinade.

In a large bowl, combine flour, cornstarch, baking powder, remaining 1/4 teaspoon salt, and cold water. Stir marinated chicken into the batter. Place 2 inches of oil in deep pan or wok and heat to 365 degrees. Add chicken, a few pieces at a time, and cook until crisp and brown, about 3 minutes. Drain chicken and arrange on a large platter with a bowl of dipping sauce in center.   Makes 6 servings.

CRANBERRY ORANGE DIPPING SAUCE:
Place 2 cups fresh cranberries in a medium saucepan. Add 1 cup orange juice and 1 cup sugar and bring to a boil. Cook about 5 minutes and puree in food processor until smooth. Add 1 tablespoon white vinegar, 1/8 teaspoon ground cinnamon, 1/8 teaspoon ground allspice, and 1/16 teaspoon salt. Serve at room temperature.

Per Serving (approx), excluding sauce:
Calories 278	*Protein 22 gm*	*Fat 12 gm*
Carbohydrate 21 gm	*Sodium 271 mg*	*Cholesterol 53 mg*

Thai Chicken Satay

This is the classic Satay that is the National dish of Thailand.

1 large skinless, boneless chicken breast, halved
2 tablespoons Southeast Asian fish sauce
1 tablespoon safflower oil
1 tablespoon lime juice
1 tablespoon minced cilantro

1 large clove garlic, minced
2 teaspoons sugar
1/4 teaspoon ground cumin
1 stalk lemon grass, finely minced, or 1 teaspoon grated lemon rind
Spicy Peanut Sauce

Place the chicken between sheets of wax paper; pound gently to flatten slightly. Cut chicken into diagonal strips about 1/2-inch thick. Thread a chicken strip onto each bamboo skewer.

In a shallow pan, combine the fish sauce, safflower oil, lime juice, cilantro, garlic, sugar, cumin, and lemon grass; stir to mix well. Dip each skewer into mixture, turning to coat the chicken. Place chicken in baking dish, cover and refrigerate at least 2 hours or overnight.

Cook chicken on prepared grill, about 3 minutes per side or until no longer pink inside. Serve with Spicy Peanut Sauce.

Makes 4 bamboo strips.

SPICY PEANUT SAUCE:
In a small skillet heat 1 tablespoon safflower oil over medium heat. Add 1/2 cup chopped red onion, 1 clove minced garlic, and 1 stalk minced lemon grass (or 1 teaspoon grated lemon rind). Cook, stirring, about 3 minutes; remove from heat.

In a food processor, chop 1/2 cup peanuts. Add onion mixture, 3/4 cup low-fat coconut milk, 1 teaspoon ground cumin, 1 tablespoon sugar, 2 tablespoons lime or lemon juice, 1/4 teaspoon salt, 1 tablespoon soy sauce, and 1/2 teaspoon chili sauce or oil. Process until smooth.

Per Serving (approx):
Calories 389
Carbohydrate 14 gm

Protein 21 gm
Sodium 1101 mg

Fat 27 gm
Cholesterol 41 mg

Chicken Nuggets and Dips

This is a really easy way to entertain. Prepare your nuggets a day or two in advance, oven-warm them just before serving, and let your guests do their own dipping.

Vegetable oil for deep frying
1 egg, beaten
1/3 cup water
1/3 cup flour
2 teaspoons sesame seeds

1 1/2 teaspoons salt
4 skinless, boneless chicken
    breast halves, cut into
    1-inch cubes
Dipping sauces

Fill a deep saucepan no more than 1/3 full of oil. Heat to 365 degrees. In a large bowl, combine egg and water, and mix well. Add flour, sesame seeds, and salt, stirring until smooth batter forms. Dip chicken in batter, draining off excess. Add chicken a few pieces at a time to hot oil. Fry about 4 minutes or until golden brown. Drain on paper towels. Serve with the sauces below.   Makes 24 nuggets.

NIPPY PINEAPPLE SAUCE:
In a small saucepan, combine 1 jar (12 ounces) pineapple preserves, 1/4 cup prepared mustard and 1/4 cup prepared horseradish. Cook over low heat about 5 minutes stirring occasionally.

DILL SAUCE:
In small bowl, combine 1/2 cup sour cream, 1/2 cup mayonnaise, 1 teaspoon dried dill weed, and 2 tablespoons minced dill pickle. Let stand at room temperature about 1 hour to allow flavors to blend.

ROYALTY SAUCE:
In a small saucepan, mix together 1 cup ketchup, 1/2 teaspoon dry mustard, 1 tablespoon brown sugar, 2 tablespoons vinegar, and 6 tablespoons margarine. Cook over low heat for 5 minutes, stirring constantly.

Per Serving (approx), excluding sauces:
Calories 598	*Protein 16 gm*	*Fat 57 gm*
Carbohydrate 4 gm	*Sodium 479 mg*	*Cholesterol 67 mg*

Glazed Teriyaki Appetizers

1 pound ground chicken
1/2 cup dry bread crumbs
1 tablespoon soy sauce
1/4 teaspoon garlic powder
1/4 teaspoon salt
1/8 teaspoon ground ginger

1 egg, beaten
1 cup prepared sweet and sour
   sauce
1 can (20 ounces) pineapple
   chunks, drained
3 tablespoons chopped red bell
   pepper

Preheat oven to 350 degrees. Spray baking sheet with nonstick cooking spray. In a medium bowl, combine chicken, bread crumbs, soy sauce, garlic powder, salt, ginger, and egg. Mix well. Form into 28 1-inch balls and place on baking sheet. Bake about 7 minutes on each side, or until no longer pink inside, and drain on paper towel. In a medium saucepan, combine sweet and sour sauce and pineapple. Heat to boiling; reduce heat. Stir in chicken balls and bell pepper. Heat through. Serve with toothpicks.   Makes 28 chicken balls.

Per Piece (approx):
Calories 51
Carbohydrate 7 gm

Protein 2 gm
Sodium 111 mg

Fat 2 gm
Cholesterol 18 mg

Creamy Tomato Chicken Dip

1 pound ground chicken
1/2 cup chopped onion
1 clove garlic, minced
1 can (8 ounces) tomato sauce
1/4 cup ketchup

3/4 teaspoon dried oregano
1 teaspoon sugar
1 package (8 ounces) cream
   cheese
1/3 cup grated Parmesan cheese

Heat a skillet and add the chicken, onion, and garlic and fry, stirring, until chicken is brown and onion is tender, about 5 minutes. Add tomato sauce, ketchup, oregano, and sugar. Stir well, cover, reduce heat to low, and simmer about 10 minutes. Add cheeses, stir, and simmer until cheese is melted and well mixed into dip, about 3 minutes. Serve in a chafing dish with chips for dipping.

Makes 3 cups dip or 12 servings.

Per Serving (approx):
Calories 140
Carbohydrate 4 gm

Protein 7 gm
Sodium 305 mg

Fat 10 gm
Cholesterol 47 mg

Oven-Fried Chicken Nuggets

If you want nuggets that are a lot lower in fat and cholesterol than those in the fast food places, here's a recipe that you'll use over and over.

1 1/3 pounds skinless,
   boneless chicken breasts
2 cups toasted whole grain,
   round oat cereal, crushed*
1 teaspoon onion salt
1/2 teaspoon pepper

1/4 teaspoon paprika
1/4 teaspoon poultry seasoning
4 tablespoons butter-flavored
   margarine, melted
Honey-Mustard Sauce

Preheat oven to 325 degrees.

With kitchen shears, cut the chicken breasts into 36 nuggets. Cover a 10 1/2 x 15 1/2 baking pan with aluminum foil; spray with vegetable cooking spray. In a medium bowl, combine crushed cereal, onion salt, pepper, paprika, and poultry seasoning. Pour mixture onto waxed paper. Roll each chicken nugget in melted margarine and then in oat cereal mixture, turning to coat.

Arrange nuggets in a single layer on prepared baking pan and bake about 25 minutes or until brown. Serve with Honey-Mustard Sauce for dipping.   Makes 36 nuggets.

HONEY-MUSTARD SAUCE:
In a small bowl, combine 1/2 cup prepared mustard, 4 tablespoons honey, and 1 teaspoon mayonnaise.

*Crush oat cereal in food processor or blender until broken into bits but not powdery.

Per Piece (approx), excluding sauce:
Calories 59
Carbohydrate 4 gm

Protein 5 gm
Sodium 89 mg

Fat 3 gm
Cholesterol 11 mg

Halloween Chicken Pizza Masks

You don't have to make these masks, but they do taste better that way.

1 pound ground chicken
1/3 cup chopped onion
1 teaspoon salt
1/2 teaspoon pepper
6 English muffins, split
2 tablespoons soft margarine
1 1/2 cups prepared pizza sauce

1 teaspoon dried oregano
1 large green bell pepper
4 ounces shredded cheddar
  cheese
4 ounces shredded mozzarella
  cheese
3 large pitted ripe olives,
  each sliced into 4 rings

Preheat oven to 450 degrees.

Heat a skillet and add ground chicken and onion; cook, stirring, until all red is gone, about 6 minutes. Stir in salt and pepper and set aside.

With aluminum foil, cover 10 1/2 x 15 1/2 baking pan. Spread each muffin half with 1/2 teaspoon of the margarine and arrange in single layer on prepared pan. Spread one heaping tablespoon pizza sauce on each muffin half. Cover generously with chicken and onion mixture; sprinkle with oregano.

Cut 12 slivers of bell pepper into "smiling" mouth shapes and set aside; chop remaining pepper and sprinkle on pizzas. Combine cheeses and sprinkle generously on pizzas. Bake about 12 minutes, or until muffins are brown and cheese bubbles.

Make mask face on each pizza by using 2 ripe olive rings for eyes and pepper slice for mouth. Turn some slices up for smiles and some down for frowns.

Makes 12 mini-pizzas.

Per Serving (approx):
Calories 216
Carbohydrate 17 gm

Protein 11 gm
Sodium 700 mg

Fat 12 gm
Cholesterol 41 mg

Island Kabobs

Here's an unusual recipe, perfect for colorful, last minute hors d'oeuvres.

3/4 pound chicken breast nuggets*
  (or 18 nuggets)
18 pieces green bell pepper,
  cut in 1-inch squares
18 canned water chestnuts,
  drained

18 canned pineapple chunks,
  drained
1 tablespoon vegetable oil
Pineapple Dipping Sauce

Preheat oven to 400 degrees.

On 6-inch bamboo skewers, thread one chicken nugget and one piece each bell pepper, water chestnut, and pineapple. Place skewers on lightly greased baking sheet and brush lightly with oil. Heat in oven until the chicken is cooked through. Test one. This could take 9 minutes or more. Serve with Pineapple Dipping Sauce.   Makes 18 appetizers.

PINEAPPLE DIPPING SAUCE:
In a small bowl, combine 1 cup pineapple preserves, 2 tablespoons soy sauce, 1 tablespoon chopped ginger (or 1 teaspoon ground ginger), and 1/8 teaspoon red pepper flakes (optional). Stir to mix well.

*Chicken nuggets are available in many markets. If not, cut skinless, boneless chicken breasts into bite-size pieces.

Per Piece (approx):
Calories 94	*Protein 5 gm*	*Fat 1 gm*
Carbohydrate 15 gm	*Sodium 129 mg*	*Cholesterol 13 mg*

In his presidential election campaign Herbert Hoover promised "a chicken in every pot and a car in every garage."

Take-Along Chicken Kabobs

1 cup tomato sauce
1/4 cup olive oil
1 medium onion, minced
2 cloves garlic, minced
1 tablespoon chopped parsley
1 teaspoon dried oregano
1 teaspoon dried thyme

1 teaspoon salt
2 pounds chicken nuggets*
Juice of 1 lemon
1/4 teaspoon pepper
8 each 1-inch chunks of green
    bell pepper, cherry tomatoes
    and small mushrooms

In a small saucepan, combine tomato sauce, olive oil, onion, garlic, parsley, oregano, thyme, and salt. Bring to a boil over medium heat; remove from heat and set aside. Sprinkle the chicken with lemon juice and pepper; place chicken in sauce mixture. Pour into bowl, cover and refrigerate at least 4 hours.

Preheat broiler to 450 degrees.

Line broiler pan with foil. Thread 4 chunks of chicken on small skewers and end with bell pepper, cherry tomato, or mushroom brushed with oil. (Varying the ending vegetables makes an attractive dish.)** Place skewers in a single layer on a lightly greased baking sheet. Broil 4 inches from heat for about 15 minutes, turning to brown on all sides. Serve hot or cold.   Makes 8 kabobs.

*Chicken nuggets are available in many areas. If they are not available in your area, cut skinless, boneless chicken breasts into bite-size pieces.

**For a main dish, use longer skewers and alternate chicken chunks with desired vegetables brushed with oil.

Per Serving (approx):
Calories 209
Carbohydrate 6 gm

Protein 29 gm
Sodium 541 mg

Fat 11 gm
Cholesterol 77 mg

Tangy Soy Chicken
with Pineapple

The grilled pineapple slices atop each portion make a very handsome presentation.

2 cans (20 ounces each) pineapple
    slices in unsweetened juice
1 cup lime juice (about 6 limes)
1 cup low-sodium soy sauce

1 tablespoon grated ginger
6 tablespoons cornstarch
20 chicken breast halves

Drain and retain juice from pineapple. This should be about 2 cups. In a medium saucepan, mix together pineapple juice, lime juice, soy sauce, and ginger. Place cornstarch in measuring cup or small bowl; add 6 tablespoons of the juice mixture and stir until smooth. Bring remaining juice mixture to boil. Add cornstarch mixture and stir until sauce is thickened and smooth. Remove from heat. Dip each pineapple slice into sauce, and place in a bowl for later use.

Dip each half of chicken breast into sauce and place on prepared grill, skin side up, about 8 inches from heat. Place remaining sauce in small saucepan and bring to boil on stovetop or grill. Grill chicken, turning and basting with sauce every 10 to 15 minutes, for about 45 minutes, or until fork can be inserted into chicken easily.

While chicken is cooking, grill pineapple slices for 1 minute each side, turning once. Arrange chicken on platter and place a pineapple slice on top of each breast. Top each piece with a teaspoon of sauce.

Makes 20 servings.

Per Serving (approx):
Calories 245
Carbohydrate 13 gm

Protein 30 gm
Sodium 459 mg

Fat 8 gm
Cholesterol 82 mg

SALADS

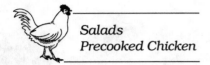

Chicken with Garden Fresh Vegetables

This is a very unusual chicken salad.

1 chicken, cooked, skinned,
   boned, and cut in strips
3 large tomatoes, cut into chunks
1 large green bell pepper, cut in
   1-inch slivers
1 cucumber, sliced

4 green onions, sliced
1 jar (12 ounces) marinated
   artichoke hearts, drained
1/2 cup sliced black olives
2 tablespoons wine vinegar
1/4 cup sesame seeds, toasted

In a large mixing bowl, combine warm chicken, tomatoes, bell pepper, cucumber, and green onions. Drain artichoke hearts and reserve marinade. Chop artichoke hearts and add with black olives to chicken-vegetable mixture; toss gently to mix well. Mix reserved marinade with wine vinegar; pour over chicken.

Cover and refrigerate until well chilled. At serving time, top with sesame seeds.
                                         Makes 6 servings.

Per Serving (approx):
Calories 313
Carbohydrate 14 gm

Protein 23 gm
Sodium 201 mg

Fat 19 gm
Cholesterol 61 mg

In the early 1960s chicken exporters of the United States became involved in a bitter tariff war with Germany. Chancellor Adenauer of Germany, after a meeting with President Kennedy, asked an aide: "Who is this President Kennedy—a chicken farmer?"

Grilled Chicken Salad

Be sure you use the mild Anaheim pepper and not the jalapeños pasillas, which are fiery hot.

2 tablespoons prepared mustard
2/3 cup pineapple juice
3 tablespoons soy sauce
2 tablespoons red wine vinegar
1 tablespoon honey
1 1/2 pounds chicken tenders
1 bunch leaf lettuce

1 can (14 ounces) pineapple tidbits
3 Anaheim peppers, stems, seeds, and membranes removed, sliced in rings
1 onion, sliced in rings
1/2 cup almond slivers, toasted
1/4 cup sesame seeds, toasted

In a small saucepan, combine mustard and pineapple juice, stirring to prevent lumping. Add soy sauce, vinegar, and honey; bring to a boil over high heat. Place chicken in a bowl and pour warm sauce over it; cover and refrigerate at least 1 hour.

Prepare grill or preheat broiler. Remove chicken from marinade. Place marinade in small saucepan and boil 3 minutes. Place chicken on prepared grill (or broiler rack) about 6 inches from heat. Cook, turning and basting with boiled marinade, about 6 minutes, or until fork can be inserted into chicken easily.

To assemble salad, arrange lettuce on 6 plates; add pineapple, pepper, and onion rings. Sprinkle with almonds and sesame seeds. Top with chicken and spoon remaining marinade over all.   Makes 6 servings.

Per Serving (approx):
Calories 364
Carbohydrate 25 gm

Protein 34 gm
Sodium 654 mg

Fat 14 gm
Cholesterol 77 mg

Chicken Salad of the Wife of Kit Carson

1 1/2 cups pineapple juice
3 tablespoons honey
2 tablespoons dark sesame oil
1/2 cup cider vinegar
2 tablespoons sugar
4 cloves garlic
4 tablespoons ground chile
1/2 teaspoon ground coriander
1/2 teaspoon ground cumin
4 skinless, boneless chicken breast halves
1 cup drained garbanzo beans
4 tablespoons chopped green chiles
2 avocados, diced
2 tomatoes, cored, seeded, and diced
1 medium head romaine lettuce, cut into thin strips
1/2 cup Spicy Lime Dressing
28 blue tortilla chips
4 teaspoons sour cream
4 tablespoons bottled tomato salsa

In a food processor or blender, combine pineapple juice, honey, sesame oil, vinegar, sugar, garlic, chile, coriander, and cumin. Blend marinade until very smooth. Place chicken in marinade and refrigerate, covered, for about 4 hours. Prepare grill. Remove chicken from marinade and place on grill. Grill about 10 minutes, turning once. Or place chicken in heavy frying pan sprayed with nonstick vegetable spray and sauté about 10 minutes, turning once.

In a large bowl, combine garbanzo beans, green chiles, avocados, tomatoes, lettuce, and Spicy Lime Dressing; toss gently to mix well. For individual salads, cut each chicken breast half into 4 or 5 strips; arrange vegetables on a plate with 6 tortilla chips around the edge. Top each with chicken strips, 1 tortilla chip, 1 teaspoon sour cream, and 1 tablespoon tomato salsa.   Makes 4 servings.

SPICY LIME DRESSING:
In a food processor or blender, combine 1/4 clove garlic, 1/2 green onion, 1/2 teaspoon ground chile, 1 1/2 tablespoons red wine vinegar, 2 tablespoons lime juice, 3/4 teaspoon Dijon mustard, 3/4 teaspoon pureed ancho chile, 1/4 teaspoon salt, and 1/8 teaspoon pepper. Process on medium speed, slowly adding 1/2 cup peanut oil in thin stream. Blend until well incorporated.

Per Serving (approx):
Calories 1006
Carbohydrate 76 gm

Protein 39 gm
Sodium 638 mg

Fat 61 gm
Cholesterol 82 mg

Fiesta Chicken-Rice Salad

This recipe is even better with brown or Basmati rice.

1 whole skinless, boneless
   chicken breast
1/2 cup salsa, divided
1 cup long-grain white rice,
   cooked according to package
   directions and cooled
1/2 cup corn kernels, frozen or fresh
1/2 cup sliced green onions

1/4 cup sliced ripe olives
2 tablespoons chopped fresh
   cilantro
Salt to taste
1/3 cup vegetable oil
1/4 cup red wine vinegar
1/2 teaspoon garlic salt
1/4 teaspoon pepper

Marinate chicken in 1/4 cup of the salsa for several hours or overnight. Grill over hot coals until cooked through and slightly charred. Remove from the grill and cut into 1/4-inch slices. Place in a large bowl with cooked rice, corn, onions, olives, and cilantro. Add salt to taste. Set aside. Toss well with the dressing (below) to coat.

In a jar with tight-fitting lid, combine oil, vinegar, garlic salt, pepper, and remaining salsa. Shake well to blend and pour over rice mixture. Toss well to coat and chill well.   Makes 4 to 6 servings.

Per Serving (approx):
Calories 259
Carbohydrate 14 gm

Protein 12 gm
Sodium 625 mg

Fat 17 gm
Cholesterol 30 mg

Wild and Brown Rice
Chicken Salad

This is a wonderful mixture of colors and textures. Simmer or microwave the chicken, or get a cooked one at your deli or supermarket.

1 box (6 ounces) long-grain
   brown and wild rice with
   seasonings
1/2 cup chicken broth
1/4 cup lemon juice
1 chicken, cooked, skinned, boned,
   and cut in pieces
1/2 teaspoon salt
1/4 teaspoon pepper

1/2 cup chopped pickled
   red bell pepper
1/2 cup minced celery
1/2 cup sliced green onion
1/2 cup pine nuts
1 package (10 ounces) frozen
   peas, thawed
Lettuce leaves

Cook rice according to package directions, omitting butter or margarine; set aside to cool. In a medium bowl, pour broth and lemon juice over warm chicken; sprinkle with salt and pepper.

In a large bowl, combine pickled bell pepper and celery. Add green onion and cooked rice and toss gently. Add chicken with juice and broth. Finally add pine nuts and green peas.

Mix well, cover and refrigerate until completely chilled. Serve on lettuce leaves.   Makes 6 servings.

Per Serving (approx):
Calories 437
Carbohydrate 17 gm

Protein 37 gm
Sodium 520 mg

Fat 24 gm
Cholesterol 102 mg

Marinated Warm Chicken Salad

2 cans (11 ounces each) mandarin
    oranges, drained; 1/2 cup syrup
    reserved
1/4 cup lime juice
1 clove garlic, minced
4 skinless, boneless chicken
    breast halves
4 teaspoons olive oil
1/4 teaspoon pepper
1/2 teaspoon salt

1 bunch romaine lettuce,
    torn into bite-size pieces
2 ribs celery, sliced thin
    diagonally
2 tomatoes, cut in thin wedges
4 mushrooms, sliced thin
1 red onion, sliced thin
1/4 cup almond slivers, toasted
1/4 cup sesame seeds, toasted
1/2 cup prepared honey Dijon
    mustard salad dressing

Preheat broiler to 500 degrees.

In a small saucepan or microwave bowl, combine 1/2 cup reserved orange syrup, lime juice, and garlic; heat to the boiling point. Place the chicken in bowl and pour on the hot marinade; let stand at least 10 minutes.

Drain the chicken. Place the marinade in the small saucepan. Let it stand.

Remove chicken to broiler pan, brush with olive oil, and sprinkle with salt and pepper. Place chicken about 4 inches from heat and broil about 7 minutes per side or until fork can be inserted into chicken easily. Reheat marinade to boiling and brush on chicken after turning.

Slice cooked chicken into about 8 pieces per breast half. On a large platter, arrange lettuce, drained oranges, celery, tomatoes, and mushrooms; top with onion slices, separated into rings. Place warm chicken on top; sprinkle with toasted almonds and sesame seeds. Serve with honey Dijon mustard dressing on the side. Makes 4 generous servings.

Per Serving (approx):
Calories 693
Carbohydrate 57 gm

Protein 39 gm
Sodium 1018 mg

Fat 34 gm
Cholesterol 80 mg

Cilantro Lime Chicken Salad with Melon Relish

1/2 cup lime juice
1/4 cup maple syrup
3 tablespoons minced cilantro
1/2 teaspoon ground cumin
1/2 teaspoon garlic salt
4 skinless, boneless chicken breast halves
1 cup diced cantaloupe
1/2 cup diced jicama
2 tablespoons minced red bell pepper

1 tablespoon seeded, minced jalapeño
1 green onion, minced
2 tablespoons prepared oil and vinegar dressing
6 cups mixed salad greens, cut small
Cilantro sprigs, for garnish
Lime slices, for garnish
Raspberries, for garnish
Cantaloupe slices, for garnish

In a zip-lock plastic bag, mix together lime juice, maple syrup, cilantro, cumin, and garlic salt. Reserve 4 tablespoons mixture and set aside. Place chicken in the bag, seal, and shake to coat. Refrigerate and marinate 30 minutes. Remove chicken from marinade; set aside.

Preheat broiler.

In a small saucepan, boil the marinade 1 minute. Place the chicken on a broiler pan about 6 inches from heat. Broil, turning and brushing with marinade, about 10 minutes or until fork can be inserted easily. Remove chicken from oven; keep warm.

In a medium bowl, combine diced cantaloupe and jicama, bell pepper, jalapeño, onion, and 1 tablespoon reserved marinade.

In a small bowl, blend the oil and vinegar dressing with 3 tablespoons of reserved marinade. In large bowl, toss salad greens with dressing mixture to coat. To serve, divide salad greens among 4 plates; cut chicken in slices and arrange over salad greens. Spoon relish over chicken. Garnish with cilantro sprigs, lime slices, raspberries, and cantaloupe slices.

Makes 4 servings.

Per Serving (approx):
Calories 449
Carbohydrate 26 gm

Protein 61 gm
Sodium 271 mg

Fat 11 gm
Cholesterol 160 mg

Portuguese Chicken Salad

3/4 cup seasoned bread crumbs
1/2 cup grated Parmesan cheese
1 bay leaf, finely crumbled
1 teaspoon paprika
1/2 teaspoon salt
1/4 teaspoon garlic powder
1/4 teaspoon pepper
1 egg white

4 skinless, boneless chicken
   breast halves, cut in 1-inch
   pieces
4 cups assorted salad greens,
   cut small
1 cup thinly sliced cabbage
1/2 red bell pepper,
   cut in thin strips
Piri Piri Vinaigrette

Preheat oven to 425 degrees.

In a shallow dish, mix together bread crumbs, cheese, bay leaf, paprika, salt, garlic powder, and pepper. In separate shallow bowl, beat egg white slightly; add chicken, stirring to coat. Dredge chicken in bread crumb mixture. Place chicken on lightly oiled baking sheet and bake for about 12 minutes or until fork can be inserted easily.

On a platter, arrange salad greens, cabbage, and bell pepper. Drizzle 1/4 cup Piri Piri Vinaigrette over greens; top with chicken. Pass remaining vinaigrette.   Makes 4 servings.

PIRI PIRI VINAIGRETTE:
In a dry small frying pan, toast 4 teaspoons red pepper flakes about 1 minute. Add 1 tablespoon olive oil, cook briefly, and remove from heat. Cool to room temperature. Whisk 1/2 cup tomato juice, 3 tablespoons red wine vinegar, 2 tablespoons fresh chopped cilantro, 1 tablespoon chopped onion, and 1/2 teaspoon salt.

Per Serving (approx):
Calories 384
Carbohydrate 23 gm

Protein 41 gm
Sodium 1172 mg

Fat 14 gm
Cholesterol 144 mg

Salads
Chicken Breasts

Chicken and Spinach Salad with Orange Vinaigrette

This colorful salad has a very different, tangy flavor.

1 pound spinach, washed and
   stemmed
2 oranges, peeled, with
   white pith removed
1 small red bell pepper, cored,
   quartered, and sliced

1/3 cup thinly sliced red onion
4 skinless, boneless chicken
   breasts
1 teaspoon olive oil
Orange Vinaigrette
1/2 cup grated Parmesan cheese

Tear spinach leaves into bite-size pieces; put in a large salad bowl. Slice peeled oranges crosswise into 1/3-inch-thick rounds, then quarter. Add the orange segments, bell pepper and onion to the spinach. Refrigerate.

Cut chicken breasts into 1-inch cubes. Heat oil in wok or large nonstick skillet. Add chicken and stir-fry 5 minutes. Remove from heat, add to spinach mixture, and toss with vinaigrette. Top with Parmesan cheese.

                                      Makes 4 servings.

ORANGE VINAIGRETTE:
Whisk together 1/4 cup fresh orange juice, 1 1/2 teaspoons grated orange rind, 1 tablespoon olive oil, 2 tablespoons red wine vinegar, 1 teaspoon Dijon mustard, 1 teaspoon Worcestershire sauce, 1 tablespoon fresh chopped parsley, 1/4 teaspoon salt, and 1/2 teaspoon pepper.

Per Serving (approx):
Calories 456
Carbohydrate 15 gm

Protein 67 gm
Sodium 610 mg

Fat 14 gm
Cholesterol 170 mg

Mesquite Chicken Salad

Although you should use mesquite charcoal for the barbecue, you can use other kinds of charcoal and it will taste nearly as good.

3 or 4 skinless, boneless chicken
   breasts
1/3 cup mesquite barbecue sauce
2 tablespoons white wine vinegar
1 tablespoon lemon juice
1 tablespoon Dijon mustard

1/4 teaspoon pepper
1 clove garlic, minced
4 tablespoons olive oil
6 cups mixed salad greens
1 pear, cored and thinly sliced

Preheat grill or broiler.

Brush chicken breasts with mesquite sauce. Grill chicken about 4 to 5 minutes on each side or until chicken is no longer pink inside. Set aside to cool.

Slice chicken into thin strips. In a small covered container, mix vinegar, lemon juice, mustard, pepper, garlic, and oil; shake well.

To serve, place salad greens on plates; top with chicken and pear slices. Sprinkle with vinaigrette. Makes 4 to 6 servings.

Per Serving (approx):
Calories 344
Carbohydrate 10 gm

Protein 41 gm
Sodium 285 mg

Fat 16 gm
Cholesterol 107 mg

Saucy Saigon Chicken Salad

2 teaspoons toasted sesame oil
8 skinless, boneless chicken
   thighs, cut in bite-size pieces
1 tablespoon soy sauce
1 cup roasted peanuts
4 cups shredded Savoy
   or Napa cabbage

1 carrot, shredded
1 red bell pepper, thinly sliced
1/2 cup finely shredded
   green onions
1/2 cup loosely packed cilantro
   leaves
Saigon Dressing

In a large skillet, heat oil and sauté chicken for 3 minutes. Add soy sauce. Lower heat and stir-fry until liquid is absorbed and chicken is well glazed. Stir in peanuts. Set aside.

In a large bowl, toss cabbage, carrot, and bell pepper with half the dressing. Place tossed salad on a platter, top with chicken and peanuts, shredded scallions, and cilantro. Drizzle remaining dressing over chicken and vegetables. Serve at room temperature or chill.   Makes 4 servings.

SAIGON DRESSING:
In a measuring cup, combine 1 tablespoon sugar; 1 large garlic clove, pressed; 1/2 teaspoon minced hot red pepper; juice of 1 large lime; 2 tablespoons fish sauce, and 2 tablespoons rice vinegar. (If fish sauce is unavailable, substitute light soy sauce.)

Per Serving (approx):
Calories 521
Carbohydrate 20 gm

Protein 39 gm
Sodium 1103 mg

Fat 32 gm
Cholesterol 99 mg

Jalapeño Tex-Mex Chicken Salad

2 teaspoons taco seasoning
1 teaspoon garlic powder
4 skinless, boneless chicken
   breast halves
1 tablespoon vegetable oil
2/3 cup canned black beans,
   rinsed and drained
1/2 cup canned corn, drained
1/4 cup mild picante sauce
1 tablespoon chopped green
   onion tops

2/3 cup seeded, chopped
   tomatoes
4 cups prepared mixed salad
   greens
8 thin slices jalapeño
Jalapeño Cream Dressing
1 plum tomato, cut in wedges,
   for garnish
Cilantro sprigs, for garnish

In a small bowl, mix taco seasoning and garlic powder; sprinkle on both sides of the chicken. Heat oil in a large skillet. Sauté chicken about 12 minutes until brown on both sides and easily pierced with fork. Remove chicken from the frying pan and set aside.

In the same frying pan, cook black beans, corn, and picante sauce until just heated through; remove from heat. Stir in green onion and tomato.

Arrange salad greens on serving platter. Cut each chicken breast in cross-wise slices (do not separate) and fan slices. Place on the salad greens and top each chicken breast with 2 slices jalapeño and 1 tablespoon Jalapeño Cream Dressing. Spoon warm bean mixture around chicken. Garnish with tomato wedges and cilantro. Pass extra dressing.

Makes 4 servings.

JALAPEÑO CREAM DRESSING:
In a small bowl, combine 1/2 cup jalapeño pepper jelly, 1/2 cup sour cream, 1 tablespoon fresh lime juice, and 1 tablespoon minced fresh cilantro.

Per Serving (approx):
Calories 474	*Protein 36 gm*	*Fat 14 gm*
Carbohydrate 50 gm	*Sodium 501 mg*	*Cholesterol 92 mg*

Santa Fe Chicken on Wild Rice Salad

1 cup low-fat yogurt
1/2 cup lime juice
1 tablespoon Dijon mustard
1 teaspoon minced garlic
1 teaspoon ground cumin
1 teaspoon curry powder
4 skinless, boneless chicken
  breast halves

Tarragon Dressing
1/2 teaspoon cumin seed
1 cup boiled wild rice
1 cup seedless green grapes
1/2 cup chopped red bell
  pepper
1/2 cup sliced green onions
Romaine lettuce leaves

In a small bowl, combine yogurt, lime juice, mustard, garlic, cumin, and curry powder. Place chicken with half of the marinade in a zip-lock bag. Reserve the other half. Let stand 15 minutes. Prepare dressing and set aside.

Preheat broiler.

Remove chicken from the marinade and place on broiler pan about 5 inches from heat. Broil about 7 minutes; turn chicken, brush with reserved marinade, and sprinkle cumin seed evenly on breast halves. Broil an additional 6 minutes or until fork can be inserted easily. Cut chicken into 1/2-inch diagonal strips. In medium bowl, mix together rice, grapes, bell pepper, and green onions. Add dressing and toss gently to mix well. To serve, line plates with lettuce leaves. Add rice mixture and arrange chicken on top.

Makes 4 servings.

TARRAGON DRESSING:
In a small bowl, combine 2 tablespoons white wine vinegar, 2 tablespoons oil, 1 tablespoon fresh lime juice, 2 teaspoons Dijon mustard, 1 teaspoon sugar, 1 teaspoon dried tarragon (or 1 tablespoon chopped fresh tarragon leaves). Mix well. Set aside.

Per Serving (approx):
Calories 466
Carbohydrate 49 gm

Protein 40 gm
Sodium 307 mg

Fat 12 gm
Cholesterol 84 mg

Chicken Salad Riviera

4 skinless, boneless chicken
  breast halves
1/4 cup flour
1 teaspoon poultry seasoning
1/2 teaspoon lemon pepper
1/2 teaspoon salt
2 tablespoons vegetable oil
1 teaspoon cornstarch
1/2 cup grapefruit juice

1/2 cup pineapple juice
2 tablespoons butter, melted
1 tablespoon honey
1 teaspoon spicy brown mustard
Assorted salad greens
1 grapefruit, cut in 8 wedges,
  for garnish
4 pineapple rings, for garnish
Chopped parsley

Between two pieces of wax paper, gently pound chicken to flatten. In a small bowl, mix together flour, poultry seasoning, lemon pepper, and salt. Dredge chicken pieces to coat. In a large frying pan, heat and add chicken. Fry about 3 minutes on each side until brown. In small bowl, mix cornstarch, grapefruit juice, and pineapple juice until smooth; add to pan and bring to low boil. Reduce heat, cover, and simmer about 10 minutes or until fork can be inserted into chicken easily.

Preheat broiler.

In a small bowl, combine butter, honey, and mustard. Dip grapefruit wedges and pineapple rings in butter mixture, one piece at a time, turning to coat. Place fruit on broiler pan and broil about 3 minutes. Keep warm.

To serve, arrange chicken on top of salad greens and pour remaining butter sauce over it. Garnish with broiled grapefruit wedges and pineapple slices and sprinkle with parsley.   Makes 4 servings.

Per Serving (approx):
Calories 1364   *Protein 38 gm*   *Fat 24 gm*
Carbohydrate 249gm   *Sodium 559 mg*   *Cholesterol 96 mg*

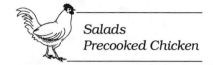
South-of-the-Border Chicken Salad

If you want a spicy change from plain chicken salad, this recipe is for you.

4 1/2 cups cooked, diced chicken
2 3/4 cups whole kernel corn,
  well drained
2 1/2 cups canned black beans,
  drained
1 cup diced red bell peppers
1 cup diced green bell peppers
1 1/2 cups thinly sliced green onions
2 tablespoons thinly sliced, seeded
  jalapeño
2/3 cup pine nuts, toasted
1/2 cup prepared barbecue sauce
3/4 cup prepared Italian salad
  dressing (not creamy)

2 tablespoons chili powder
1 tablespoon cumin
2 1/2 tablespoons lime juice
2 1/2 tablespoons chopped
  cilantro
1 1/2 teaspoon prepared
  hot pepper sauce
1 head iceberg lettuce, shredded
Sour cream (optional),
  for garnish
Chopped black olives (optional),
  for garnish
Cheddar cheese, shredded
  (optional), for garnish

In a large bowl, combine chicken, corn, black beans, red and green bell peppers, green onions, jalapeño, and pine nuts; toss gently. In another bowl, combine barbecue sauce, Italian dressing, chili powder, cumin, lime juice, cilantro, and hot pepper sauce; mix well. Pour dressing mixture over chicken mixture and toss to coat evenly. Cover and refrigerate for 3 hours or overnight.

Serve over a bed of shredded lettuce. If desired, garnish with dollops of sour cream, chopped black olives, and shredded Cheddar cheese.

                                          Makes 6 servings.

Per Serving (approx):
Calories 624
Carbohydrate 49 gm

Protein 41 gm
Sodium 964 mg

Fat 29 gm
Cholesterol 79 mg

Warm Chicken and Watercress Salad

This special salad is low in fat, easy to prepare, and inexpensive. And look at the nutritional analysis!

1/3 cup lemon juice
1 tablespoon vegetable oil
1 tablespoon minced rosemary or
   or 1 teaspoon dried rosemary
2 garlic cloves, minced

1/2 teaspoon salt
1/4 teaspoon pepper
1 1/4 pounds skinless, boneless
   chicken thighs
2 bunches watercress, well
   rinsed

In a shallow bowl, combine all ingredients except watercress and chicken. Place the chicken in marinade and let stand at least 30 minutes.

Preheat broiler. In a small saucepan heat the marinade to boiling. Place chicken on broiler pan and broil 6 to 8 inches from heat source for 15 to 20 minutes on each side. After first 10 minutes, turn and brush occasionally with marinade.

To serve, arrange watercress on individual dinner plates. Slice chicken and arrange on watercress. Spoon pan juices and any remaining hot marinade (bring it to a boil first) over watercress and chicken. Serve hot.

Makes 4 servings.

Per Serving (approx):
Calories 256
Carbohydrate 2 gm

Protein 28 gm
Sodium 385 mg

Fat 15 gm
Cholesterol 101 mg

Salads
Chicken Breasts

Sonora Sunset Chicken Salad

2 skinless, boneless chicken
  breast halves
1/4 teaspoon garlic powder
1/4 teaspoon lemon pepper
1/8 teaspoon cayenne
6 cups salad greens
1 tomato, peeled and chopped
1 avocado, sliced
1/2 cup sliced carrots
1/2 cup diced celery

1/2 cup sliced cucumber
1/2 cup sliced red onion
1 cup grated cheddar cheese
1 can (15 ounces) pinto beans,
  drained, liquid reserved
Sonora Spice Mix
Sonora Dressing
4 tortillas, cut in strips,
  fried crisp

Preheat oven to 400 degrees.

Place chicken in a baking pan. In a small bowl or cup, mix garlic powder, lemon pepper, and cayenne. Sprinkle over chicken. Bake for 30 minutes or until a fork can be inserted easily. Remove from oven, cool, cut into long strips and set aside. In a large salad bowl, toss greens with tomato, avocado, carrots, celery, cucumber, onion, and grated cheese.

In a saucepan, place beans with 1/4 cup reserved bean liquid and simmer. Stir in 2 teaspoons Sonora Spice Mix. Place bean mixture and chicken on top of salad ingredients. Add Sonora Dressing and toss gently. Top with tortilla strips. Makes 4 servings.

SONORA SPICE MIX:
Combine the following ingredients: 1/4 teaspoon chili powder, 1/4 teaspoon ground cloves, 1/4 teaspoon paprika, 1/4 teaspoon salt, 1/8 teaspoon ground coriander, 1/8 teaspoon garlic powder, 1/8 teaspoon onion powder, 1/8 teaspoon dried oregano, 1/8 teaspoon pepper, 1/8 teaspoon cayenne, 1/8 teaspoon white pepper, and 1/8 teaspoon dried thyme.

SONORA DRESSING:
Whisk together 3 tablespoons sugar, 3 tablespoons cooking oil, 3 tablespoons ketchup, and 3 teaspoons red wine vinegar.

Per Serving (approx):
Calories 657
Carbohydrate 60 gm

Protein 33 gm
Sodium 959 mg

Fat 31 gm
Cholesterol 70 mg

Hot or Cold
Indonesian Chicken Salad

Be sure to prepare vegetables and measure all ingredients before starting to cook, so the vegetables will be crisp.

1 tablespoon peanut oil
2 skinless, boneless chicken
   breasts (about 1 1/2 pounds),
   cut in 1-inch strips
1 teaspoon grated ginger
1 clove garlic, minced
1 cup diagonally cut string beans
1 cup matchstick-sliced carrots
1/2 teaspoon salt
1 tablespoon sugar
1/4 cup cider vinegar

1/4 teaspoon turmeric
1/4 cup water
1/4 cup canned unsweetened
   coconut milk
1 cup peeled and sliced
   cucumbers
1/3 cup sliced green onion
1/2 teaspoon pepper
1/4 chopped honey-roasted
   peanuts

In a large skillet or wok, heat oil. Add chicken, ginger, and garlic; stir-fry about 3 minutes. Add string beans and cook 3 minutes more. Add carrots, salt, sugar, vinegar, turmeric, and water; stir-fry 3 minutes more. Stir in coconut milk, cucumbers, green onion, and pepper; stir-fry about 1 minute to heat through.

To serve hot, top with peanuts and accompany with rice. To serve cold, refrigerate in shallow dish at least 2 hours or overnight; arrange on lettuce and sprinkle with peanuts.   Makes 4 servings.

Per Serving (approx):
Calories 314
Carbohydrate 13 gm

Protein 33 gm
Sodium 415 mg

Fat 15 gm
Cholesterol 80 mg

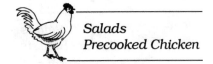

Chicken and Pasta Salad

1 package (16 ounces) frozen broccoli
1/4 teaspoon salt
1 chicken, cooked, skinned, boned, and cut into chunks
1/2 pound shell macaroni, cooked according to package directions

2 tomatoes, cut into large cubes
1/2 cup coarsely chopped red onion
1/2 teaspoon pepper
1 cup Italian salad dressing
Seasoned croutons (optional)
Black olives (optional)

In a saucepan, steam broccoli for about 5 minutes. Drain the broccoli and sprinkle with salt. In a large bowl combine warm chicken, broccoli, shell macaroni, tomatoes, and onion. Sprinkle with pepper. Add Italian dressing and mix gently. Chill in refrigerator. If desired, sprinkle with seasoned croutons and black olives.   Makes 6 servings.

Per Serving (approx):
Calories 502
Carbohydrate 40 gm

Protein 32 gm
Sodium 476 mg

Fat 24 gm
Cholesterol 65 mg

Chicken and Fruit Salad

4 cups cooked chicken breast, chopped into 1-inch pieces
1 cup apple, chopped into 1-inch pieces
1 cup seedless grapes
1 cup pineapple tidbits

1 cup chopped walnuts
1/2 cup mayonnaise
1 teaspoon curry powder
1 tablespoon lemon juice
Maraschino cherries (optional)

In a large bowl combine chicken, fruit, and nuts. In a small bowl, thoroughly mix mayonnaise, curry powder, and lemon juice. Add dressing to chicken and fruit, and refrigerate for at least 1 hour before serving. If desired at serving time, add maraschino cherries. Makes 6 to 8 servings.

Per Serving (approx):
Calories 334
Carbohydrate 10 gm

Protein 21 gm
Sodium 118 mg

Fat 23 gm
Cholesterol 58 mg

44

Chicken in Melon

This makes a stunning dish for a summer buffet.

4 cantaloupes
2 cups cooked diced chicken

1 cup seedless grapes, peeled
1/2 cup mayonnaise

Halve the melons and discard the seeds. Scoop out flesh with a melon baller and set aside. Turn the empty melon halves upside down to drain.

Mix together diced chicken, melon balls, grapes, and mayonnaise. Pile mixture into drained melon shells. Chill well brfore serving.

Makes 8 servings.

Per Serving (approx):
Calories 264
Carbohydrate 24 gm

Protein 12 gm
Sodium 123 mg

Fat 13 gm
Cholesterol 31 mg

Layered Chicken Salad

1 chicken, cooked, boned, skinned
  and cut in pieces
1 can (8 ounces) water chestnuts,
  drained and sliced
2 cups alfalfa sprouts

1 red onion, thinly sliced,
  broken into rings
1/2 cup oil-free Italian dressing,
  divided
1/2 teaspoon pepper, divided

In a glass bowl, layer half each of the following ingredients in this order: chicken, water chestnuts, alfalfa sprouts, and onion rings. Sprinkle with half of the dressing and half of the pepper. Repeat layers and sprinkle with remaining dressing and pepper. Cover and refrigerate at least 2 hours. Serve cold.

Makes 4 servings.

Per Serving (approx):
Calories 261
Carbohydrate 16 gm

Protein 37 gm
Sodium 552 mg

Fat 6 gm
Cholesterol 98 mg

Peppery Grilled Salad

Grilled salads have become stars on restaurant menus. They're easy to prepare at home, fresh from the grill, or made with leftover chicken and warmed in the microwave.

1 1/4 pounds skinless,
   boneless chicken thighs
1 teaspoon pepper
3 tablespoons Worcestershire sauce
6 tablespoons olive oil, divided
Salt to taste
1 tablespoon Dijon mustard
2 tablespoons wine vinegar
1 tablespoon minced green onion
1 small head Bibb or Boston
   lettuce, torn into pieces

1 bunch arugula, well rinsed,
   torn into pieces
1 head Belgian endive,
   torn into pieces
1/2 pound string beans,
   cooked tender-crisp
1 cup cherry tomatoes
1 tablespoon minced basil
1 tablespoon minced parsley

Open the chicken thighs and pound to flatten evenly. Press pepper into both sides of chicken and place in a shallow baking dish. Add 2 tablespoons of the Worcestershire sauce; turn chicken to coat well. Cover and refrigerate 1 hour or longer.

Prepare grill for cooking. Brush chicken with 1 tablespoon oil and sprinkle lightly with salt. Grill chicken for 25 to 30 minutes, or until cooked through, turning occasionally.

In a salad bowl, combine mustard, vinegar, green onion, and remaining tablespoon of Worcestershire sauce. Gradually whisk in remaining 5 tablespoons of oil. Slice warm chicken and add any meat juices to dressing. Arrange greens around edges of 4 dinner plates. Toss chicken, string beans, and tomatoes with dressing and mound equal portions in middle of greens. To serve, drizzle salads with any remaining dressing and sprinkle with minced basil and parsley. Makes 4 servings.

Per Serving (approx):
Calories 476
Carbohydrate 9 gm

Protein 30 gm
Sodium 299 mg

Fat 35 gm
Cholesterol 101 mg

Walnut Chicken Salad

You can prepare the chicken the day before, and serve it warm on a cold salad, or serve it cold on a cold salad.

2 whole skinless, boneless chicken
   breasts, halved, and cut into strips
1/4 cup white wine vinegar
3 tablespoons olive oil, divided
1/4 cup orange juice
1 garlic clove, minced
1/2 teaspoon white pepper
1/2 teaspoon salt

Cilantro Vinaigrette
1/2 pound mixed greens
   (spinach, romaine and
   butter lettuce)
2 large tomatoes, chopped
1/2 red bell pepper, julienned
Orange slices, for garnish

Place chicken in a glass dish with cover. In a small bowl, whisk together vinegar, 2 tablespoons of the olive oil, orange juice, garlic, white pepper, and salt; pour over chicken, cover, and refrigerate 1 hour. Meanwhile, prepare Cilantro Vinaigrette.

Drain chicken and discard marinade. In a large skillet, heat the remaining 1 tablespoon olive oil. Add the chicken and fry, stirring, until fork can be inserted easily.

In a large serving bowl, gently toss mixed greens, tomatoes, and bell pepper with half the vinaigrette and spoon onto 4 salad plates. Arrange chicken strips on top; spoon remaining vinaigrette over chicken. Garnish with orange slices.   Makes 4 servings.

CILANTRO VINAIGRETTE:
In a small jar with a lid, combine 1/4 cup chopped cilantro, 2 tablespoons minced red onion, 2 tablespoons white wine vinegar, 6 tablespoons orange juice, 2 teaspoons grated orange rind, 2 teaspoons honey, 1/4 cup plain yogurt, 1 tablespoon walnut oil, 1/8 teaspoon salt, 1/8 teaspoon white pepper, and 1/8 teaspoon cardamon. Refrigerate. Before serving, add 1/4 cup walnut pieces.

Per Serving (approx):
Calories 541
Carbohydrate 35 gm

Protein 36 gm
Sodium 683 mg

Fat 29 gm
Cholesterol 82 mg

Confetti Chicken Salad

3/4 cup bulgur wheat
3/4 cup boiling water
2 skinless, boneless chicken
   breast halves
1 teaspoon dried dill
1/2 teaspoon dried mint leaves
1/2 teaspoon dried marjoram
2 tablespoons olive oil
2 medium carrots, shredded
1 green bell pepper, minced

1 red bell pepper, minced
2 green onions, chopped
1/2 pint quartered cherry
   tomatoes
1/2 teaspoon salt
1/4 teaspoon pepper
2 tablespoons lemon juice
1 tablespoon red wine vinegar
1/4 cup mayonnaise

Preheat broiler.

In a small bowl, combine bulgur and water; cover and set aside for about 20 minutes until fluffy and soft. In a shallow baking pan, arrange chicken in single layer. In a small bowl, combine the dill, mint, marjoram, and oil; brush half of mixture over chicken. With rack about 6 inches from heat, broil chicken 5 minutes. Turn chicken and brush with remaining oil-herb mixture. Broil about 4 minutes more, or until fork can be inserted into chicken easily. Remove from oven and set aside to cool.

In a large bowl, combine carrot, green and red bell peppers, green onions, and cherry tomatoes. Cut chicken in 1/2-inch-square pieces and add to vegetables. Stir in bulgur. In small bowl, combine salt, pepper, lemon juice, vinegar, and mayonnaise. Add to chicken and vegetables and toss gently to mix.   Makes 6 servings.

Per Serving (approx):
Calories 257   *Protein 13 gm*   *Fat 14 gm*
Carbohydrate 19 gm   *Sodium 286 mg*   *Cholesterol 30 mg*

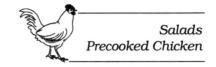

Thai Chicken Salad

Thai cuisine has come into its own in the past few years. Here is a very traditional Thai salad with a refreshing minty ginger flavor.

1 chicken, cooked, boned, skinned
    and cut into thin shreds
1 cucumber, peeled, seeded,
    shredded
2 cups fresh bean sprouts
2 fresh green chiles, seeded,
    shredded

1/2 red onion, sliced thin
    and broken into rings
1 tablespoon grated ginger
1/2 cup chopped cilantro
    (stems and leaves)
Lime-Mint Dressing
1/4 cup chopped roasted
    peanuts

In a large bowl, combine chicken and cucumber. In another bowl, combine bean sprouts, chiles, onion, and ginger. If not serving immediately, cover and refrigerate ingredients.

At serving time, combine chicken-cucumber mixture, bean sprout mixture, cilantro, and Lime-Mint Dressing. Sprinkle with chopped peanuts and serve. Makes 4 to 6 servings.

LIME-MINT DRESSING:
Combine 1/4 cup lime juice, 3 tablespoons fish sauce, 2 tablespoons vegetable oil, 5 teaspoons sugar, 1 tablespoon chopped mint leaves, 2 cloves garlic (minced), and 1/2 teaspoon salt. Stir until sugar dissolves.

Per Serving (approx):
Calories 439
Carbohydrate 14 gm

Protein 39 gm
Sodium 899 mg

Fat 25 gm
Cholesterol 140 mg

Grilled Chicken Satay Salad

Usually we suggest alternatives for ingredients that may be hard to find in certain areas of the country, but this recipe simply doesn't work without the ingredients listed. Asian grocery stores have them.

2 1/4 pounds skinless, boneless chicken breast, cut into strips
2 cups Thai peanut sauce, divided
1 pound mixed salad greens, torn apart (spinach, radicchio, Boston, butter lettuce or romaine)
3/4 cup prepared sesame-soy salad dressing

1 papaya, peeled, seeded, sliced
1 avocado, sliced
1 cucumber, peeled, seeded, and diced
1 red bell pepper, julienned
1/4 cup chopped roasted peanuts
3 ounces Enoki mushrooms

Thread 1 or 2 chicken strips on each of 24 bamboo skewers; place in a flat baking pan; 10 1/2 x 15 1/2 is okay. Pour 1 cup of Thai peanut sauce over chicken and marinate in refrigerator for at least 1 hour.

Arrange the skewers on a lightly oiled broiler pan and broil about 2 minutes per side, basting with reserved 1 cup Thai peanut sauce. (Chicken may also be grilled.) Toss mixed salad greens with sesame-soy salad dressing and arrange on 6 individual plates.

On each plate, place 4 chicken skewers in criss-cross fashion on top of greens. Between spokes of skewers, arrange slices of papaya, avocado, cucumber, and bell pepper strips. Sprinkle with the roasted peanuts. Place sprig of Enoki mushrooms in center of salad.

Makes 6 servings.

Per Serving (approx):
Calories 839
Carbohydrate 32 gm

Protein 64 gm
Sodium 1280 mg

Fat 51 gm
Cholesterol 116 mg

Chicken Bulgur Salad

We don't know why bulgar wheat isn't more popular, but it should be. It's easy to prepare and goes well with practically anything. This warm salad is proof of its versatility.

3/4 cup bulgur wheat
3/4 cup boiling water
1 pound skinless, boneless
  chicken breast
2 tomatoes, peeled, seeded,
  and chopped
1/4 cup chopped basil
2 tablespoons olive oil

2 tablespoons red wine vinegar
1 garlic clove, minced
1 tablespoon chopped mint
  leaves
Salt and pepper to taste
1 head romaine lettuce,
  separated into leaves
1/2 cup minced parsley,
  for garnish

Prepare bulgur in boiling water according to directions on page 48. Meanwhile, in a large saucepan boil 2 inches of water. Add chicken tenders; reduce heat, cover, and simmer 7 to 10 minutes until chicken is cooked through. Let tenders cool in liquid about 10 minutes. Drain the chicken and shred into bite-sized pieces.

In a salad bowl, toss bulgur with chicken, tomatoes, basil, oil, vinegar, garlic, and mint; season with salt and pepper to taste.

To serve, mound salad on a bed of romaine lettuce; garnish with parsley.
Makes 4 to 6 servings.

Per Serving (approx):
Calories 240
Carbohydrate 21 gm

Protein 22 gm
Sodium 56 mg

Fat 7 gm
Cholesterol 51 mg

Hot Chinese Chicken Salad

Like so many Chinese salads, this one should be served hot, or, in our opinion, better still, at room temperature.

8 skinless, boneless chicken thighs, cut into bite-size pieces
1/4 cup cornstarch
1/4 cup vegetable oil
1 tomato, cut into chunks
1 can (4 ounces) water chestnuts, drained, sliced
1 can (4 ounces) sliced mushrooms, drained
1 cup coarsely chopped green onions
1 cup diagonally sliced celery
1/8 teaspoon garlic powder
1/4 cup soy sauce
2 cups finely shredded iceberg lettuce

Dredge chicken in cornstarch. In a wok or frying pan, heat oil. Add the chicken and fry about 3 minutes or until brown. Keep turning the chicken. Add the tomato, water chestnuts, mushrooms, green onion, celery, garlic powder, and soy sauce. Stir gently. Cover and simmer about 5 minutes.

In a large serving bowl, add chicken and vegetable mixture to lettuce and toss lightly. Serve hot with rice.   Makes 4 servings.

Per Serving (approx):
Calories 423   *Protein 30 gm*   *Fat 25 gm*
Carbohydrate 19 gm   *Sodium 1160 mg*   *Cholesterol 98 mg*

> You can put everything, and the more things the better, into a salad, as into a conversation; but everything depends upon the skill of mixing.

Chicken Salad Oriental

We suggest that you cook the chicken breasts the day before so they are nicely chilled before you combine them with the other ingredients.

1 head iceberg lettuce, shredded
3/4 cup chopped celery
1 cup chow mein noodles
1/4 cup vegetable oil
4 skinless, boneless chicken breast
    halves, cut in 2-inch strips
1 can (8 ounces) water chestnuts,
    drained and sliced

1 1/2 cups snow peas
Chow mein noodles
Curry Dressing
1/4 cup cashews, for garnish
5 radishes, thinly sliced,
    for garnish
2 green onions, minced,
    for garnish

In a salad bowl, mix lettuce and celery; sprinkle chow mein noodles on top. In a frying pan, heat oil. Add chicken and stir-fry about 10 minutes or until lightly browned. Add water chestnuts and snow peas; stir-fry 1 minute. Remove chicken mixture from frying pan and arrange over chow mein noodles. Add 1 cup Curry Dressing and toss to mix. Garnish with cashew nuts, radishes, and onion. Serve remaining dressing on the side.

Makes 4 servings.

CURRY DRESSING:
In a medium bowl, combine 3 tablespoons pineapple juice, 2 tablespoons lemon juice, 1 tablespoon light brown sugar, 2 teaspoons curry powder, 2 teaspoons soy sauce, 1/2 teaspoon onion powder, 1/4 teaspoon garlic powder, 1 cup mayonnaise, and 1/2 cup sour cream. Stir until smooth. Refrigerate until serving time.

Per Serving (approx):
Calories 921
Carbohydrate 32 gm

Protein 36 gm
Sodium 720 mg

Fat 72 gm
Cholesterol 112 mg

Chicken and Wild Rice Salad

4 skinless, boneless chicken
   breast halves
1 1/2 cups unsweetened apple juice
3 cups cooked wild rice,
   prepared according to package
   directions
1 1/2 cups halved seedless
   green grapes

1 cup chopped unpeeled apple
1/2 cup chopped celery
3/4 cup slivered almonds,
   divided
1/2 cup chopped water
   chestnuts
Mayonnaise Dressing
Spinach leaves

In a large saucepan, combine chicken with apple juice. Cook over medium heat about 15 minutes, or until fork can be inserted into chicken easily. Remove chicken from pan and, if desired, reserve broth for another use. Dice chicken and chill.

Gently toss chicken with wild rice, grapes, apple, celery, 1/2 cup almonds, and water chestnuts. Add dressing and toss again. Cover and chill about 30 minutes to blend flavors.

To serve, place spinach leaves on platter and spoon chicken mixture on top. Sprinkle with remaining 1/4 cup almonds.   Makes 4 servings.

MAYONNAISE DRESSING:
Combine 1 cup mayonnaise, 1/2 teaspoon seasoned salt, and 1/4 teaspoon cinnamon. Mix well.

Per Serving (approx):
Calories 961
Carbohydrate 58 gm

Protein 42 gm
Sodium 986 mg

Fat 62 gm
Cholesterol 100 mg

SOUPS & CHILIS

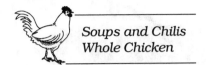

Curried Chicken and Olive Soup

Admittedly a very unusual combination of ingredients, this very good soup is well worth the effort. It can be a main course when served with a mixed green salad and crusty French bread.

1 whole chicken
4 cups water
1 onion, cut in pieces
2 stalks celery, chopped
2 large onions, sliced thin
2 tart apples, cored and sliced
1/4 pound margarine or butter
1/2 teaspoon salt

1 teaspoon chili powder
1 teaspoon curry powder
1/2 cup flour
1 package (12 ounces) frozen
  peas
3 cups milk
2/3 cup stuffed green olives
1 cup light cream

Boil chicken in water with onion and celery, for 1 hour, or until tender. Cool and drain. Strain broth and set aside 3 cups. Keep anything over this quantity for another purpose.

Bone and skin the cooked chicken. Dice chicken (approximately 1 1/2 to 2 cups). Sauté onion and apple slices in margarine. Add salt, chili powder, curry powder, and flour. Stir until flour is cooked, approximately 2 minutes.

Add chicken broth and peas. Cook until peas are tender, stirring frequently. Add milk, diced chicken, and chopped olives. Bring to boil and add cream. Serve immediately.   Makes 6 to 8 servings.

Per Serving (approx):
Calories 426
Carbohydrate 42 gm

Protein 10 gm
Sodium 810 mg

Fat 24 gm
Cholesterol 39 mg

Crockpot Moroccan Soup

A favorite meal in Morocco, this hearty, spicy soup is called "Harira." This crockpot version can simmer away all day and be ready at dinner time.

2 1/4 pounds chicken thighs
1 1/2 cups lentils, rinsed and
  picked over
1 cup chopped onions
1 cup chopped celery
  (including leaves)

2 tablespoons tomato paste
1 teaspoon turmeric
3/4 teaspoon ground cinnamon
7 cups chicken broth or water
2 to 3 tablespoons lemon juice
Salt and pepper to taste
Oranges with Cinnamon

In a crockpot combine chicken thighs, lentils, onion, celery, tomato paste, turmeric, cinnamon, and chicken broth. Place lid on pot and set temperature to high or low. Allow soup to cook until thighs are tender (3 to 5 hours on high; 7 to 9 hours on low).

Transfer thighs from soup to cutting board; remove and discard skin and bones. Cut meat into bite-size pieces and return to soup. Season to taste with lemon juice, salt, and pepper. Serve hot with Oranges with Cinnamon on the side. Makes 6 servings.

ORANGES WITH CINNAMON:
Peel and section 6 small oranges. Add 2 teaspoons lemon juice and sprinkle with sugar and ground cinnamon to taste. Chill and serve.

Per Serving (approx), excluding oranges:
Calories 477	*Protein 44 gm*	*Fat 19 gm*
Carbohydrate 32 gm	*Sodium 175 mg*	*Cholesterol 111 mg*

Chicken-Asparagus Chowder

4 tablespoons butter-flavored
  margarine
5 tablespoons minced onion
6 tablespoons flour
5 cups low-sodium chicken
  broth

1 cup sour cream
2 tablespoons white wine
1 small box frozen asparagus,
  thawed
1 chicken, cooked, skinned,
  boned, and chopped

In a Dutch oven, melt margarine. Add onion and sauté until golden brown, about 3 minutes. Add flour, stirring, and cook about 2 minutes. Slowly add chicken broth, stirring constantly until mixture boils, about 3 minutes.

Reduce heat to low. Place sour cream in small bowl; slowly stir in 1 cup of hot broth. Add sour cream and broth mixture to Dutch oven, stirring until smooth. Add wine. Chop asparagus into bite-size pieces. Add chicken and asparagus to Dutch oven, gently stirring until heated.

Makes 4 servings.

Per Serving (approx):
Calories 496
Carbohydrate 17 gm

Protein 41 gm
Sodium 227 mg

Fat 30 gm
Cholesterol 120 mg

Freeze extra chicken broth in ice cube trays. Remove cubes from the trays. Place the cubes in plastic bags and return the bags to the freezer. To use them, thaw in microwave first, if you wish.

Tex-Mex Chicken Chowder

This recipe is ideal for easy, informal entertaining, and if you're lucky enough to have any leftovers, it tastes even better the second day.

1 tablespoon canola oil
2 pounds skinless, boneless
   chicken breast, cut in cubes
1 clove garlic, minced
1 onion, sliced
1/2 cup chopped green bell pepper
3 tomatillos, peeled and cut in wedges
1 can (14 1/2 ounces) low-sodium
   chicken broth

1 1/2 cups corn, cut from cob
1 can (14 1/2 ounces) tomato
   wedges, drained, juice reserved
3 summer squash, sliced thin
1 teaspoon ground cumin
1/2 teaspoon salt
1/4 teaspoon pepper
1 cup sliced jicama
1 tablespoon chopped cilantro

In a large Dutch oven, heat oil and add chicken and garlic. Turn chicken to brown on all sides, about 3 minutes. Add onion and bell pepper; cook about 5 minutes, stirring. Add tomatillos and chicken broth; simmer about 10 minutes. Add corn and tomato liquid.

Cover and cook on low heat about 10 minutes. Add squash, cumin, salt, pepper, and tomato wedges. Cover and simmer about 5 minutes. Add jicama and cilantro and cook 5 minutes more.   Makes 6 servings.

Per Serving (approx):
Calories 319
Carbohydrate 22 gm

Protein 41 gm
Sodium 297 mg

Fat 7 gm
Cholesterol 103 mg

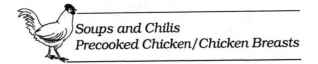
Creamy Chicken, Leek, and Potato Soup

2 large leeks, thinly sliced
6 potatoes, peeled and diced
4 cups chicken broth
1 teaspoon salt

1 1/2 cups cooked chicken, cubed or shredded
1 cup sour cream
2 cups milk
1 tablespoon chopped chives

In a large saucepan, combine leeks, potatoes, chicken broth, and salt. Boil, then simmer 15 minutes until potatoes are tender. Puree mixture in a blender or food processor. Return to saucepan. Add chicken. Stir in sour cream, milk, and chives. Heat gently.   Makes 4 servings.

Per Serving (approx):
Calories 877
Carbohydrate 90 gm

Protein 61 gm
Sodium 806 mg

Fat 30 gm
Cholesterol 202 mg

East-West Broth

Having this broth on hand allows a busy cook to make many different soups simply by adding different combinations of vegetables and spices. The next two recipes are samples.

2 cans (46 to 49 1/2 ounces each) chicken broth or water

2 1/3 pounds skinless, chicken breast halves

Skim fat from top of chicken broth. In a Dutch oven, bring broth to a boil. Add chicken; reduce heat and simmer, uncovered, about 20 minutes or until chicken is cooked through. If time permits, allow chicken to cool in broth. Remove chicken from broth; shred meat and discard bones. Pour broth through strainer lined with cheesecloth into clean saucepan. (May be made ahead to this point and refrigerated up to one week before serving.) Use half of the broth (about 6 cups) and half of the shredded chicken (about 2 cups) in the following two recipes. Both recipes may be doubled.   Makes 12 servings.

Per Serving (approx):
Calories 17
Carbohydrate 1 gm

Protein 1 gm
Sodium 1209 mg

Fat 1 gm
Cholesterol 0 mg

Italian Chicken Noodle Soup

6 cups East-West Broth (page 60)
2 cups cooked, shredded chicken
1/2 medium zucchini, diced
1 can (19 ounces) cannellini
   (white kidney) beans
1/4 pound thin egg noodles

2 carrots, diced
2 green onions, thinly sliced
1/4 cup grated Parmesan cheese
2 tablespoons chopped basil
   or 1 tablespoon prepared pesto

Bring broth to boil in a saucepan. Add chicken and remaining ingredients except cheese and basil. Cook about 5 minutes until noodles are cooked and vegetables are tender-crisp. To serve, stir in Parmesan and basil; pour into bowls.   Makes 4 servings.

Per Serving (approx):
Calories 485
Carbohydrate 62 gm

Protein 40 gm
Sodium 2681 mg

Fat 9 gm
Cholesterol 84 mg

Far East Chicken Noodle Soup

This soup includes Chinese chili paste and Japanese curly noodles.

6 cups East-West Broth (page 60)
2 cups cooked, shredded chicken
1/4 pound snow peas, cut in
   half on an angle
2 carrots, cut into julienne strips
2 to 3 green onions, thinly sliced

2 tablespoons minced cilantro
1 tablespoon grated ginger
1 to 2 teaspoons Chinese chili
   paste with garlic
1 package (5 ounces) Japanese
   curly noodles (chucka soba)
Cilantro sprigs (optional),
   for garnish

Bring broth to boil in a medium saucepan. Add chicken and remaining ingredients except noodles and cilantro. Add noodles and boil about 5 minutes until noodles are cooked and vegetables are tender-crisp. To serve, pour into bowls and garnish with cilantro sprigs.

    Makes 4 servings.

Per Serving (approx):
Calories 164
Carbohydrate 8 gm

Protein 22 gm
Sodium 2253 mg

Fat 5 gm
Cholesterol 53 mg

Korean Chicken Wing Soup

These are the wings, not the drumettes, and you know how inexpensive they are. But, what you probably didn't know is that they make a great soup!

8 chicken wings
1 tablespoon toasted sesame oil
1 tablespoon peanut oil
1 carrot, sliced thin
2 small zucchini, sliced
1/4 cup chopped green onion

1 clove garlic, minced
1/2 teaspoon grated ginger
1/2 teaspoon chili powder
4 cups warm low-sodium
   chicken broth
2 tablespoons soy sauce

Brush chicken wings with sesame oil. In a large Dutch oven, heat peanut oil and add chicken. Cook, turning, about every 5 minutes, until brown on all sides. Add carrot, stir for about 3 minutes, then add zucchini, green onion, garlic, ginger, and chili powder.

Continue to stir gently, about 3 minutes. Add chicken broth and soy sauce. Bring to boil, reduce heat to low, and simmer about 10 minutes until fork can be inserted into chicken easily.   Makes 4 servings.

Serve soup over cooked rice, if desired.

Per Serving (approx):
Calories 320
Carbohydrate 7 gm

Protein 23 gm
Sodium 587 mg

Fat 22 gm
Cholesterol 62 mg

> Soldiers returning from World War II brought many new ways of cooking chicken from Europe, the Far East, and the South Pacific. Chicken was not just for Sunday anymore.

White Bean Chicken Chili

1 pound chicken drumettes
1 cup chopped onion
2 cloves garlic, minced
1 1/2 teaspoons chili powder
1/8 to 1/4 teaspoon cayenne
1 red bell pepper, chopped
1 can (15 ounces) chicken broth

2 cans (15 ounces each) butter
  or white beans, rinsed and
  drained
1 can (4 ounces) chopped green
  chiles
Grated cheddar cheese

In a 4-quart saucepan sprayed with vegetable oil, brown chicken on all sides. Add onion and garlic, cook until tender. Add remaining ingredients except cheese. Heat to boiling; reduce heat. Uncover and simmer, stirring occasionally, for 20 to 25 minutes or until chicken is no longer pink inside. Sprinkle with cheese.

Makes 5 servings.

Per Serving (approx):
Calories 519
Carbohydrate 50 gm

Protein 38 gm
Sodium 1112 mg

Fat 19 gm
Cholesterol 69 mg

Each wing weighs slightly over 3 ounces
and has about an ounce of meat on it.

Crockpot Chili

As all chili fans know, chili can range from mild to volcanic. This one is middling-to-hot, meant to simmer all day, ready for your evening meal. Try it with cornbread and a green salad.

1 1/4 pounds skinless, boneless chicken thighs
1 can (16 ounces) pinto, red kidney or black beans, drained
1 can (14 ounces) Italian plum tomatoes
1/2 cup chopped onion
1/2 cup chopped green bell pepper

3 tablespoons chili powder
1 tablespoon ground cumin
2 garlic cloves, minced
1/2 to 1 teaspoon hot pepper sauce (optional)
Salt and pepper to taste
Sour cream (optional)
Chopped green onions (optional)

Trim chicken and cut into 1-inch pieces. In a crockpot combine chicken, beans, undrained tomatoes, onion, bell pepper, chili powder, cumin, garlic, and hot pepper sauce. Cover pot and set temperature control to high or low. Allow chili to cook until meat is tender (3 to 5 hours on high; 7 to 9 hours on low). Season with salt and pepper to taste.

Serve chili topped with a dollop of sour cream and chopped green onions, if desired. Makes 4 to 6 servings.

*For a thicker chili, use only half the tomato juice.

Per Serving (approx):
Calories 252
Carbohydrate 19 gm

Protein 24 gm
Sodium 360 mg

Fat 9 gm
Cholesterol 67 mg

ASIAN & INDIAN

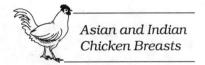
Broccoli Chicken
with Plum Sherry Sauce

Despite its elegant title, this tasty colorful meal takes only a few minutes to prepare.

2 tablespoons canola oil
4 skinless, boneless chicken
   breast halves, cut into thin strips
4 cups broccoli florets
1 cup low-sodium chicken broth,
   warm, divided
1/4 cup sliced green onion
2/3 cup diagonally sliced celery
1/4 pound mushrooms, sliced

1 can (8 ounces) water
   chestnuts, sliced
1/4 teaspoon pepper
2 tablespoons cornstarch
1/4 cup low-sodium soy sauce
1/2 cup red plum jam
2 tablespoons dry sherry
3 tablespoons sesame seeds,
   toasted

In a large frying pan or wok, heat oil, chicken strips, and stir-fry about 2 minutes. Add broccoli, stirring and cooking 2 minutes more. Add 2 table-spoons chicken broth and stir in onion and celery, cooking 2 minutes more. Add mushrooms and 2 tablespoons more chicken broth, cooking 2 minutes. Add water chestnuts, salt, and pepper, stirring and cooking 1 minute.

In a small bowl, stir together cornstarch and soy sauce until smooth. Add remaining 3/4 cup broth to chicken and vegetables, pushing them to side of pan. Slowly stir soy mixture into broth until it thickens; then stir everything in pan together.

In a small saucepan, mix plum jam and sherry; heat just until jam melts. Place chicken mixture in shallow serving bowl; drizzle plum-sherry sauce over all and sprinkle with sesame seeds.   Makes 4 servings.

Per Serving (approx):

Calories 478	*Protein 37 gm*	*Fat 15 gm*
Carbohydrate 48 gm	*Sodium 964 mg*	*Cholesterol 80 mg*

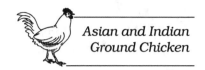

Japanese Hibachi Chicken

This recipe gets its name from the Japanese portable barbecue. Of course, you can use any kind of barbecue, or just your stovetop.

1 pound ground chicken
1 tablespoon vegetable oil
1/2 pound pea pods, halved at
   an angle

1/2 pound mushrooms, halved
1/2 pound zucchini, julienned
Teriyaki Glaze

Sauté chicken in oiled skillet on the stove or over the hot coals of your hibachi. Make sure the chicken is uniformly light brown. Remove from pan. Coat bottom of pan with oil, add pea pods, mushrooms, and zucchini. Stir-fry until cooked. Return chicken to pan, pour Teriyaki Glaze over and cook, stirring until thickened and glossy.   Makes 4 servings.

TERIYAKI GLAZE:
Mix 2 tablespoons cornstarch with 1/4 cup each light soy sauce, water, and brown sugar (packed) and 1 tablespoon grated ginger.

Per Serving (approx):
Calories 294
Carbohydrate 33 gm

Protein 21 gm
Sodium 950 mg

Fat 9 gm
Cholesterol 71 mg

Japan and Hong Kong are major importers of chicken parts from the United States. The largest importer, however, is the Russian Federation.

Mint and Ginger Chicken

Thailand is the home country of this unusual recipe that combines cubed, marinated chicken with cabbage. It is surprisingly tasty.

1 1/2 pounds skinless, boneless
   chicken breast cut into
   1/2-inch cubes
2 tablespoons flour
2 tablespoons fish sauce
2 tablespoons dark soy sauce, divided
1 1/2-inch piece ginger, peeled
1 jalapeño chile, seeded and minced

1 tablespoon vinegar
1 tablespoon sugar
1 lime, peel grated and juiced
2 tablespoons peanut oil
3 cups chopped Napa cabbage
4 green onions, chopped
1/4 cup chopped mint

In a bowl sprinkle chicken with flour, turning to coat it. Add fish sauce and 1 tablespoon of the soy sauce and turn it some more; set aside.

Place ginger in a blender or food processor and mince for about 30 seconds; add chile, remaining 1 tablespoon soy sauce, vinegar, sugar, and 1/2 teaspoon grated lime peel. Blend or process for about 1 minute; set aside.

Heat the oil in a wok. Add chicken, cabbage, and onion and stir-fry about 4 minutes until chicken turns white. Pour ginger sauce over chicken and continue to stir-fry over high heat until the sauce thickens, about 2 minutes. Sprinkle with lime juice and top with the mint.

Makes 4 servings.

Per Serving (approx):
Calories 320
Carbohydrate 13 gm

Protein 43 gm
Sodium 1196 mg

Fat 11 gm
Cholesterol 115 mg

Thai Thigh Kabobs

8 skinless, boneless chicken thighs
1/2 cup hot garlic soy sauce
1/4 cup brown sugar
1/4 cup ketchup
2 tablespoons lime juice
1 large green onion, chopped
1 tablespoon peanut butter

1 large white onion
1 each large red, orange,
   and yellow bell peppers,
   cut in 1 1/2-inch chunks
Thai Rice Pilaf
Cilantro sprigs, for garnish
Lime slices, for garnish

Gently pound chicken to 1/2-inch thickness. Cut each thigh in half and place in a glass bowl. In a blender, combine hot garlic soy sauce, brown sugar, ketchup, lime juice, green onion, and peanut butter. Process on high speed until smooth. Pour mixture over chicken, cover and refrigerate 15 minutes.

Drain the chicken; pour the leftover marinade into a saucepan and heat about 6 minutes, stirring occasionally, until marinade is thickened. Reduce heat, cover, and keep warm.

Preheat the broiler and arrange rack so kabobs will be about 8 inches from heat. Cut onion into 8 wedges and separate each wedge in half. On each of 4 long metal skewers alternately thread chicken, onion, and peppers. Place on broiler pan. Coat kabobs evenly with vegetable spray. Broil 8 minutes; turning and brushing liberally with the leftover marinade until kabobs begin to glaze. To serve, place skewers on a bed of Thai Rice Pilaf. Garnish with cilantro and lime slices. Makes 4 servings.

THAI RICE PILAF:
Heat 2 tablespoons canola oil. Add 1 package (7 ounces) curry rice mix. Sauté until rice is lightly toasted. Add 2 1/2 cups low-sodium chicken broth and 1/2 teaspoon seasoned salt. Bring to a boil, cover, and reduce heat. Simmer about 25 minutes until all liquid is absorbed. Gently fold in 3 tablespoons chopped cilantro, 2 tablespoons lime juice, and 1/2 teaspoon finely grated lime peel.

Per Serving (approx):
Calories 625
Carbohydrate 74 gm

Protein 35 gm
Sodium 2859 mg

Fat 21 gm
Cholesterol 98 mg

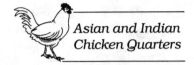

Thai Barbecued Chicken

Unfortunately, there are no equivalents for fish sauce and coconut milk. If you have an Asian grocery store in your area (or a mail-order source) for these items, you have a great recipe; without them, the recipe won't work.

32 cilantro stems, chopped
3 garlic cloves, chopped
2 tablespoons fish sauce
1 teaspoon turmeric
1 teaspoon white pepper

1/4 teaspoon salt
1/2 cup tamarind nectar
1/2 cup coconut milk
4 chicken leg quarters

In blender container, combine cilantro, garlic, fish sauce, turmeric, white pepper, and salt; blend 45 seconds; add tamarind nectar and blend 1 more minute. Add coconut milk and blend 1 minute. Arrange chicken in a large bowl in a single layer. Pierce chicken with a fork and pour marinade over it, making sure the marinade goes under the skin. Pierce again several times with fork. Cover, refrigerate, and marinate at least 2 hours or overnight.

Preheat oven to 350 degrees.

Remove chicken from marinade and place in single layer in baking dish; brush with marinade. Pour remaining marinade into small ovenproof container and place both chicken and marinade in oven for 25 minutes.

Remove chicken to prepared charcoal grill, skin side up, about 6 inches from heat. Grill, turning and basting with heated sauce, about 10 minutes per side or until brown and fork pierces chicken easily. If desired, for hotter taste, serve with red curry sauce (available in powder form at food specialty shops).   Makes 4 servings.

Per Serving (approx):
Calories 811   *Protein 62 gm*   *Fat 37 gm*
Carbohydrate 57 gm   *Sodium 937 mg*   *Cholesterol 207 mg*

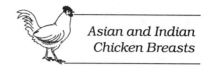

Thai Chicken Stir-Fry with Ginger

If you like Thai food, you should find a source for fish sauce. They use it in everything. If there isn't an Asian grocery store available, try one of the mail-order catalogs advertised in various food magazines.

1 1/2 cups low-sodium chicken broth
3/4 cup coconut milk
1/2 cup grated ginger, divided
1 cup uncooked soft jasmine rice*
2 cloves garlic, minced
3 tablespoons fish sauce
2 teaspoons sugar
1 teaspoon soy sauce

1 cup warm water
1/4 cup vegetable oil
1 1/2 cups onion, cut into
   vertical strips
1 1/2 pounds skinless, boneless
   chicken breasts, cut in 2-inch
   strips
1/2 teaspoon white pepper

In a saucepan, combine broth, coconut milk, and 1 teaspoon of the ginger. Add jasmine rice and bring to a boil. Stir, reduce heat to low, cover and cook 20 minutes. Turn off heat and let sit 10 minutes without removing the cover. While the rice is cooking, in a small bowl mix the remaining ginger and minced garlic. In another bowl, combine fish sauce, sugar, and soy sauce; stir until sugar is dissolved; add warm water and set aside.

In a large, heavy frying pan or wok, heat oil. Add onion and stir-fry until it begins to change color and is slightly crisp, about 3 minutes. Remove with slotted spoon; keep warm. To pan, add ginger-garlic mixture and cook until light brown, about 2 minutes. Add chicken and stir-fry until no longer pink, about 5 minutes. Add fish sauce mixture and pepper; cook 3 minutes more. Serve over jasmine rice.   Makes 6 servings.

*Jasmine rice is a type of rice grown in Thailand. If you don't have it in your area, use short-grain white rice.

Per Serving (approx):
Calories 373
Carbohydrate 19 gm

Protein 31 gm
Sodium 703 mg

Fat 19 gm
Cholesterol 78 mg

Key Lime Thai Chicken

6 skinless, boneless chicken
  breast halves
1/2 cup key lime juice
1/4 cup vegetable oil
1 tablespoon honey
4 garlic cloves, minced
1/4 cup chopped green onion

1/2 cup chopped cilantro
1 teaspoon dried mint
1/2 teaspoon red pepper flakes
1/2 teaspoon pepper
Cilantro sprigs, for garnish
Key Lime Thai Cucumber Salsa

Place chicken in a shallow glass dish. In a small bowl, whisk together lime juice, oil, honey, garlic, onion, cilantro, mint, bell pepper, and pepper. Pour over chicken breasts, turning to coat. Refrigerate and marinate 15 minutes.

Remove chicken from marinade; reserve marinade. Place chicken on broiler pan about 6 inches from heat. Broil, turning and basting with reserved marinade, about 10 minutes or until fork pierces chicken easily. Garnish with cilantro sprigs. Serve with Key Lime Thai Cucumber Salsa.   Makes 6 servings.

KEY LIME THAI CUCUMBER SALSA:
In medium bowl, combine 1/2 cup key lime juice, 1/4 cup vegetable oil, 1/4 cup sugar, 1/2 teaspoon salt, 2 teaspoons Thai chili sauce, 1/2 cup chopped green onion, 2 peeled and diced small cucumbers, and 1/4 cup chopped cilantro. Cover and refrigerate. Before serving, sprinkle with 1/4 cup minced roasted peanuts.

Per Serving (approx):
Calories 428   *Protein 32 gm*   *Fat 25 gm*
Carbohydrate 20 gm   *Sodium 313 mg*   *Cholesterol 80 mg*

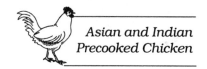

Pan Chicken with Jasmine Rice

*If jasmine rice is not readily available, use Uncle You-Know-Who kind. The
Anaheim green pepper may not be available where you live; if so, use the
New Mexico Red Chile pepper, which is just as good.*

1 cup cooked soft jasmine rice (see page 71)	1/4 cup chopped Anaheim pepper
1 whole chicken, cooked, skinned, boned, and chopped	2 tablespoons low-sodium soy sauce
4 tablespoons lemon juice, divided	1 tablespoon fish sauce
2 cloves garlic, minced	1/2 teaspoon cinnamon
1 tablespoon canola oil	1/3 cup low-sodium chicken broth, warmed
1/2 cup minced onion	

While rice is still warm, sprinkle with 1 tablespoon of the lemon juice
and toss to mix well. Sprinkle warm chicken with remaining 3 tablespoons lemon juice and the garlic.

In a large nonstick frying pan heat oil. Add onion and pepper, stirring
constantly for about 1 minute. Add chicken and stir-fry about 1 minute.
Add cooked rice and stir-fry. Add soy sauce, fish sauce, and cinnamon,
cooking and stirring until heated through, about 1 minute. Pour chicken
broth over all and cook 1 minute more. Serve with chutney, if desired.

Makes 6 servings.

Per Serving (approx):
Calories 75
Carbohydrate 12 gm

Protein 2 gm
Sodium 351 mg

Fat 2 gm
Cholesterol 0 mg

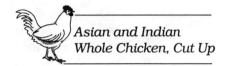
Coriander Chicken with Peanut Sauce

1 whole chicken, cut up
6 tablespoons low-sodium soy sauce
2 tablespoons honey
1 tablespoon ground coriander

2 garlic cloves, crushed
2 teaspoons finely grated ginger
1/4 teaspoon turmeric
1/4 teaspoon cayenne
Peanut Sauce

Cut each breast half crosswise into 2 pieces. Cut 2 parallel diagonal slits on meat side of each piece of breast, thighs and drumsticks, cutting almost all the way through to the bone.

In a large bowl, combine soy sauce, honey, coriander, garlic, ginger, turmeric, and cayenne. Add chicken, turning to coat. Refrigerate and marinate at least 45 minutes. Preheat broiler and arrange the oven rack so chicken is about 6 inches from heat.

Remove chicken from marinade and place, skin side down, on oiled rack of broiler pan. Broil, turning once and basting with marinade, about 15 minutes or until golden brown and fork pierces chicken easily. Remove from oven and place on serving platter. Pass the Peanut Sauce.

Makes 4 servings

PEANUT SAUCE:
In a small bowl, combine 4 tablespoons smooth peanut butter, 4 tablespoons low-sodium soy sauce, 2 tablespoons lemon juice, 3 tablespoons brown sugar, 1 1/2 teaspoons cayenne, and 2 tablespoons honey. Stir to blend.

Per Serving (approx):
Calories 676	*Protein 60 gm*	*Fat 34 gm*
Carbohydrate 32 gm	*Sodium 1597 mg*	*Cholesterol 210 mg*

Peanutty Chicken Breasts with Ginger Butter

This is a fun recipe with an Asian flavor, using ingredients that you already have in your cupboard.

4 skinless, boneless chicken
   breast halves
1/2 cup buttermilk
1/2 teaspoon hot pepper sauce
3 tablespoons butter
1 tablespoon honey
1/2 teaspoon minced ginger

1/2 cup minced roasted peanuts, not salted
1 cup flour
1/4 teaspoon garlic powder
1 teaspoon seasoned salt
1/4 teaspoon pepper
2 tablespoons peanut oil

Place chicken breasts between 2 sheets of wax paper and pound gently to flatten. In a shallow dish, combine buttermilk and pepper sauce; add chicken and marinate 30 minutes, or cover and refrigerate for several hours.

In a small bowl, cream butter, honey, and ginger; set aside. In a shallow dish, combine peanuts, flour, garlic powder, seasoned salt, and pepper. Remove chicken from marinade; drain well and dredge in flour mixture to coat evenly.

In a large frying pan, heat oil and add chicken. Sauté about 3 minutes until it is lightly browned. Turn and cook about 5 minutes more until golden brown and no longer pink inside. Top each breast half with a small dollop of ginger butter.　　　　　Makes 4 servings.

Per Serving (approx):
Calories 544
Carbohydrate 34 gm

Protein 39 gm
Sodium 1234 mg

Fat 28 gm
Cholesterol 105 mg

Chicken Thighs with Ginger Pears

The ingredients and flavors of East and West have merged into piquant, colorful, and easy dishes such as this.

2 teaspoons vegetable oil
3 tablespoons soy sauce
2 tablespoons lemon juice, divided
4 teaspoons minced, peeled ginger
   or 1 teaspoon ground ginger
1 tablespoon Dijon mustard
1 garlic clove, minced

Salt and pepper to taste
2 pounds skinless chicken
   thighs
2 teaspoons cornstarch
1 can (16 ounces) sliced pears
   in heavy syrup
Chopped parsley (optional)

Coat a 12 x 8 baking pan with oil. Add soy sauce, 1 tablespoon of the lemon juice, ginger, mustard, garlic, and salt and pepper to taste; stir to combine. Add thighs and coat well. Cover; marinate in refrigerator at least 30 minutes.

Preheat oven to 375 degrees.

Bake chicken in the marinade 30 minutes. Meanwhile, in a medium bowl, dissolve the cornstarch in remaining lemon juice; stir in undrained pears. Remove thighs from baking pan and set aside. Skim off and discard as much clear fat as possible. Add pear mixture to pan and stir to combine with pan juices. Return thighs to pan, smooth side up. Bake 20 minutes longer until sauce thickens and chicken is cooked through. Sprinkle with chopped parsley, if desired.   Makes 4 to 6 servings.

Per Serving (approx):

Calories 436	*Protein 33 gm*	*Fat 15 gm*
Carbohydrate 43 gm	*Sodium 677 mg*	*Cholesterol 108 mg*

Lemon-Thyme Chicken Thighs

3 tablespoons vegetable oil
16 chicken thighs
3 teaspoons garlic salt
1 1/2 cups flour, divided
3 teaspoons dried thyme
3 tablespoons honey
1 tablespoon prepared mustard

2 tablespoons horseradish
3 tablespoons lemon juice
1 cup buttermilk, divided
1 teaspoon salt
1/2 teaspoon pepper
2 lemons, sliced, for garnish
3 sprigs mint, for garnish

Preheat oven to 375 degrees.

In a large frying pan heat oil. Sprinkle each chicken thigh with garlic salt. Mix 1 1/4 cups flour and thyme in a wide bowl. Roll chicken in flour mixture to coat. Add chicken to frying pan and fry about 6 minutes on each side until brown.

Remove chicken from the frying pan and arrange in 9 x 13 baking pan. Combine honey, mustard, horseradish, lemon juice, and 1/2 cup buttermilk. Drizzle mixture over chicken. Bake about 45 minutes or until a fork can be inserted easily.

Meanwhile, drain all but 2 tablespoons oil from the pan in which you fried the chicken and place it over medium heat. Add the salt, pepper, and remaining 1/4 cup flour and 1/2 cup buttermilk. Cook, stirring, until sauce thickens.

Arrange chicken on a platter and drizzle with sauce. Garnish with lemon slices and mint sprigs.   Makes 8 servings.

Per Serving (approx):
Calories 465
Carbohydrate 40 gm

Protein 29 gm
Sodium 449 mg

Fat 21 gm
Cholesterol 91 mg

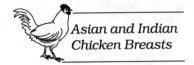
Raspberry Chicken

1/2 cup prepared fat-free
   raspberry vinaigrette
4 skinless, boneless chicken
   breast halves
4 garlic cloves, minced
1 tablespoon minced ginger

1/2 teaspoon crushed anise seed
1/2 cup water
1/4 cup soy sauce
2/3 cup raspberries, for garnish
1/2 pound snow peas, cooked,
   for garnish

In a small bowl, combine raspberry vinaigrette, garlic, ginger, anise seed, water, and soy sauce. Place chicken in a skillet and pour the vinaigrette mixture over the chicken. Boil, then simmer covered about 25 minutes until a fork can be inserted into chicken easily.

Preheat broiler.

Remove chicken from frying pan and place on broiler pan rack sprayed with vegetable spray. Arrange oven rack so chicken is about 4 inches from heat. Broil about 3 minutes on each side. Remove chicken to heated platter, cover and set aside.

Bring sauce in frying pan to a boil and cook about 15 minutes or until thickened and reduced by about half. To serve, pour a portion of sauce on each of 4 individual plates. Thinly slice each chicken breast half across the grain and fan out slices on one side of plate. Garnish with raspberries. Fan out a portion of pea pods on other side of each plate.

Makes 4 servings.

Per Serving (approx):
Calories 280
Carbohydrate 11 gm

Protein 32 gm
Sodium 1187 mg

Fat 12 gm
Cholesterol 80 mg

Golden Harvest Chicken

2 chicken breasts, skinned
  and halved
Golden Harvest Marinade
2 tablespoons vegetable oil
1 red apple, cored,
  cut in 1/4-inch slices

2 teaspoons cornstarch
2 tablespoons cold water
4 green onions, cut in 1/2-inch
  pieces
Steamed broccoli florets

With a sharp knife make diagonal cuts 1 inch apart in thickest part of each chicken breast. Place chicken, uncut side down, in container with marinade. Cover and refrigerate 30 minutes.

Remove the chicken from marinade; reserve marinade. In a frying pan, heat oil. Add chicken, uncut side down, and fry about 5 minutes or until brown. Drain oil from frying pan. Turn chicken, cover with reserved marinade, place apples on top of chicken, and simmer over low heat about 30 minutes or until fork can be inserted easily.

Remove the chicken and apples to a serving plate. Over high heat without a cover, reduce marinade by half. In a small dish, mix cornstarch and water until smooth. Add cornstarch mixture and green onions to frying pan and cook, stirring constantly, until thickened. Spoon sauce over chicken. Garnish with steamed broccoli florets.   Makes 4 servings.

GOLDEN HARVEST MARINADE:
In a large nonmetallic container, combine 2 cups apple juice, 1/4 cup teriyaki sauce, 1 teaspoon minced garlic, 1 teaspoon ground ginger, 1 1/2 teaspoons ground turmeric, and 1 tablespoon chicken bouillon granules.

Per Serving (approx):
Calories 333
Carbohydrate 29 gm

Protein 30 gm
Sodium 960 mg

Fat 11 gm
Cholesterol 77 mg

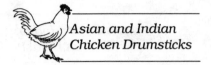

Indonesian Spiced Chicken

If you can't find tamarind nectar, use unsweetened grapefruit juice.

1/4 cup chopped green onion
1 clove garlic
1/2 cup tamarind nectar
2 tablespoons lemon juice
1/2 teaspoon salt
1 teaspoon ground coriander
1/2 teaspoon pepper
1 teaspoon ground cumin
1/4 teaspoon ground cloves

1/4 teaspoon ground nutmeg
1/2 teaspoon ground cinnamon
1/4 teaspoon turmeric
1 tablespoon peanut oil
4 chicken drumsticks, skinned
1/2 teaspoon grated ginger
1/2 cup canned unsweetened
   coconut milk

In a blender, process green onion, garlic, tamarind nectar, lemon juice, and salt until smooth, about 1 minute. Fry coriander, pepper, cumin, cloves, nutmeg, cinnamon, and turmeric in a dry frying pan for about 2 minutes. Add oil and stir to mix well with spices.

Add chicken, turning to coat each piece with oil-spice mixture. Add ginger and cook about 2 minutes on each side. Stir in the blender mixture, scraping pan to release pan drippings. Stir in coconut milk and continue to cook, uncovered, over medium heat, 20 minutes. Turn chicken, reduce heat to low and cook about 20 minutes more or until fork pierces chicken easily. Makes 4 servings.

Per Serving (approx):
Calories 368
Carbohydrate 13 gm

Protein 36 gm
Sodium 417 mg

Fat 19 gm
Cholesterol 116 mg

The average drumstick weighs 4 ounces, of which about half is edible meat. The average thigh section weighs 5 ounces and has more than 2 ounces of edible meat.

Spicy Balinese Chicken

4 skinless, boneless chicken
  breast halves
3 tablespoons Dijon mustard
1/2 cup gingersnap crumbs

Spicy Pineapple Sauce
Red bell pepper strips,
  for garnish
Basil sprigs, for garnish

Preheat oven to 350 degrees.

Between 2 sheets of plastic wrap, place chicken and gently pound to uniform thickness; brush with mustard. Put gingersnap crumbs in a dish and dredge the chicken in the crumbs.

In shallow baking dish lightly sprayed with vegetable oil, place chicken and refrigerate 20 minutes. Bake about 20 minutes or until juices run clear and fork pierces chicken easily. Prepare Spicy Pineapple Sauce. On 4 individual plates, spoon 1/4 of Spicy Pineapple Sauce, and top with chicken breast half. Garnish with bell pepper strips and basil sprigs.

Makes 4 servings.

SPICY PINEAPPLE SAUCE:
In a frying pan, heat 1 tablespoon peanut oil. Add 1 minced garlic clove and 1 chopped red onion. Sauté about 2 minutes. Stir in 1/4 cup rice vinegar and 1 can (8 ounces) crushed pineapple with juice. Add 1/4 teaspoon allspice, 1/4 teaspoon red pepper flakes, and 2 1/2 teaspoons Dijon mustard. Heat, stirring, about 4 minutes or until bubbly and slightly thickened. In a blender, puree pineapple mixture until smooth; keep warm. Just before serving, stir in 2 tablespoons minced basil and 1/4 cup diced red bell pepper.

Per Serving (approx):

Calories 272	*Protein 32 gm*	*Fat 8 gm*
Carbohydrate 17 gm	*Sodium 639 mg*	*Cholesterol 80 mg*

Chicken Adobo with Island Beans and Peppers

Many consider this to be the national dish of the Philippines. If it isn't, we think it should be.

1 1/2 teaspoons dried oregano	1/3 cup lime juice
1 1/2 teaspoons onion powder	2 garlic cloves, peeled and
1/4 teaspoon salt	crushed
1/8 teaspoon pepper	Island Beans and Peppers
8 skinless, boneless chicken	1/2 teaspoon grated lime peel
thighs	Cilantro sprigs, for garnish
	Lime slices, for garnish

In a small bowl, combine oregano, onion powder, salt, and pepper. Rub mixture over both sides of chicken; set aside. In a large frying pan, combine lime juice and garlic; simmer for 2 minutes. Remove garlic from frying pan and discard.

Add chicken to the pan and fry, covered, over medium heat, turning once, for about 10 minutes or until fork can be inserted easily.

Place Island Beans and Peppers on a serving dish, arrange the chicken on top, and sprinkle with lime peel. Garnish with cilantro sprigs and lime slices.   Makes 6 servings.

ISLAND BEANS AND PEPPERS:
In a large frying pan, combine 1 red bell pepper (cut in thin strips), 1/2 cup chopped green pepper, 3 tablespoons chopped onion, 1 teaspoon chopped cilantro, 1 tablespoon vegetable oil, 2 tablespoons lime juice, 1/8 teaspoon salt, and 1/8 teaspoon pepper. Cook, stirring, over medium low heat, 3 minutes. Stir in 2 cans (15 ounces each) rinsed and drained black beans. Cook over low heat, stirring, about 3 minutes, or until beans are hot.

Per Serving (approx):
Calories 376   *Protein 31 gm*   *Fat 11 gm*
Carbohydrate 39 gm   *Sodium 592 mg*   *Cholesterol 66 mg*

Chicken with Melon

4 skinless, boneless chicken breasts
1 teaspoon salt
1/2 teaspoon pepper
1/4 honeydew melon
1/4 cantaloupe
2 tablespoons vegetable oil
3/4 cup sake or Riesling

1/4 cup chicken broth
1 teaspoon grated ginger
2 teaspoons cornstarch
1/4 cup rice wine vinegar
1 tablespoon honey
1 tablespoon butter
1 tablespoon chopped parsley

Cut each chicken breast in half and slightly flatten with hand. Sprinkle with salt and pepper. Peel melons and slice into thin strips (or cut into melon balls). Heat the oil in a large frying pan. Add chicken and sauté about 5 minutes on each side until golden brown. Add sake (or wine), chicken broth, and ginger; simmer for several minutes. Dissolve cornstarch in rice wine vinegar. Remove chicken to serving platter. To frying pan, add vinegar mixture, honey, and melon, stirring gently. Add butter and parsley and dribble sauce over chicken.   Makes 8 servings.

Per Serving (approx):
Calories 253   *Protein 31 gm*   *Fat 9 gm*
Carbohydrate 7 gm   *Sodium 384 mg*   *Cholesterol 87 mg*

Vietnamese Tomato Chicken

1 1/4 pounds skinless,
    boneless chicken breast,
    cut into strips
2 green onions, cut into 1-inch
    pieces
1 can (8 ounces) bamboo shoots,
    drained and rinsed
1/2 teaspoon garlic salt

1/8 teaspoon pepper
2 tablespoons vegetable oil
1/2 cup Spanish style tomato
    sauce
1/2 cup water
1 1/2 tablespoons fish sauce
2 tablespoons sesame
    seeds, toasted and crushed

Combine chicken, green onion, bamboo shoots, garlic salt, and pepper. Cover and refrigerate about 15 minutes. In frying pan, heat oil and add chicken mixture. Cook, stirring, for about 10 minutes until chicken is no longer pink. In a small bowl, combine tomato sauce, water, and fish sauce; pour over chicken. Bring to a boil, cover, and simmer about 10 minutes more. Sprinkle with crushed sesame seeds.   Makes 6 servings.

Per Serving (approx):
Calories 201   *Protein 25 gm*   *Fat 9 gm*
Carbohydrate 4 gm   *Sodium 473 mg*   *Cholesterol 65 mg*

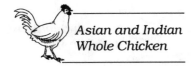
Vietnamese Lemon Grass Baked Chicken

Don't let the lemon grass in this recipe stop you. Most supermarket produce departments carry it these days.

1 whole chicken, cut up
2 stalks lemon grass, bottom 6 inches only, sliced diagonally
1/2 cup low-sodium soy sauce
2 tablespoons canola oil
1 tablespoon fish sauce

2 cloves garlic, minced
1 teaspoon sugar
2 unripe bananas, sliced in quarters
4 slices fresh pineapple, halved

Take the skin off the cut up chicken. In a small bowl, mix together lemon grass, soy sauce, oil, fish sauce, garlic, and sugar. In another bowl, place chicken and pour mixture over all. Cover and refrigerate at least 3 hours or overnight.

Preheat oven to 350 degrees.

In a baking dish, arrange chicken, undrained, in a single layer. Add banana and pineapple slices; pour remaining marinade over all. Cover and bake about 30 minutes. Remove cover and turn chicken. Return to oven and bake, uncovered, about 30 minutes more or until a fork pierces chicken easily.   Makes 4 servings.

Per Serving (approx):
Calories 1434
Carbohydrate 243gm

Protein 55 gm
Sodium 1395 mg

Fat 27 gm
Cholesterol 134 mg

Garlic Chicken and Grapes

12 chicken thighs
3 tablespoons Dijon mustard
3 tablespoons soy sauce
2 tablespoons white wine vinegar
2 tablespoons honey
2 garlic cloves, minced

1/16 teaspoon cayenne
1 tablespoon sesame seeds
2 cups red seedless grapes
1 cup hazelnuts, coarsely
   chopped and toasted
Parsley, for garnish

Preheat oven to 400 degrees.

Coat a large baking pan with vegetable spray. Place chicken in pan; cover with foil. Bake for 35 minutes. In a small bowl, mix together mustard, soy sauce, vinegar, honey, garlic, and cayenne. Remove chicken from oven and uncover; drain excess liquid, leaving about 2 tablespoons in the pan. Spoon mustard mixture over chicken and sprinkle with sesame seeds.

Return chicken to oven and bake, uncovered, for about 15 minutes or until a fork can be inserted in chicken easily, basting chicken with sauce halfway through cooking. Place grapes and hazelnuts around chicken and bake about 3 minutes or until grapes are heated through. To serve, place chicken and grapes on a platter and spoon sauce over both. Garnish with parsley.   Makes 6 servings.

Per Serving (approx):
Calories 433
Carbohydrate 16 gm

Protein 28 gm
Sodium 787 mg

Fat 28 gm
Cholesterol 90 mg

> "The true cook is the perfect blend, the only perfect blend, of artist and philosopher. He knows his worth: he holds in his palm the happiness of mankind, the welfare of generations yet unborn."
> Norman Douglas, "An Almanac"

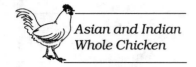
Roast Chicken Tandoori

As you probably don't have a mud and clay tandoori oven in your home or backyard, you'll have to make do with this recipe, using a conventional electric or gas range.

1 teaspoon salt	1 teaspoon paprika
Juice of 1 lemon	1/2 cup yogurt
2 garlic cloves, minced	1 whole chicken
2 tablespoons minced ginger	1 teaspoon pepper
1 teaspoon ground cumin	2 teaspoons salt
1 teaspoon ground cardamom seeds	1 tablespoon olive oil
2 teaspoons curry powder	1/2 cup lemon juice

Preheat oven to 400 degrees.

In a small bowl, combine first 9 ingredients. Set aside.

Remove giblets from chicken, wash them, and place in the bottom of a roasting pan. Rinse chicken thoroughly inside and out, and pat dry. Mix pepper and salt and rub into cavity. Run your fingers under skin of breast and legs, separating it gently from the meat underneath.

Distribute herb mixture as evenly as possible between skin and meat, then rub olive oil over skin of chicken.

Place chicken, breast down, on top of giblets and roast for 30 minutes, basting after 15 minutes with lemon juice.

Reduce heat to 375 degrees, turn chicken breast up, baste once more and roast 15 minutes longer, until the skin is golden brown and a thermometer inserted into thickest part of thigh registers between 170 and 175 degrees.

Let rest 10 minutes before carving. Discard the giblets.

Makes 4 to 6 servings.

Per Serving (approx):
Calories 570   *Protein 62 gm*   *Fat 34 gm*
Carbohydrate 5 gm   *Sodium 965 mg*   *Cholesterol 246 mg*

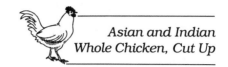

Almost Indian Chicken

2 tablespoons olive oil
1 whole chicken, cut up
1 1-inch piece ginger, cut in slivers
2 cloves garlic, crushed
1 onion, sliced thin
1 teaspoon ground cumin
1 teaspoon ground coriander

1 teaspoon dried parsley flakes
1/2 teaspoon curry powder
1/8 teaspoon pepper
3/4 cup yogurt
1/2 cup chicken broth, divided
1 1/2 tablespoons cornstarch
2 teaspoons soy sauce

In a frying pan, heat oil. Add chicken, ginger, garlic, and onion. Sauté about 10 minutes, or until chicken is brown on all sides and onion is translucent. Drain oil from pan.

Combine cumin, coriander, parsley flakes, curry powder, pepper, yogurt, and 1/4 cup of the chicken broth in a small bowl or cup. Pour mixture over chicken in the frying pan and simmer, covered, about 40 minutes, or until done. Remove chicken to a serving dish.

In a small bowl, combine cornstarch, soy sauce, and remaining 1/4 cup chicken broth. Add to frying pan and cook, stirring, about 2 minutes or until thickened. Pour sauce over chicken. Makes 4 servings.

Per Serving (approx):
Calories 577
Carbohydrate 9 gm

Protein 55 gm
Sodium 532 mg

Fat 36 gm
Cholesterol 215 mg

Curried Chicken with Apricots

The dried fruit, reconstituted by orange juice and milk, are bursting with flavor in this delightful dish.

3/4 cup dried apricots, cut in half
1/4 cup raisins
1 cup orange juice
1 tablespoon butter
2 tablespoons minced onion
1 clove garlic, minced
1 1/2 teaspoons curry powder

1/2 teaspoon cinnamon
1/2 teaspoon chili powder
1/2 teaspoon salt
1/4 teaspoon ground ginger
1 bay leaf, broken
6 chicken breast halves, skinned
1/4 cup skim milk

Preheat oven to 350 degrees.

In a small bowl, combine apricots and raisins with orange juice and let sit 15 minutes, stirring occasionally. In a small dish, combine butter, onion, garlic, curry powder, cinnamon, chili powder, salt, ginger, and bay leaf; mix well.

In a greased shallow baking dish, arrange chicken in a single layer. Spread spice mixture evenly over chicken. Drain the apricots and raisins and arrange in dish with chicken. Save the orange juice. To the orange juice, add skim milk; pour over chicken. Cover and bake about 1 hour. Remove the cover after 45 minutes and cook uncovered for the final 15 minutes.

Makes 6 servings.

Per Serving (approx):
Calories 287
Carbohydrate 29 gm

Protein 30 gm
Sodium 295 mg

Fat 6 gm
Cholesterol 77 mg

ITALIAN &
MEDITERRANEAN

Easy Antipasto Chicken

4 chicken quarters
1/2 cup Italian dressing, divided
4 slices tomato
4 onion rings
4 green bell pepper rings

4 mushrooms
1/2 teaspoon salt
1/2 teaspoon pepper
2 tablespoons grated Parmesan
 cheese

Preheat oven to 350 degrees.

In a 9 x 13 pan, arrange chicken quarters. Pour half of the Italian dressing evenly over chicken. On each piece of chicken, place one slice tomato, one onion ring and one ring of bell pepper.

Place mushrooms, cap side down, in bottom of pan around chicken. Pour remaining dressing over chicken and vegetables. Sprinkle with salt, pepper, and cheese.

Bake 30 minutes and baste with pan juices; continue cooking about 30 minutes more, until done. To serve, place the mushrooms on top of the bell pepper rings.   Makes 4 servings.

Per Serving (approx):
Calories 804
Carbohydrate 32 gm

Protein 64 gm
Sodium 800 mg

Fat 47 gm
Cholesterol 209 mg

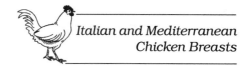

Chicken in Tomato Mushroom Sauce

4 skinless, boneless chicken
   breasts
1/3 cup flour, divided
1 teaspoon salt
1/2 teaspoon pepper
1/4 cup olive oil
5 white onions, minced

1 clove garlic, chopped
1 cup sliced mushrooms
2 teaspoons minced parsley
1 can (16 ounces) tomatoes
1 cup dry white wine
1 tablespoon brandy
1 tablespoon tomato paste

Cut chicken breasts in half. Combine 1/4 cup of the flour, salt, and pepper and dust lightly over chicken. In a large frying pan, heat oil. Add chicken and sauté about 6 minutes until brown on all sides. Remove chicken and keep warm.

To pan, add onions, garlic, mushrooms, and parsley; sauté until onions are opaque, about 5 minutes. Add tomatoes, wine, brandy, tomato paste, and remaining 1 tablespoon flour. Stir and simmer on low heat about 15 minutes. Return chicken to pan, cover and cook until done, about 30 minutes.   Makes 6 servings.

Per Serving (approx):
Calories 453
Carbohydrate 27 gm

Protein 43 gm
Sodium 499 mg

Fat 16 gm
Cholesterol 107 mg

Chicken Pepperoncini

1 teaspoon salt
1/2 teaspoon pepper
1 cup flour
4 each chicken drumsticks,
   thighs, and breast halves
1/2 cup vegetable oil
1/2 cup dry white wine

3 lemons, 2 1/2 juiced
   and 1/2 thinly sliced
3/4 cup bottled pepper-
   oncini peppers, 1/3 cup
   liquid reserved
6 slices Swiss cheese, halved
3 tablespoons grated Romano
   cheese
Lemon slices, for garnish

Preheat oven to 350 degrees.

In a paper bag, combine salt, pepper, and flour. Add chicken and shake to coat.

In a large frying pan, heat oil. Add chicken and sauté until chicken is brown on all sides. Remove chicken and drain on paper towels. Arrange chicken in a large baking pan. Pour wine, lemon juice, and reserved pepperoncini liquid over the chicken.

Place 1 slice of Swiss cheese on each piece of chicken; arrange pepperoncini on top, and sprinkle evenly with Romano cheese. Cover the pan and bake for 45 minutes. Remove the cover and cook 15 minutes more until chicken is done.

To serve, place chicken on platter; spoon pan juices over all and garnish with lemon slices.   Makes 8 servings.

Per Serving (approx):
Calories 360	*Protein 23 gm*	*Fat 22 gm*
Carbohydrate 15 gm	*Sodium 376 mg*	*Cholesterol 65 mg*

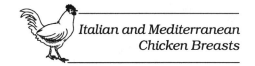

Italian Salsa Chicken

1 1/2 pounds skinless
  chicken breast, halved
1/2 cup reduced calorie Italian
  salad dressing, divided
2 tomatoes, seeded and
  chopped

2 tablespoons chopped green
  onions
1/4 cup chopped parsley
1 tablespoon chopped
  basil

Preheat broiler. In a rectangular baking pan coated with vegetable spray, place chicken breasts cut side up. Reserve 1/4 cup of the Italian salad dressing. Brush chicken with the other 1/4 cup of dressing. Broil 4 to 6 inches from heat for about 5 to 7 minutes on each side, brushing often with dressing, until chicken is no longer pink inside. In bowl with reserved Italian dressing, mix tomatoes, onions, parsley, and basil. Serve with chicken.   Makes 3 to 4 servings.

Per Serving (approx):
Calories 305
Carbohydrate 9 gm

Protein 43 gm
Sodium 262 mg

Fat 11 gm
Cholesterol 123 mg

Chicken Veronique

1 pound skinless, boneless
  chicken breast
1 lemon wedge
Pepper to taste
1 tablespoon unsalted margarine

1 1/2 teaspoons cornstarch
1/2 cup low-sodium chicken
  broth or bouillon
1/4 cup dry white wine
1 cup halved seedless green
  grapes

Rub chicken with lemon and sprinkle lightly with pepper. In a large skillet, melt the margarine. Add the chicken pieces so that they do not touch. Sauté 4 minutes, turning once, until chicken is lightly browned on both sides. Remove from skillet; keep warm.

In a small bowl, mix cornstarch, broth, and wine until smooth; add to the skillet and boil for 1 minute, stirring constantly. Stir in grapes and heat through.   Makes 3 to 4 servings.

Per Serving (approx):
Calories 201
Carbohydrate 5 gm

Protein 28 gm
Sodium 70 mg

Fat 6 gm
Cholesterol 77 mg

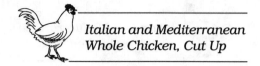

Chicken Tuscany

From Tuscany, in the heart of Italy, comes this peasant recipe for chicken cooked with mushrooms and potatoes.

6 red potatoes, scrubbed and
   sliced 1/8-inch thick
3/4 pound shiitake, chanterelle,
   or white mushrooms (or a mixture),
   sliced
1/4 cup olive oil, divided
1/4 cup grated Parmesan cheese,
   divided

1 tablespoon minced garlic,
   divided
1 tablespoon minced rose-
   mary or 1/2 teaspoon dried
   rosemary, divided
Salt and pepper to taste
1 whole chicken, cut up

Preheat oven to 425 degrees.

Pat potato slices dry with paper towels. In a large bowl, toss potatoes and mushrooms with 2 1/2 tablespoons of the olive oil, 2 tablespoons Parmesan, 2 teaspoons garlic, 2 teaspoons rosemary, 1/2 teaspoon salt, and 1/4 teaspoon pepper. In a 13 x 9 dish, arrange potatoes in one layer; top with remaining cheese. Bake for 15 minutes until potatoes are lightly browned.

Meanwhile, in a large skillet, heat remaining 1 1/2 tablespoons oil. Add chicken pieces; season lightly with salt and pepper and sprinkle with remaining rosemary and garlic. Cook 5 to 6 minutes on each side until browned; do not crowd pan. (If necessary, brown the chicken in two batches.)

Remove baking dish from oven. Arrange chicken on top of potato mixture; drizzle with any oil from skillet and return to oven. Bake 20 to 25 minutes longer, or until chicken is cooked through.   Makes 6 servings.

Per Serving (approx):
Calories 917
Carbohydrate 93 gm

Protein 58 gm
Sodium 236 mg

Fat 35 gm
Cholesterol 186 mg

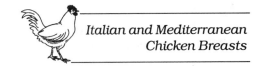

Chicken Parmesan

This dish is elegant, but easy-to-make. You'll have lots of the Italian sauce left over. Store in your refrigerator to use in other dishes.

6 boneless chicken breasts
2 eggs, beaten and seasoned
  with garlic powder, salt, and pepper
1/2 cup seasoned bread crumbs

2 tablespoons olive oil
1 pound mozzarella cheese,
  sliced very thin
Italian Sauce

Dip chicken breasts in the beaten eggs, then in bread crumbs to coat. Sauté in hot oil until firm. Arrange in a broiler pan that has been lined with greased foil. Top each breast with mozzarella cheese and 2 tablespoons of Italian sauce. Broil 3 inches from heat until cheese is melted. Serve with extra sauce.   Makes 6 servings.

ITALIAN SAUCE:
Sauté 1 medium chopped onion and 1/2 cup sliced mushrooms separately in 2 tablespoons oil each. Set aside. In a saucepan, combine 1 can (12 ounces) Italian tomatoes with basil, 1 can (6 ounces) tomato paste, 3/4 cup Burgundy, 2 cloves crushed garlic, 1 tablespoon oregano, 1 tablespoon fresh basil, 1 tablespoon sugar, and 3 tablespoons Parmesan cheese. Add mushrooms and onions, stir, simmer, and add salt and pepper to taste.

Per Serving (approx):
Calories 901
Carbohydrate 24 gm

Protein 78 gm
Sodium 724 mg

Fat 53 gm
Cholesterol 292 mg

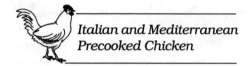

Chicken Cacciatore

This makes a very special dinner for two in less than 15 minutes.

1 tablespoon olive oil	1/2 cup dry white wine
1 onion, chopped	1/2 cup water
1 green bell pepper, chopped	1/2 pound oven-roasted
1 teaspoon dried Italian herb	chicken drumsticks or thighs
seasoning	Salt and pepper to taste
1 can (8 ounces) stewed or whole	1/2 pound ziti pasta, cooked
tomatoes, undrained	and drained

In a skillet heat oil and add onion, bell pepper, and Italian seasoning; sauté 3 to 4 minutes until vegetables are tender-crisp. Add tomatoes and their liquid, wine, and water; cook 3 minutes longer, stirring to break up tomatoes.

Add chicken; continue cooking 3 to 5 minutes until chicken is heated through. Season with salt and pepper to taste.

This is very good served hot over ziti.   Makes 2 servings.

Per Serving (approx):
Calories 516   *Protein 15 gm*   *Fat 9 gm*
Carbohydrate 83 gm   *Sodium 302 mg*   *Cholesterol 0 mg*

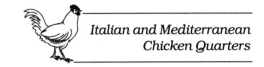
Italian Chicken with Salsa

4 chicken quarters, skinned
1 cup zesty Italian dressing
1 cup garlic and onion croutons
1 tablespoon olive oil

Italian Salsa
1/2 cup grated Parmesan cheese
Tomato wedges, for garnish

Preheat oven to 400 degrees.

Place the chicken in a large zip-lock bag. Pour dressing over it. Seal bag and marinate in the refrigerator for 15 minutes. Remove chicken from the marinade and drain. Discard the marinade. Crush croutons to fine crumbs; place on a flat dish. Add chicken one piece at a time, dredging it carefully. In a large rectangular glass baking dish coated with olive oil, place chicken and bake for 25 minutes. Prepare Italian Salsa.

Remove chicken from oven and spoon salsa over it. Return to oven and bake about 15 minutes longer until vegetables are tender-crisp.

To serve, spoon salsa on and around the chicken. Sprinkle with cheese and garnish with tomato wedges.   Makes 4 servings.

ITALIAN SALSA:
In a bowl, combine 2 Roma tomatoes, 1 small zucchini, chopped, 1 cup sliced mushrooms, 1 cup chopped onion, 1 1/2 teaspoons dried oregano, 1 teaspoon dried basil, and 1 teaspoon garlic powder. Let stand for 1/2 hour before using to let the flavors mingle.

Per Serving (approx):
Calories 1044
Carbohydrate 32 gm

Protein 70 gm
Sodium 1129 mg

Fat 71 gm
Cholesterol 217 mg

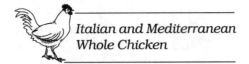

Roast Chicken Florentine

The concept of serving roast chicken on a bed of spinach, with a garlicky sauce, comes from Florence, Italy.

1 whole chicken
Salt and pepper to taste
1/3 cup olive oil, divided
3 sprigs rosemary, divided,
   or 1 tablespoon dried rosemary

2 lemons, divided
10 garlic cloves, unpeeled
2 bags (10 ounces each)
   spinach, stemmed,
   rinsed and dried

Preheat oven to 350 degrees.

Remove giblets from chicken. Season cavity with salt and pepper to taste, 1 tablespoon oil, and 1 sprig (or 1/3 tablespoon dried) rosemary. Squeeze in juice of half a lemon; add the lemon half to the cavity. Truss chicken and place in a roasting pan. Squeeze juice from remaining 1 1/2 lemons over chicken; season with salt and pepper, and drizzle with 1 tablespoon olive oil. Add garlic and remaining rosemary to pan.

Roast in oven for 1 to 1 1/4 hours until chicken registers 180 degrees on a meat thermometer inserted in the thickest part of thigh, and juices run clear. Baste occasionally with pan juices.

Remove chicken to a serving platter and keep warm. Strain pan juices and extract garlic pulp by pressing cloves (which you had placed in the roasting pan) against a strainer. Add the garlic pulp to the pan juices. Skim fat from pan juices; whisk remaining oil into juices.

To serve, arrange the raw spinach on a platter. Carve chicken into serving pieces. Place chicken on spinach and drizzle with warm garlic sauce from roasting pan.   Makes 4 to 5 servings.

Per Serving (approx):

Calories 646	*Protein 59 gm*	*Fat 42 gm*
Carbohydrate 8 gm	*Sodium 253 mg*	*Cholesterol 219 mg*

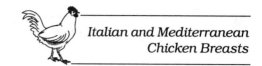

Chicken and Dried Tomatoes

1/4 pound dried tomato halves
Warm water to cover
1 1/2 tablespoons butter
4 skinless, boneless chicken breast
   halves, each cut in 6 pieces
1 large green onion, diced,
   or 2 tablespoons minced onion

1 tablespoon Dijon mustard
2/3 cup whipping cream
2 tablespoons dry vermouth
   or white wine
1 to 2 tablespoons dried tarragon

Soak tomato halves in warm water to soften and cut into narrow strips. In a skillet melt butter; add chicken pieces and sauté 4 to 5 minutes. Remove chicken to a platter. Add green onion and sauté for 1 minute. Add remaining ingredients to skillet. Simmer and stir until sauce thickens slightly. Return chicken to skillet and simmer until heated through.

Makes 4 to 6 servings.

Per Serving (approx):
Calories 306
Carbohydrate 12 gm

Protein 22 gm
Sodium 170 mg

Fat 16 gm
Cholesterol 98 mg

Fontina Mushroom Chicken

1/4 cup olive oil
3 tablespoons balsamic vinegar
4 boneless chicken breast halves
Salt and pepper to taste
3 tablespoons minced tarragon
1 teaspoon lemon pepper

3 tablespoons minced parsley
1 pound mushrooms, chopped
1 cup chopped onion
1/2 pound Fontina cheese,
   thinly sliced

Preheat oven to 350 degrees. In a large frying pan, heat oil and vinegar. Add chicken and cook about 6 minutes or until the chicken is brown and tender. Remove chicken to ungreased ovenproof dish; sprinkle with salt and pepper. To the same frying pan, add tarragon, lemon pepper, parsley, mushrooms, and onion. Cook, stirring frequently to loosen brown bits from bottom of frying pan, about 3 minutes or until the onion and mushrooms are tender. Spoon mushroom mixture over chicken and place cheese on top to cover completely. Place in oven for about 2 minutes or until cheese melts.

Makes 4 servings.

Per Serving (approx):
Calories 732
Carbohydrate 12 gm

Protein 71 gm
Sodium 1127 mg

Fat 44 gm
Cholesterol 208 mg

Chicken Saltimbocca

Literally translated, saltimbocca means "jumps into the mouth." Named after the famous veal dish, this chicken version also cooks quickly and is eaten rapidly.

1 1/4 pounds skinless, boneless
    chicken breast, sliced into cutlets
Ground dried sage to taste
Salt and pepper to taste
5 to 6 slices ham
1 tablespoon olive oil

1/3 cup Marsala or Madeira
    wine
1 tablespoon butter
2 teaspoons minced parsley
Sage leaves, for garnish

Season chicken with ground sage, salt and pepper to taste. Top each cutlet with a slice of ham, pressing lightly so that it sticks to chicken, In a skillet heat the olive oil; place cutlets ham side down in the skillet.

Cook 2 minutes on each side or until cooked through and lightly browned. Remove to warm serving platter.

Add Marsala to the skillet; cook 2 minutes or until liquid is reduced to about one-third, stirring often. Whisk in butter. To serve, pour pan sauce over cutlets; sprinkle with parsley and garnish with fresh sage leaves.

Makes 4 servings.

Per Serving (approx):
Calories 278
Carbohydrate 3 gm

Protein 41 gm
Sodium 488 mg

Fat 7 gm
Cholesterol 119 mg

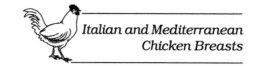

Mediterranean Chicken

1 teaspoon olive oil
2 1/2 pounds chicken breast halves
1 cup sliced mushrooms
1/2 cup chopped onion
15 ounces prepared marinara sauce

1 package (9 ounces) frozen
 artichoke hearts, thawed and
 drained
2 3/4 ounces sliced olives,
 drained
Fettuccine noodles
Grated Parmesan cheese

In a skillet, heat oil and brown chicken on all sides. Remove chicken. Drain all but 1 tablespoon of oil from the skillet. Add the mushrooms and onion and fry until they are tender. Stir in marinara sauce, artichokes, and olives. Return chicken to skillet.

Cover; cook about 25 minutes, stirring occasionally, until chicken is done. Serve chicken over cooked fettuccine; sprinkle with cheese.

Makes 3 to 4 servings.

Per Serving (approx):
Calories 656
Carbohydrate 27 gm

Protein 76 gm
Sodium 1151 mg

Fat 27 gm
Cholesterol 205 mg

Poultry Made a Pleasure and a Profit was considered scandalous and nearly banned because it advocated crossing two breeds of chickens for profit.

Chicken Breasts with Green Olive Sauce

1/2 cup flour
1 teaspoon salt
1 teaspoon pepper
1/8 teaspoon cayenne
4 skinless, boneless chicken breasts,
    pounded flat
1/2 stick of butter
4 tablespoons olive oil

1 cup fumé blanc
1 cup chopped onion
2/3 cup stuffed green olives,
    sliced
3/4 cup half-and-half
2 large cloves garlic, minced
10 halves sun-dried tomatoes
    in olive oil, drained

Mix flour, salt, pepper, and cayenne in a plastic bag. Add prepared chicken breasts and shake to coat well. Heat butter and olive oil in a skillet. Sauté chicken until golden brown on both sides.

Add wine, cover, and simmer for 1 minute. Remove chicken and keep it warm; add onions and olives to the skillet, and sauté until onions are translucent. Add half-and-half, garlic, and sundried tomatoes. Reduce sauce by half, stirring often.

Pour 3/4 of the sauce on a warm platter, top with chicken breasts, and pour remaining sauce over breasts.   Makes 4 servings.

Per Serving (approx):
Calories 563
Carbohydrate 26 gm

Protein 34 gm
Sodium 1271 mg

Fat 32 gm
Cholesterol 101 mg

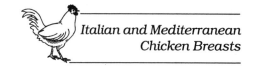
Chicken with Tomatoes and White Wine

2 tablespoons butter
2 tablespoons olive oil
5 skinless, boneless chicken
  breast halves, pounded flat
Salt and pepper to taste
1 tablespoon chopped rosemary
2 garlic cloves, crushed

2 tablespoons chopped green
  onion
1 can (14 ounces) plum Italian
  tomatoes
3/4 pound mushrooms,
  quartered
1/2 cup chicken broth
3/4 cup chardonnay

In a large skillet, heat butter and oil and brown flattened chicken breasts. Season with salt and pepper to taste and rosemary. Remove chicken from skillet and keep warm. In the same skillet, sauté garlic and green onion; add tomatoes and mushrooms and cook 5 minutes.

Add chicken broth and wine; cook sauce until it is reduced, about 10 minutes; return chicken to the skillet and let it absorb flavor for 3 minutes.   Makes 5 servings.

Per Serving (approx):
Calories 317
Carbohydrate 8 gm

Protein 32 gm
Sodium 275 mg

Fat 15 gm
Cholesterol 93 mg

> "If there is need for an elegant and groaning board, you have, in the chicken the most praiseworthy meat."
> Aldrovani, 16th century
> Italian scientist

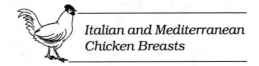
Chicken in Lemon Sauce

1/4 cup margarine
8 skinless, boneless chicken
   breast halves
2 tablespoons white wine
1/2 teaspoon grated lemon peel
2 tablespoons lemon juice
1/4 teaspoon salt

1/8 teaspoon white pepper
1 cup sliced mushrooms
1 cup light cream
1/3 cup grated Parmesan cheese
Lemon wedges, for garnish
Parsley, for garnish

In a skillet, heat the margarine and add the chicken. Sauté about 10 minutes until chicken is brown and tender. Remove the chicken to a baking dish. Discard the margarine. Add wine, lemon peel, and lemon juice to the skillet. Cook 1 minute; add salt and pepper. Add the mushrooms and cook for 1 minute. Pour in the cream, stirring constantly, and simmer.

Preheat broiler.

Pour sauce over chicken and sprinkle with Parmesan cheese. With chicken about 6 inches from heat, broil until lightly browned. Garnish with lemon wedges and parsley. Makes 8 servings.

Per Serving (approx):
Calories 299
Carbohydrate 2 gm

Protein 32 gm
Sodium 299 mg

Fat 18 gm
Cholesterol 110 mg

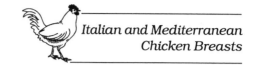
Chicken Ratatouille

This dish, from the Provence region of France, can be made and served in many different ways. The ingredients can be cooked together or separately; it can be served hot, cold, or at room temperature; and it works well as a main course or as an appetizer.

1/4 cup olive oil
2 skinless, boneless chicken breasts,
  cut into 1-inch pieces
2 small zucchini, thinly sliced
1 small eggplant, peeled and
  cut into 1-inch cubes
1 green bell pepper, cut into
  1-inch pieces

1 large onion, thinly sliced
1/2 pound mushrooms, sliced
1 can (16 ounces) tomato wedges
2 teaspoons garlic salt
1 teaspoon dried basil
1 teaspoon dried parsley
1/2 teaspoon pepper

In a large frying pan, heat oil. Add chicken and sauté, stirring, about 2 minutes. Add zucchini, eggplant, bell pepper, onion, and mushrooms. Cook, stirring occasionally, about 15 minutes or until they are tender. Add tomatoes, stirring gently. Add garlic salt, basil, parsley, and pepper.

Simmer, uncovered, about 5 minutes or until a fork pierces chicken easily. Serve the chicken on a large platter with a mound of rice in the center.
          Makes 4 servings.

Per Serving (approx):
Calories 389
Carbohydrate 22 gm

Protein 34 gm
Sodium 307 mg

Fat 18 gm
Cholesterol 80 mg

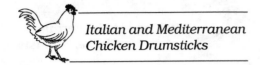

Spanish Chicken and Rice

1 1/2 pounds drumsticks
Salt and pepper to taste
1 tablespoon vegetable oil
1 onion, chopped
1 red bell pepper, cut into thin strips
2 cloves garlic, minced
1 cup long grain rice

1 can (14 1/2 ounces) diced
  tomatoes
1 1/2 teaspoons chili powder
8 pimento-stuffed olives, sliced
1 cup frozen peas
Salt and pepper to taste

Sprinkle the chicken with salt and pepper. In a skillet, heat oil and brown the chicken on all sides for about 10 minutes; remove. Add onion, bell pepper, and garlic to the skillet, and cook until tender, about 5 minutes; stir often.

Drain tomatoes; reserve juice. Add enough water to tomato juice to make 2 cups. Add rice, tomatoes, reserved tomato juice, chili powder, and olives to skillet; mix well. Return chicken to skillet.

Cover skillet tightly; simmer gently 25 to 35 minutes until chicken is no longer pink inside and liquid is absorbed. Stir in peas, let stand 5 minutes. Add salt and pepper to taste.   Makes 4 servings.

Per Serving (approx):
Calories 532   *Protein 39 gm*   *Fat 22 gm*
Carbohydrate 43 gm   *Sodium 492 mg*   *Cholesterol 118 mg*

"It is sheer foolhardiness to be arrogant
to a cook."
                    Agnes Reppelier,
                "Americans and Others"

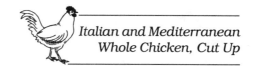
Spanish Chicken Stew

Spanish cuisine depends on the ingredients for flavor rather than on the seasonings. In Spain this dish is served in bowls with hard rolls to dip into the stew.

1/4 cup olive oil
1 whole chicken, cut up
1 teaspoon salt
1 teaspoon paprika
1/4 teaspoon pepper
2 onions, cut in wedges
1 red bell pepper, cut in large chunks

2 cups warm chicken broth
4 potatoes, cut in quarters
1/2 pound button mushrooms
1 can (15 1/2 ounces)
    garbanzo beans*
1 bay leaf

In Dutch oven, heat oil and add chicken. Sauté, turning, about 10 minutes until brown on all sides. Drain off oil and discard. Sprinkle chicken with salt, paprika, and pepper. Add onion and bell pepper to the pan.

Pour warm broth over all and bring to boil. Add potatoes, mushrooms, garbanzo beans, and bay leaf. Return to boil; reduce heat and simmer, uncovered, until the chicken and vegetables are tender, about 40 minutes. Remove bay leaf.   Makes 6 servings.

*Garbanzo beans are also know as chickpeas.

Per Serving (approx):
Calories 706
Carbohydrate 61 gm

Protein 47 gm
Sodium 1165 mg

Fat 30 gm
Cholesterol 140 mg

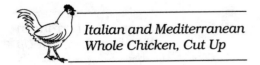

Spanish Olive Chicken

A very satisfactory one-dish meal that is about as authentically Spanish as they come.

3 tablespoons olive oil
1 whole chicken, cut up
1 teaspoon salt
1 teaspoon cinnamon
1/4 teaspoon pepper
3 tomatoes, cut in wedges

3 green bell peppers, cut in
  wedges
1/2 cup sliced black olives
1/2 cup white wine
3 tablespoons tomato paste
Parsley, for garnish

In a Dutch oven, heat olive oil. Add chicken and sauté it, turning, about 10 minutes until brown on all sides. Drain off oil and discard. Combine salt, cinnamon, and pepper; sprinkle on all sides of chicken in pan. Add tomatoes, bell peppers, and olives; pour wine over all. Cover and simmer on low about 40 minutes or until a fork pierces the chicken easily.

Remove chicken to a warm serving bowl. Add tomato paste to the ingredients in the pan; boil, uncovered, about 1 minute more. Pour sauce over chicken, garnish with chopped parsley.   Makes 4 servings.

Per Serving (approx):
Calories 648
Carbohydrate 12 gm

Protein 54 gm
Sodium 918 mg

Fat 40 gm
Cholesterol 210 mg

Arroz Con Pollo

This is Spain's national dish. Coupled with turkey sausage, it's improved in our opinion.

2 1/3 pounds skinless chicken
    breasts, halved
2 teaspoons olive oil
4 links hot Italian turkey
    sausage (8 ounces), cut into
    1-inch chunks
1 onion, chopped
1 red bell pepper, chopped
1 garlic clove, minced
1 cup long-grain rice

1 teaspoon dried oregano
1/2 teaspoon paprika
1/8 teaspoon saffron threads
    (optional)
1 package (9 ounces) frozen
    artichoke hearts, thawed
1 1/3 cups reduced-sodium
    chicken broth
1/4 cup dry sherry
Salt and pepper to taste

With a heavy knife, cut each breast piece crosswise in half. In a Dutch oven, heat oil. Add chicken breasts, meat-side down, in batches; do not crowd. Cook about 3 minutes or until lightly browned. Remove breasts and set aside.

To the drippings in the Dutch oven, add sausage, onion, bell pepper, and garlic. Cook about 4 minutes or until onions are softened, stirring often. Add rice, oregano, paprika, and saffron; stir about 1 minute or until rice turns opaque. Add artichoke hearts, broth, sherry, and salt and pepper to taste; bring to a boil. Return the chicken breasts to the Dutch oven. Cover tightly; simmer about 30 minutes or until rice is tender and liquid almost absorbed. Let stand, covered, 5 minutes. Season with salt and pepper to taste and serve hot.   Makes 6 to 8 servings.

Per Serving (approx):
Calories 316
Carbohydrate 21 gm

Protein 38 gm
Sodium 229 mg

Fat 8 gm
Cholesterol 105 mg

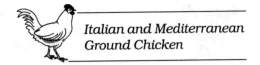

Moussaka

Moussaka, a traditional Greek dish, is usually made with lamb or beef. We like the chicken better because it is lighter. See for yourself.

1 eggplant (1 1/4 pounds)
6 tablespoons olive oil
1 pound ground chicken
1/2 pound mushrooms, sliced
1 teaspoon cinnamon

1 teaspoon dried oregano
1 teaspoon garlic salt
Bechamel Sauce
2 tablespoons grated Parmesan
  cheese

Preheat broiler.

Slice eggplant crosswise into 1/2-inch-thick slices. In a baking pan, arrange slices in single layer. Brush with half the olive oil. Broil about 2 inches from heat for 4 to 5 minutes or until lightly browned. Turn slices, brushing again with the rest of the oil, and broil 5 to 10 minutes or until soft and tender.

While eggplant is broiling, sauté chicken with mushrooms until it is uniformly light brown. Stir in cinnamon, oregano, and garlic salt.

Change oven temperature to 350 degrees. Prepare Bechamel Sauce.

Oil a 2-quart baking dish and fill with half the eggplant slices. Top with chicken mixture, then remaining eggplant. Spread Bechamel Sauce on top and sprinkle with cheese. Bake for 30 minutes or until hot in center.
Makes 4 servings.

BECHAMEL SAUCE:
Mix 1 can (10 ounces) white sauce with 1/4 cup grated Parmesan cheese and 1 egg yolk, beating with wire whisk until smooth.

Per Serving (approx):
Calories 562
Carbohydrate 19 gm

Protein 22 gm
Sodium 485 mg

Fat 44 gm
Cholesterol 156 mg

Greek Baked
Lemon Oregano Chicken

This recipe captures all the flavor and ease of preparation of Mediterranean cooking.

1 lemon
4 chicken quarters
1 teaspoon dried oregano
1/2 teaspoon salt
1/4 teaspoon pepper
1 tablespoon olive oil

1 tablespoon butter-flavored
    light margarine
1/2 cup sliced celery
6 small new potatoes, halved
1/2 cup warm water

Preheat oven to 300 degrees.

Grate the peel of the lemon. Set the peel aside. Slice the lemon in half; squeeze its juice and reserve it in a cup. Rub all sides of chicken with the lemon from which you have squeezed the juice. Combine oregano, salt, and pepper; sprinkle over chicken.

In a skillet, heat olive oil and margarine and add chicken, skin side down. Sprinkle celery and reserved lemon peel evenly over the chicken. Fry for about 5 minutes, turn the chicken, and cook 5 minutes more until brown on all sides. Put the skillet in reserve.

Arrange the chicken in a lightly greased 2-quart baking dish. With a slotted spoon, remove the celery mixture from pan and arrange around chicken. Add potatoes around chicken.

Add the reserved lemon juice and water to the skillet, stirring and scraping up pan drippings. Bring to a boil and pour over the chicken and potatoes. Bake uncovered, basting occasionally with pan juices, for about 1 hour 15 minutes.   Makes 4 servings.

Per Serving (approx):
Calories 572
Carbohydrate 20 gm

Protein 55 gm
Sodium 468 mg

Fat 30 gm
Cholesterol 210 mg

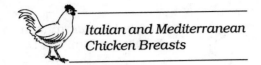

Pruned Chicken

1 head garlic, cloves peeled and minced	1/3 cup olive oil
2 tablespoons dried oregano	1/2 teaspoon salt
1 cup chopped pitted prunes	1/4 teaspoon pepper
1 cup Spanish olives	8 boneless chicken breasts, cut into large cubes
3/4 cup capers and juice	1 cup brown sugar
2 bay leaves	1 cup white wine
1/2 cup red wine vinegar	1/2 cup chopped parsley

Make marinade by combining garlic, oregano, prunes, olives, capers and juice, bay leaves, vinegar, olive oil, salt, and pepper. Pour over chicken and marinate, covered, in the refrigerator overnight.

Preheat oven to 350 degrees.

Arrange chicken in a shallow baking pan, spoon marinade over chicken and sprinkle with brown sugar. Pour wine around the chicken. Bake 50 minutes, basting the chicken frequently with pan juices. Sprinkle with parsley and serve.   Makes 10 servings.

Per Serving (approx):
Calories 501   *Protein 46 gm*   *Fat 22 gm*
Carbohydrate 24 gm   *Sodium 699 mg*   *Cholesterol 127 mg*

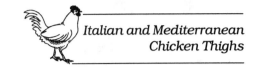

Grecian Chicken Pilaf

These ingredients suggest a whole new group of flavors for cooking chicken.

3 tablespoons tomato paste
1/4 cup red wine
8 skinless chicken thighs
1/2 teaspoon salt
1/4 teaspoon pepper
1 tablespoon olive oil
1 tablespoon butter-flavored
  margarine
1 large onion, minced

1 clove garlic, minced
1/2 teaspoon ground cinnamon
1/4 teaspoon ground allspice
2 cups warm low-sodium
  chicken broth
6 whole cloves
1 cup rice
1/2 cup nonfat yogurt

In a small bowl, dissolve tomato paste in wine. Sprinkle chicken with salt and pepper. In a Dutch oven, heat olive oil and margarine. Add chicken and cook about 7 minutes until brown on all sides. Remove chicken to platter.

Add onion and garlic to pan; cook about 5 minutes until tender and translucent. Add cinnamon and allspice. Stir tomato paste mixture into pan; add broth, stirring until smooth. Return chicken to pan in a single layer; add cloves, cover, and simmer on low about 15 minutes.

Stir in rice, submerging completely in liquid. Cover, cook about 15 minutes, and stir. Cook about 10 minutes more until rice is done and fork pierces chicken easily. Remove cloves. To serve, place 1 tablespoon yogurt on each piece of chicken.   Makes 4 servings.

Per Serving (approx):
Calories 518
Carbohydrate 51 gm

Protein 33 gm
Sodium 452 mg

Fat 19 gm
Cholesterol 99 mg

Athenian Chicken

1 tablespoon chili powder
Juice of 1/2 lime
3 skinless, boneless chicken
   breasts, cut lengthwise
   in 1/2-inch strips
2 cups cooked brown rice
1 large tomato, cut in 1/4-inch slices

1/4 cup stuffed green olives,
   halved
1/2 pound feta cheese,
   grated
10 round Ritz crackers,
   crumbled

Preheat oven to 350 degrees.

In a bowl, mix chili powder and lime juice. Add chicken and stir it to coat. Refrigerate until ready to use. Spray a 9 x 13 casserole dish with vegetable spray. Place rice in dish and level it. Arrange tomato slices on rice. Sprinkle olive halves evenly over tomato and rice.

Arrange chicken strips lengthwise on top. Sprinkle feta cheese over chicken and top with cracker crumbs. Cover with foil and bake about 45 minutes until tender.   Makes 8 servings.

Per Serving (approx):
Calories 278
Carbohydrate 17 gm

Protein 28 gm
Sodium 518 mg

Fat 11 gm
Cholesterol 85 mg

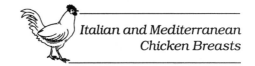

Chicken à la Nancy

This is a recipe that is ideal for entertaining, yet takes only fifteen or twenty minutes to prepare.

1 1/4 pounds skinless,
   boneless chicken breasts
1/4 cup vegetable oil
1/2 pound mushrooms, sliced
1/2 lemon, sliced thin
1 garlic clove, crushed
1 tablespoon flour

1 can (14 ounces) artichoke
   hearts, drained and
   quartered
1/2 cup dry white wine
Salt and pepper to taste
1/2 teaspoon dried oregano

Pound chicken breasts to 1/4-inch thickness. Cut into 2-inch squares.

In a skillet, heat oil. Add mushrooms, lemon, and garlic. Sauté 1 to 2 minutes until golden. Blend flour into pan juices. Stir in chicken, artichokes, wine, flour, salt, pepper, and oregano. Cook 10 to 12 minutes until chicken is tender, stirring frequently.   Makes 4 servings.

Per Serving (approx):
Calories 406
Carbohydrate 16 gm

Protein 40 gm
Sodium 386 mg

Fat 18 gm
Cholesterol 97 mg

"There is no spectacle on earth more appealing than a beautiful woman in the act of cooking dinner for someone she loves."
Thomas Wolfe, *The Web and the Rock*

North African Chicken and Saffron Rice

In Tangiers they use goat milk, but cow milk works just as well.

4 skinless, boneless chicken
  breast halves
2 tablespoons lime juice, divided
1/2 teaspoon salt, divided
1/4 teaspoon pepper
2 tablespoons olive oil
2 onions, sliced
1 tablespoon crushed cumin seed
  in 2 tablespoons water

4 small tomatoes, quartered
1/2 cup minced green bell
  pepper
1 tablespoon grated ginger
1 teaspoon curry powder
1 package (5 ounces) long-grain
  saffron rice
1/2 teaspoon dried mint
1/4 cup skim milk

Preheat oven to 325 degrees.

Sprinkle chicken with 1 tablespoon lime juice, 1/4 teaspoon salt, and pepper; set aside.

In a skillet, heat olive oil. Add onions, stirring and cooking until translucent, about 5 minutes; remove from pan and keep warm. Place chicken in frying pan and cook about 3 minutes on each side or until opaque; remove and keep warm. To frying pan, add cumin seed in water, tomatoes, bell pepper, ginger, curry powder, remaining 1 tablespoon lime juice and remaining salt. Cook about 5 minutes; add chicken. Cook, uncovered, about 10 minutes more. Cook rice according to package directions, using no fat and shortest cooking time.

Arrange chicken in 2-quart baking dish. Top with half the saffron rice, onions, and half of sauce in frying pan. Sprinkle with mint. Add remaining rice and sauce; pour milk over all. Cover and bake about 30 minutes or until chicken is tender and most of liquid is absorbed.

Makes 4 servings.

Per Serving (approx):
Calories 459
Carbohydrate 52 gm

Protein 35 gm
Sodium 386 mg

Fat 12 gm
Cholesterol 81 mg

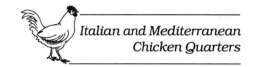
Chicken Couscous

Lime Sauce
4 skinless chicken drumsticks
4 skinless chicken thighs
2 tablespoons olive oil
1 onion, chopped
5 cloves garlic, minced
3 cups low-sodium chicken
  broth

2 tablespoons lime juice
3 carrots, sliced
2 ribs celery, sliced
1 can (15 ounces) garbanzo
  beans, drained well
1 can (14 ounces) artichoke
  hearts, drained
Raisin Couscous

Prepare Lime Sauce. Spread it over chicken pieces and set aside for about 15 minutes. In a Dutch oven, heat oil. Drain the chicken; reserve the sauce. Add chicken and sauté about 5 minutes. Turn chicken; add onion and garlic, stirring as chicken continues to brown, about 5 minutes. Pour chicken broth and reserved lime juice over chicken; stir to loosen pan drippings. Add carrots.

Cover and simmer until chicken is tender, about 20 minutes. Add celery and boil. Stir in beans and gently place artichoke hearts across top. Cover, reduce heat to low and simmer 5 minutes more. With a slotted spoon, remove chicken and vegetables to a warm serving bowl. Skim off any fat in pan, boil juices about 5 minutes and pour into a gravy boat. To serve, mound Raisin Couscous in a wide serving bowl, top with chicken and vegetables, and pour juices over all.   Makes 4 servings.

LIME SAUCE:
In a cup, mix together 1 tablespoon lime juice, 1 teaspoon coriander and 1/2 teaspoon each of cinnamon, ginger, turmeric, and pepper.

RAISIN COUSCOUS:
In a saucepan, combine 1 3/4 cups chicken broth, 1/3 cup raisins, 2 tablespoons butter, 1/4 teaspoon cinnamon, and 1/4 teaspoon nutmeg. Boil 2 minutes over high heat. Stir in 1 cup couscous, cover, and remove from heat. Let stand 5 minutes, fluff with fork, and serve immediately.

Per Serving (approx):
Calories 990
Carbohydrate 144gm

Protein 62 gm
Sodium 1553 mg

Fat 29 gm
Cholesterol 144 mg

Moroccan Chicken Breasts

The diet-conscious will find a squeeze of lemon a very satisfying substitute for the mayonnaise sauce.

3 skinless, boneless chicken breasts,
   cut in half
1 clove garlic (about 1 teaspoon)
2 tablespoons Italian (flat leaf)
   parsley
2 tablespoons cilantro
1 teaspoon salt

3 teaspoons ground cumin
3 teaspoons sweet paprika
1/2 teaspoon cayenne
4 tablespoons lemon juice
4 tablespoons olive oil
1 cup mayonnaise
Cilantro sprigs, for garnish

Arrange chicken in glass or ceramic dish. In a food processor fitted with steel blade, mince garlic. Add remaining herbs and spices and process. Add lemon juice and olive oil and puree. Spread half of the spice mixture over all surfaces of chicken. Cover and marinate, refrigerated, 2 to 12 hours. Refrigerate balance of spice mixture.

Preheat grill or broiler. Grill or broil chicken about 3 minutes per side. Mix reserved spice mixture with mayonnaise to make a sauce, to be served on the side.

Serve each piece of chicken with a dollop of sauce, garnished with cilantro sprigs. This dish is equally good served hot or at room temperature.

Makes 4 to 6 servings.

Per Serving (approx):
Calories 521
Carbohydrate 2 gm

Protein 30 gm
Sodium 675 mg

Fat 44 gm
Cholesterol 94 mg

CONTINENTAL

Parisian Chicken Stew

While most of us think of Paris as the center of elegant cuisine, there are many hearty, no-nonsense dishes in Paris, particularly in the small neighborhood restaurants. This recipe is from one such restaurant.

1 3/4 pounds skinless chicken thighs
Salt and pepper to taste
1/4 cup flour
1 teaspoon dried thyme
3 tablespoons canola oil
1 can (14 1/2 ounces) beef broth
1/4 cup white wine
2 tablespoons tomato paste

1 garlic clove, minced
1 pound small red potatoes, scrubbed and quartered
1 package (16 ounces) frozen baby carrots
1 package (10 ounces) frozen peas and onions
Thyme sprigs or chopped parsley, for garnish

Sprinkle chicken lightly with salt and pepper to taste. On a plate, combine flour and thyme. Coat thighs lightly with flour, reserving any excess.

In a Dutch oven, heat oil. Add chicken; cook 3 to 4 minutes on each side until browned. Remove and keep warm. Add reserved flour to pot; cook 3 to 4 minutes, until flour has deepened to a rich brown, stirring constantly.

With a wire whisk, stir in the broth, wine, tomato paste, and garlic. Return chicken to pot and add potatoes. Reduce heat, cover, and cook 15 to 20 minutes until potatoes are tender but not mushy. Stir in frozen vegetables; simmer 5 to 10 minutes longer, or until chicken is cooked through and vegetables are tender.

Garnish with thyme sprigs or chopped parsley.   Makes 3 to 4 servings.

Per Serving (approx):
Calories 673
Carbohydrate 55 gm

Protein 49 gm
Sodium 617 mg

Fat 27 gm
Cholesterol 142 mg

Chicken Daube au Cassis

This is a classic French dish in which chicken is slowly simmered in wine.

3 pounds skinless, boneless
  chicken thighs
1/3 cup flour
1 teaspoon salt
1/2 teaspoon pepper
2 to 3 tablespoons vegetable oil
2 tablespoons butter or margarine
1/2 cup chopped onion

1 1/2 cups dry red wine
1 can (14 ounces) beef broth
2 to 3 tablespoons crême
  de cassis or Madeira
1/4 cup currants
1 tablespoon tomato paste
1/2 teaspoon dried thyme

Cut chicken into 1-inch cubes. On a plate, combine flour with salt and pepper; dredge chicken in mixture, reserving excess. In a Dutch oven, heat 2 tablespoons oil. Sauté chicken 10 minutes until brown, adding more oil if necessary. With a slotted spoon, remove chicken and set aside.

Add butter, onion, and reserved flour to the Dutch oven. Reduce heat and stir for 10 minutes until the mixture is brown. Add remaining ingredients except chicken and bring to boil, stirring up brown bits from pan.

Add chicken, simmer, partially covered, 30 to 40 minutes until chicken is tender and sauce has thickened. Season to taste with salt and pepper. (May be made 2 days in advance. Cover and reheat in 350 degree oven for 35 minutes.) Makes 12 servings.

Per Serving (approx):
Calories 244   *Protein 23 gm*   *Fat 14 gm*
Carbohydrate 7 gm   *Sodium 206 mg*   *Cholesterol 86 mg*

The French were the first to see the potential in raising chickens for profit. A manual, published in 1751 detailed the methods of raising chickens the year round.

Coq au Vin

This classic French dish has been modified to use prepared chicken broth and frozen vegetables.

1/4 cup vegetable oil, divided
3 1/2 pounds skinless whole
   chicken, cut up
1/2 pound mushrooms,
   quartered
1 onion, diced
2 carrots, diced
1/4 pound turkey ham, cubed
1/4 cup flour
2 cups dry red or white wine

2 cups reduced-sodium chicken
   broth
2 teaspoons no-salt-added
   tomato paste
1 teaspoon dried thyme
1 bay leaf
1 package (10 ounces) frozen
   pearl onions, thawed and
   drained
Salt and pepper to taste

In a large skillet, heat 2 tablespoons oil. Add chicken pieces; brown lightly on all sides. Remove chicken and set aside. To skillet, add mushrooms and sauté 1 to 2 minutes until golden. With a slotted spoon, remove mushrooms and set aside.

Add remaining 2 tablespoons oil to skillet and stir in onion, carrots, and ham. Sprinkle with flour; sauté, stirring often, 5 minutes until vegetables are soft and flour is a nutty brown color. Gradually stir in wine and broth. Add tomato paste, thyme, and bay leaf. Return chicken to pan and stir in pearl onions. Cover and simmer 40 minutes or until chicken is tender. Stir in reserved sautéed mushrooms and cook until heated through. Season with salt and pepper to taste; serve with crusty French bread.
Makes 6 servings.

Per Serving (approx):
Calories 522
Carbohydrate 18 gm

Protein 72 gm
Sodium 363 mg

Fat 18 gm
Cholesterol 191 mg

Braised Chicken "Coq au Vin" with Fresh Glazed Carrots and Tarragon

4 chicken legs, cut at joint
Salt and pepper to taste
2 tablespoons vegetable oil
2 tablespoon flour
4 cups dry red wine
1 cup minced onions
1/4 cup brandy
2 tablespoons tomato paste
2 teaspoons peppercorns, cracked

2 cloves
1 bay leaf
Nutmeg to taste
2 cups carrots, cut into
   3/4-inch pieces
1 tablespoon peanut oil
1 teaspoon sugar
1 tablespoon tarragon
Thyme sprigs, for garnish

Season chicken with salt and pepper. In a Dutch oven, heat oil. Add chicken, cook 4 to 5 minutes on each side or until well browned. Transfer to a plate. Pour off and discard all but 2 tablespoons of fat; stir in flour. Add wine, onions, brandy, tomato paste, peppercorns, cloves, and bay leaf. Mix well. Bring to a boil. Add chicken; cover and simmer 30 to 40 minutes or until chicken is done. Season to taste with salt and nutmeg.

Meanwhile, boil carrots in lightly salted water until tender. Drain; add peanut oil and sugar. Cook over medium heat until sugar melts and carrots are glazed, stirring constantly. Sprinkle with tarragon; stir gently.

Serve chicken and sauce on a bed of mashed potatoes. Arrange glazed carrots on top. Garnish with sprig of thyme.   Makes 4 servings.

Per Serving (approx):
Calories 567
Carbohydrate 20 gm

Protein 25 gm
Sodium 186 mg

Fat 22 gm
Cholesterol 78 mg

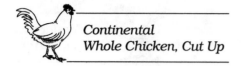

Chicken Pot-au-Feu

"Pot on fire" is the what the name means. The French make two courses of this one-pot dish, serving the liquid as a soup with croutons, and the meat and vegetables as a main course. You can use any vegetables that you like.

1/4 cup corn oil	3 sprigs parsley
1 whole chicken, cut up	1/2 teaspoon salt
1 quart water	2 small heads cabbage,
1 onion, halved	cut in wedges
2 carrots, sliced	1 package (10 ounces) frozen peas
2 ribs celery, sliced	1 tablespoon cornstarch
2 chicken bouillon cubes	1 tablespoon water

In a large Dutch oven, heat oil. Add chicken and cook, turning, about 10 minutes until brown on all sides. Add water, onion, carrots, celery, bouillon cubes, parsley, and salt. Cover and simmer about 30 minutes or until fork pierces chicken easily. Remove parsley. Add cabbage and peas. Cover and simmer about 15 minutes until vegetables are tender. Remove chicken and vegetables; keep warm.

In a small bowl, combine cornstarch and water, stirring until smooth. Add cornstarch mixture to juices in Dutch oven, stirring until slightly thickened. Return chicken and vegetables to Dutch oven until heated through.   Makes 4 servings.

Per Serving (approx):
Calories 891
Carbohydrate 62 gm

Protein 67 gm
Sodium 1577 mg

Fat 42 gm
Cholesterol 210 mg

> "I hope to make France so prosperous that every peasant will have a chicken in his pot on Sunday."
> Henry IV, King of France, 1553

Capon Flanders Style

The farm wives of Flanders, in France, put this on the stove when they go out in the fields, at harvest time. It's ready to serve in about two and a half hours.

1 capon or roasting chicken
   (6 to 7 pounds)
1 bottle sauterne or chablis
Boiling water to cover
1 tablespoon salt

1/8 teaspoon ground mace
2 tablespoons sugar
6 carrots, cut lengthwise in
  strips

Cut capon in pieces for serving. Place in a large kettle and add 2 1/2 cups of the wine and boiling water to cover. Add salt, mace, and sugar. Cover and simmer for 2 to 2 1/2 hours or until almost tender. Add carrots. Cook until carrots are tender.

Remove chicken and carrots to hot platter and keep warm. Make a gravy from stock, using butter and flour and 1/2 cup wine to flavor. Pour gravy over chicken and carrots. Makes 8 servings.

Per Serving (approx):
Calories 679
Carbohydrate 9 gm

Protein 69 gm
Sodium 371 mg

Fat 34 gm
Cholesterol 273 mg

Chicken Thighs Montmorency

Tart, fleshy Montmorency cherries give their name and taste to this very special way of preparing chicken.

1 3/4 pounds skinless chicken thighs
1 tablespoon vegetable oil
Salt and pepper to taste
1 jar (10 ounces) cherry preserves
1/4 cup orange juice

2 tablespoons Madeira or
   dry sherry
1 tablespoon grated orange peel
1/2 teaspoon dry mustard
1/2 teaspoon ground ginger

Preheat oven to 375 degrees.

Place thighs in shallow roasting pan; brush with oil, and sprinkle with salt and pepper to taste. Cover with foil and bake 30 minutes.

Meanwhile, in a bowl, combine preserves, orange juice, Madeira, orange peel, mustard, and ginger; mix well. Pour cherry mixture over thighs; cover loosely with foil.

Bake about 15 minutes or until chicken is cooked through and tender.

Makes 3 to 4 servings.

Per Serving (approx):
Calories 639   *Protein 43 gm*   *Fat 20 gm*
Carbohydrate 70 gm   *Sodium 143 mg*   *Cholesterol 142 mg*

Swiss Chicken Breasts

2 tablespoons olive oil
4 chicken breast halves
1 onion, chopped
2 garlic cloves, crushed
1 can (16 ounces) stewed
   tomatoes
1 cup dry white wine

2 teaspoons dried thyme
1/2 teaspoon salt
1/4 teaspoon pepper
1/2 pound mushrooms, sliced
1/4 cup chopped parsley
4 slices Swiss cheese

In a large skillet, heat oil. Add chicken, onion, and garlic; cook about 10 minutes or until chicken is brown on all sides. Remove chicken from pan and set aside.

To the same pan, add tomatoes, wine, and thyme. Remove skin from chicken and return chicken to pan. Add salt, pepper, mushrooms, and 1/2 of parsley. Cook about 20 minutes longer or until the chicken is tender. Place 1 slice of cheese on each breast half, sprinkle with remaining parsley, cover and simmer until cheese melts.   Makes 4 servings.

Per Serving (approx):
Calories 383
Carbohydrate 18 gm

Protein 32 gm
Sodium 663 mg

Fat 16 gm
Cholesterol 80 mg

127

Chicken Goulash

If you don't use the sour cream and sauerkraut, this is just chicken stew. If you use this recipe as it appears here, you have made real Hungarian goulash.

1 1/4 pounds boneless chicken thighs
2 tablespoons vegetable oil
3/4 cup chopped onions
4 teaspoons paprika
1 can (14 ounces) chicken broth
1 can (8 ounces) sauerkraut, drained

2 tablespoons tomato paste
1/4 teaspoon caraway seeds
Salt and pepper to taste
1/2 cup sour cream
Chopped parsley

Trim chicken and cut into 2-inch pieces. In a Dutch oven, heat oil. Add chicken in batches if necessary to avoid crowding; sauté 6 to 8 minutes until well browned on all sides. Remove chicken and set aside. Stir the onions into the pan; sauté about 2 minutes or until they are soft. Add paprika and stir well. Stir in broth, sauerkraut, tomato paste, caraway seeds, and salt and pepper.

Toss chicken with sauerkraut. Partially cover, reduce heat to very low, and simmer 40 to 50 minutes until the chicken is tender; stir the goulash occasionally. Just before serving, stir in sour cream; do not boil.

This is good over noodles sprinkled with parsley.

Makes 3 to 4 servings

Per Serving (approx) excluding salad:
Calories 391   *Protein 31 gm*   *Fat 26 gm*
Carbohydrate 10 gm   *Sodium 1092 mg*   *Cholesterol 113 mg*

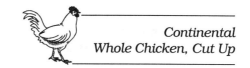

Hungarian Chicken

1 tablespoon peanut oil
1 cup yogurt (at room temperature)
1 whole chicken, cut up
1 cup chopped onion
1 teaspoon caraway seed

1 teaspoon garlic salt
1/2 teaspoon dried dill
1/2 teaspoon paprika
1/4 teaspoon pepper
1/2 cup white wine

Heat oil in a skillet. Place chicken in the pan and sauté about 10 minutes, until brown on all sides. Add onion and fry about 5 minutes more. Push chicken and onion aside and drain oil from pan. Discard the oil.

Arrange chicken in the skillet and sprinkle with caraway seed, garlic salt, dill, paprika, and pepper. Pour wine over all. Cover and simmer about 30 minutes or until chicken is tender. Stir yogurt into the pan and heat slowly, about 5 minutes. Serve over egg noodles. Makes 4 servings.

Per Serving (approx):
Calories 550
Carbohydrate 7 gm

Protein 55 gm
Sodium 205 mg

Fat 31 gm
Cholesterol 217 mg

Mushroom Chicken

1 whole chicken, cut up
  (2 1/2 pounds)
8 mushrooms, sliced
1 onion, minced
1 tablespoon paprika
1 clove garlic, minced
1 teaspoon dried marjoram
1/4 teaspoon salt

1/8 teaspoon pepper
3/4 cup white wine
1 teaspoon cornstarch
2 tablespoons water
2/3 cup low-fat yogurt
  (at room temperature)
1 tablespoon minced parsley

Remove skin from chicken. In a skillet, heat the oil and brown the chicken on all sides. Add mushrooms, onion, paprika, garlic, marjoram, salt, pepper, and wine. Simmer covered until chicken juices run clear when pierced with a sharp knife, about 35 minutes. Blend cornstarch with water; stir into skillet. Cook and stir until thickened, about 2 minutes. Stir yogurt with a fork until smooth. Blend into liquid in skillet. Cook over low heat until hot. Serve sprinkled with parsley. Makes 4 servings.

Per Serving (approx):
Calories 578
Carbohydrate 11 gm

Protein 61 gm
Sodium 347 mg

Fat 29 gm
Cholesterol 230 mg

Raspberry-Sauced Chicken Breast

3 skinless, boneless chicken
  breasts, halved
3 tablespoons butter
1 onion, coarsely chopped
2 cloves garlic, minced
2 tablespoons white wine vinegar
1/2 cup raspberry wine*

1/2 cup chicken broth
1/2 cup whipping cream
1 small tomato, peeled,
  seeded and chopped
1/2 pint raspberries
Salt and pepper to taste

Flatten chicken breasts to half original thickness. In a large skillet, heat the butter and brown chicken on both sides over moderate heat. Remove and set aside. Add onions and garlic to skillet and cook until tender, 8 to 10 minutes. Add vinegar and wine and bring to a boil, stirring constantly. Simmer, uncovered, to reduce liquid to about two tablespoons. Add chicken broth, cream, and tomato and whisk for a minute or two.

Return the chicken to pan and simmer until it is hot and sauce is reduced by half, 5 minutes or so. Remove chicken to a warm platter.

Add raspberries to sauce, swirling them around by shaking the skillet. Add salt and pepper to taste and pour over chicken breasts.

Makes 6 servings.

*Or white wine with 2 teaspoons raspberry preserves.

Per Serving (approx):
Calories 323
Carbohydrate 9 gm

Protein 31 gm
Sodium 262 mg

Fat 17 gm
Cholesterol 123 mg

Glazed Lemon Sherried Chicken

2 tablespoons butter
8 skinless, boneless chicken thighs
1 tablespoon lemon juice
1/2 cup dry sherry

1/4 cup chicken broth
1 tablespoon grated lemon peel
8 lemon slices, for garnish
Watercress, for garnish

In a frying pan, melt butter and add chicken. Sauté about 8 minutes until brown on all sides. Add lemon juice, 1/4 cup sherry, and chicken broth. Cover and simmer about 15 minutes or until chicken is done. Remove chicken to a serving platter and keep warm.

Add the remaining 1/4 cup sherry and lemon peel to the frying pan. Bring to boil, reduce heat and cook until the sauce coats back of a spoon. Drizzle sauce over chicken and garnish with lemon slices and water-cress.   Makes 4 servings.

Per Serving (approx):
Calories 302
Carbohydrate 2 gm

Protein 27 gm
Sodium 244 mg

Fat 17 gm
Cholesterol 114 mg

It is reliably predicted that the average American will eat more than 85 pounds of chicken a year by 2000. In 1995 the annual per capita consumption was 78 pounds.

*Continental
Chicken Thighs*

Spiced Chicken with Apricots

The recipe calls for dried apricots, but dried prunes, peaches, or apples will work well, too.

8 skinless chicken thighs
1/4 cup honey
1 onion, chopped
3 cloves garlic, minced

2 sticks cinnamon
Juice of 1 lemon
2 teaspoons ground turmeric
1/2 cup dried apricots,
    quartered

Preheat oven to 350 degrees. Arrange chicken thighs in Dutch oven. Pour honey over chicken; sprinkle with onion and minced garlic. Add cinnamon sticks, and sprinkle with lemon juice and turmeric. Top with apricot quarters. Cover and bake for about 2 hours or until fork can be inserted into chicken easily. Remove cinnamon sticks from chicken mixture and serve.   Makes 4 servings.

Per Serving (approx):
Calories 357
Carbohydrate 35 gm

Protein 28 gm
Sodium 96 mg

Fat 12 gm
Cholesterol 98 mg

Chicken and Onions

4 tablespoons canola oil, divided
6 boneless chicken thighs, cut
   into 3/4-inch cubes
2 onions, cut in half and sliced thin
1/2 cup Gamay Beaujolais

2 cans (12 ounces each) chopped
   tomatoes in juice
1 bay leaf
1 1/2 teaspoons saffron powder
Salt and pepper to taste
Italian (flat leaf) parsley, chopped

In a large skillet, heat 2 tablespoons of oil. Sauté chicken pieces until brown, then remove from pan and set aside. In the same pan, heat the remaining 2 tablespoons canola oil and fry the onions until softened and translucent. Add wine and reduce the liquid almost completely. Pour tomatoes into the pan, and add bay leaf and saffron. Simmer for 20 minutes. Add the chicken and simmer 5 more minutes. Remove the bay leaf. Season with salt and pepper and parsley.   Makes 6 servings.

Per Serving (approx):
Calories 275
Carbohydrate 13 gm

Protein 14 gm
Sodium 279 mg

Fat 17 gm
Cholesterol 45 mg

Flemish Drumsticks

3 tablespoons vegetable oil
2 to 2 1/4 pounds skinless
   chicken drumsticks
4 medium leeks
1/4 cup unsalted margarine
1 pound small red potatoes,
   thinly sliced

1/2 cup grated Parmesan cheese
1/2 teaspoon minced garlic
1/2 teaspoon dried thyme
Salt to taste
1/4 teaspoon pepper
1/2 cup dry white wine
1/2 cup chicken broth

In a Dutch oven, heat oil. Add drumsticks; sauté 15 minutes until brown, turning occasionally. Trim the root ends from leeks, cutting carefully so leeks hold together. Trim tops, leaving 2 inches of green; slit tops lengthwise 3 or 4 times to expose any sand. Rinse leeks well under cold water.

Preheat oven to 375 degrees.

Remove chicken from the Dutch oven and reserve; discard the oil. In the same Dutch oven, melt the margarine. Stir in the leeks, potatoes, cheese, garlic, thyme, salt to taste, and pepper; toss vegetables to coat well. Add wine and broth. Return drumsticks to the pot and arrange vegetables around them. Cover and bake 1 hour until drumsticks and potatoes are tender.   Makes 4 to 5 servings.

Per Serving (approx):
Calories 691   *Protein 44 gm*   *Fat 39 gm*
Carbohydrate 37 gm   *Sodium 482 mg*   *Cholesterol 133 mg*

"Bush Legs" is what chicken drumsticks are called in Russia. Why? Because the legislation permitting the export of chicken to Russia was passed during the Bush administration.

*Continental
Chicken Breasts*

Dilled Chicken

2 large skinless, boneless chicken
   breasts, halved
4 tablespoons vegetable oil, divided
1 cucumber, peeled and
   thinly sliced
1 cup sliced green onions

1/2 cup minced dill, divided
1/8 teaspoon salt
1 cup mushrooms, halved
1/8 teaspoon pepper
1/2 cup white wine
1 pint sour cream

Cut chicken breasts part way through and flatten. In a skillet, heat 1 tablespoon of oil. Add cucumber, scallions, and 1 tablespoon of dill. Cook, stirring, about 1 minute or until cucumber is translucent. Remove from pan and sprinkle with salt. In same frying pan, heat 1 tablespoon of oil over medium temperature. Add mushrooms and 1 tablespoon dill; stir and fry for 2 minutes and remove from pan.

In the same frying pan, heat remaining 2 tablespoons oil. Add chicken and cook about 6 minutes until chicken is brown on both sides. Add remaining dill, pepper, and wine. Simmer, turning occasionally, until a fork pierces the chicken easily. Remove chicken from pan and place on a serving platter. To pan drippings, add sour cream, cucumber mixture and mushrooms. Stir until heated through. Pour over chicken.

Makes 4 servings.

Per Serving (approx):
Calories 437
Carbohydrate 7 gm

Protein 32 gm
Sodium 174 mg

Fat 29 gm
Cholesterol 102 mg

CARIBBEAN & HAWAIIAN

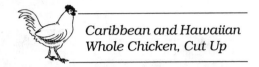

Hawaiian Chicken

The cuisine of Hawaii is a wonderful blend of native and foreign cultures.

3 tablespoons vegetable oil
1 whole chicken, cut up
3/4 cup chopped onion
2 garlic cloves, minced
3 tomatoes, peeled and chopped
3 cups fresh or canned
   pineapple chunks
1/4 cup pineapple juice

1 hot red pepper, seeded and
   chopped
3/4 teaspoon salt
1/4 teaspoon pepper
1 can (8 ounces) sliced water
   chestnuts, drained
1/2 pound snow peas
1 tablespoon chopped chives

In a skillet heat the oil and fry the chicken until it is brown on all sides. Remove the chicken to a platter. Set aside. Add onion and garlic to the skillet. Add tomatoes, pineapple, pineapple juice, hot pepper, salt, pepper, and water chestnuts. Return chicken to pan, cover, and simmer for 45 minutes. Add peas and chives; cover and simmer for 10 to 15 minutes until peas are tender and chicken juices run clear. Thicken the pan juices if desired with cornstarch and a bit of water.   Makes 6 servings.

Per Serving (approx):

Calories 330	*Protein 5 gm*	*Fat 8 gm*
Carbohydrate 60 gm	*Sodium 303 mg*	*Cholesterol 0 mg*

Luau Chicken

1 whole chicken, cut up
1/4 cup pineapple juice
1/4 cup dark corn syrup
1/4 cup chili sauce

2 tablespoons lime juice
2 cloves garlic, minced
2 tablespoons soy sauce
1 teaspoon grated ginger

In a zip-lock bag, mix remaining ingredients. Add chicken, seal the bag, and marinate for at least 8 hours, but no longer than 24 hours. Preheat oven to 350 degrees. Spray jelly roll pan with nonstick cooking spray. Place the chicken in the pan. Reserve the marinade. Roast chicken, brushing occasionally with marinade, for 50 to 60 minutes or until chicken is no longer pink inside.   Makes 4 servings.

Per Serving (approx):

Calories 761	*Protein 81 gm*	*Fat 40 gm*
Carbohydrate 20 gm	*Sodium 768 mg*	*Cholesterol 319 mg*

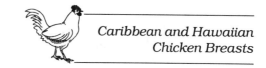

Chicken Waikiki

Hawaii claims credit for this recipe, which combines pineapple, nuts, and coconut with chicken.

3 1/2 cups pineapple juice
1 cup rice
1 cup crushed pineapple
1/2 cup bread crumbs
1/2 cup minced macadamia nuts

2 tablespoons shredded coconut
2 skinless, boneless chicken
 breasts, halved
1/4 cup honey
1/4 cup butter

In a large saucepan, boil pineapple juice, reduce heat, and stir in rice. Cover and simmer for 20 minutes. Turn off heat and add crushed pineapple.*

In a shallow dish, combine bread crumbs, nuts, and coconut; set aside. Brush both sides of chicken pieces with honey. Roll chicken in breadcrumb mixture, pressing mixture into the chicken to coat thoroughly.

Preheat oven to 350 degrees.

In a large frying pan, melt butter. Add chicken and cook about 3 minutes on each side or until brown. Spray a casserole dish with vegetable spray. Add rice mixture and arrange chicken on top. Cover and bake about 30 minutes or until fork pierces chicken easily.   Makes 4 servings.

*Rice may appear too moist, but moisture will be absorbed in baking.

Per Serving (approx):
Calories 777
Carbohydrate 95 gm

Protein 33 gm
Sodium 295 mg

Fat 29 gm
Cholesterol 112 mg

137

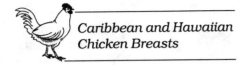

Polynesian Chicken

1/4 cup reduced-sodium soy sauce
2 tablespoons brown sugar
1 tablespoon lemon juice
2 teaspoons cornstarch
1/2 teaspoon ground ginger
1 clove garlic, minced
1 can (15 1/2 ounces) pineapple
   chunks

1 1/2 pounds chicken breasts,
   halved
2 tablespoons vegetable oil
3 green onions, cut in
   1-inch pieces
1 red bell pepper, cut in
   1-inch pieces

In a bowl, combine soy sauce, brown sugar, lemon juice, cornstarch, ginger, garlic, and 1/4 cup pineapple juice from the can. Add chicken; marinate at least 30 minutes. Drain; reserve marinade. In a large skillet, heat oil and add chicken. Cover and cook 7 to 10 minutes on each side. Add onions, bell pepper, pineapple chunks, and 1/2 cup reserved marinade. Cook 3 minutes more or until chicken is done.   Makes 4 servings.

Per Serving (approx):
Calories 427
Carbohydrate 25 gm

Protein 43 gm
Sodium 578 mg

Fat 18 gm
Cholesterol 115 mg

Chicken in Papaya Sauce

4 skinless, boneless chicken breast
   halves
2 papayas (2 cups)
1/2 cup orange juice

2 tablespoons Dijon mustard
1/4 cup lemon juice
1/2 teaspoon salt

Peel and remove seeds of papayas; reserve 1 teaspoon of seeds. Slice one papaya lengthwise in 1/2-inch slices; reserve. Dice remaining papaya and place in blender; add orange juice, mustard, and reserved papaya seeds. Blend until seeds are minced, about 1 minute. Spray a skillet with vegetable spray. Add chicken and cook, turning, about 10 minutes or until brown. Pour lemon juice over chicken and sprinkle with salt. Spoon blended papaya over chicken, reduce heat to low, cover and cook about 25 minutes, turning and spooning with sauce after 15 minutes. Add reserved papaya slices and cook 5 minutes more, covered. Turn off heat and let sit 5 minutes.   Makes 4 servings.

Per Serving (approx):
Calories 236
Carbohydrate 20 gm

Protein 30 gm
Sodium 552 mg

Fat 4 gm
Cholesterol 77 mg

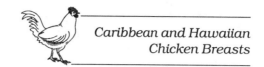
Zesty Orange-Banana Chicken

4 skinless, boneless chicken
  breast halves
1/2 teaspoon salt
1/4 teaspoon pepper
1 tablespoon butter
4 tablespoons orange juice
1/2 cup canned tomato sauce
3 green onions, chopped
2 garlic cloves, minced

1 teaspoon ground cumin
1 teaspoon dried oregano
1/2 teaspoon cayenne
1 firm, ripe banana, peeled
  and cut in 1-inch slices
1 orange, peeled, membrane
  removed, cut crosswise in 4
  slices
4 tablespoons yogurt
Cilantro sprigs, for garnish

Preheat oven to 350 degrees.

Sprinkle chicken with salt and pepper. Pound chicken to 1/4-inch thickness. Coat an 8-inch square baking pan with butter and arrange the chicken.

In a large bowl, combine orange juice, tomato sauce, onion, garlic, cumin, oregano, and cayenne. Pour over chicken. Add banana slices and bake, basting occasionally, for 15 minutes, or until fork can be inserted into chicken easily.

Remove to a serving platter and spoon sauce over chicken. Place 1 orange slice and 1 tablespoon yogurt on each breast half. Garnish with cilantro sprigs.   Makes 4 servings.

Per Serving (approx):
Calories 254
Carbohydrate 16 gm

Protein 31 gm
Sodium 580 mg

Fat 7 gm
Cholesterol 90 mg

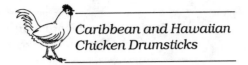

Chile-Stuffed Chicken Legs
with Bananas

4 green onions, cut in 1-inch pieces
1 can (4 ounces) chopped green
　 chile peppers
2 tablespoons lime juice, divided
1 tablespoon vegetable oil
2 tablespoons ketchup
1/4 teaspoon salt
6 chicken drumsticks

4 tablespoons margarine, divided
1/4 teaspoon hot pepper sauce
1/4 cup honey
1/2 teaspoon ground cinnamon
1/4 cup brown sugar
2 tablespoons dry sherry
3 bananas, sliced in half
　 crosswise, then lengthwise

Preheat oven to 400 degrees.

In a blender, combine onions, chiles with liquid, 1 tablespoon lime juice, oil, ketchup, and salt; blend at medium speed until smooth. Carefully loosen skin on each drumstick by pushing fingers between skin and meat. Spread 2 tablespoons chile mixture under skin of each drumstick; tuck skin under leg to hold securely. Place chicken skin side up in baking pan. Bake uncovered for 30 minutes, until almost tender.

Meanwhile, in a small saucepan, combine 1 tablespoon margarine, hot pepper sauce, and honey; heat until the margarine melts. Remove chicken from oven, brush with honey mixture and bake about 15 minutes more or until a fork can be inserted easily.

In a square baking dish, combine remaining 3 tablespoons margarine, cinnamon, brown sugar, sherry, and remaining 1 tablespoon lime juice; heat in the oven until the margarine melts. Place bananas in butter mixture and turn to coat. Place in the oven while the chicken is baking. Test the chicken to see if it is done. If it is, arrange with bananas on a platter.
Makes 6 servings.

Per Serving (approx):
Calories 424　　　　　*Protein 23 gm*　　　　*Fat 22 gm*
Carbohydrate 33 gm　　*Sodium 368 mg*　　　*Cholesterol 78 mg*

Rum Raisin Chicken

3 tablespoons light rum
2 tablespoons dark seedless raisins
1/4 cup butter
1/3 cup slivered almonds
6 skinless, boneless chicken breast
   halves

3/4 teaspoon salt
1/4 teaspoon pepper
3/4 cup chicken broth
1 tablespoon cornstarch
1/2 cup half-and-half
Curly mustard greens,
   for garnish

In a small bowl, combine raisins and rum; set aside. In a large frying pan, melt butter. Add almonds and cook, stirring, until almonds are toasted. With a slotted spoon, remove almonds to a small dish. Place chicken in same pan and sprinkle evenly with salt and pepper. Cook over medium heat, turning often, for about 20 minutes or until a fork pierces chicken easily. Remove chicken to a platter and keep warm.

Add broth to pan juices and bring to a boil. In a small bowl, mix cornstarch and half-and-half until smooth; slowly add to broth, whisking it until smooth. Reduce heat and simmer 2 minutes. Stir in rum and raisins; cook 1 minute.

To serve, pour sauce over chicken; top with toasted almonds. Garnish with mustard greens.   Makes 6 servings.

Per Serving (approx):
Calories 337	*Protein 33 gm*	*Fat 18 gm*
Carbohydrate 8 gm	*Sodium 638 mg*	*Cholesterol 108 mg*

Most chickens are raised by independent contractors who care for the birds from birth to maturity. So demanding is their responsibility that many wear beepers day and night to warn them if temperatures in the chicken houses rise or fall beyond prescribed limits.

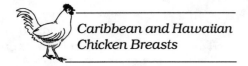

Tangy Mango Chicken

Be sure to use ripe mangos—but be sure they are not too mushy.

4 chicken breasts	2 teaspoons ground ginger
3/4 cup wine vinegar, divided	1 clove garlic, minced
1 teaspoon dried thyme	2 tablespoons chopped onion
1/2 teaspoon salt	2 mangos, flesh coarsely
1/2 cup brown sugar	chopped

Place chicken in a large glass bowl. Combine 1/2 cup vinegar and thyme; pour over chicken. Cover and refrigerate 2 hours, turning occasionally.

Preheat oven to 325 degrees.

Remove chicken from marinade and arrange in a shallow baking pan; sprinkle with salt. In a small saucepan, combine brown sugar, ginger, garlic, onion, and remaining 1/4 cup vinegar. Add chopped mangos and simmer and stir; pour over chicken. Bake for about 50 minutes or until a fork pierces the chicken easily.

Remove chicken to a warm serving dish and keep warm. Pour liquid from baking pan into a saucepan and simmer about 4 minutes, stirring until slightly thickened; pour over chicken. Makes 4 servings.

Per Serving (approx):

Calories 507	*Protein 57 gm*	*Fat 15 gm*
Carbohydrate 36 gm	*Sodium 433 mg*	*Cholesterol 159 mg*

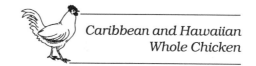
Spicy Cuban Rotisserie Chicken

We hope that someday soon you can savor the chicken of the street vendors in Havana, but until then this recipe is a nice alternative.

1 whole chicken	2 teaspoon dried oregano
1/4 cup lime juice	1 teaspoon salt
3 tablespoons olive oil	1 teaspoon ground cumin
1 green onion, minced	1/4 teaspoon pepper
2 cloves garlic, minced	Lime slices, for garnish
1 teaspoon grated lime peel	Cilantro sprigs, for garnish

Truss chicken or just tie drumsticks together. In a large glass or ceramic bowl, combine lime juice, oil, green onion, garlic, lime peel, oregano, salt, cumin, and pepper. Place chicken in this mixture, turning to coat it completely. Cover and refrigerate several hours or overnight, turning chicken several times.

Pour off the marinade and place chicken on a rotisserie spit. You can also have the marinated chicken in a rectangular baking pan for an hour. Cook about 1 1/2 hours or until drumsticks move easily in sockets and juices run clear. When done, a meat thermometer inserted into thigh will register 180 degrees. Remove chicken from rotisserie and place on rack; let sit about 10 minutes. Move chicken to platter and discard the string. Garnish with lime slices and cilantro sprigs.   Makes 4 servings.

Per Serving (approx):
Calories 893
Carbohydrate 3 gm

Protein 92 gm
Sodium 852 mg

Fat 57 gm
Cholesterol 356 mg

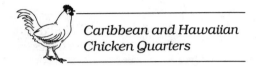

*Caribbean and Hawaiian
Chicken Quarters*

Nuevo Cubano Chicken Roast

Homesick Cubans, living in Miami, Florida, created this recipe.

4 chicken quarters
1 tablespoon chopped cilantro
1 teaspoon poultry seasoning
3/4 teaspoon garlic salt
1/2 teaspoon paprika
1/2 teaspoon pepper

1/4 teaspoon red pepper flakes
1 1/2 teaspoons olive oil
Spicy Avocado Creme
Cilantro sprigs, for garnish
Lemon peel strips, for garnish
Roasted red bell pepper,*
    cut in strips, for garnish

Preheat oven to 425 degrees.

In a small bowl, combine cilantro, poultry seasoning, garlic salt, paprika, black pepper, red pepper flakes, and olive oil. Rub mixture on each chicken piece. Place chicken, skin side up, on a rack in a large roasting pan. Roast without turning about 40 minutes or until golden brown and a fork pierces chicken easily.

Prepare Spicy Avocado Creme. To serve, arrange chicken on a large platter and drizzle with Spicy Avocado Creme, reserving some. Garnish with cilantro sprigs, lemon peel strips, and roasted bell pepper strips. Pass extra Avocado Creme.   Makes 4 servings.

SPICY AVOCADO CREME:
In a saucepan, combine 1 can (14 1/2 ounces) chicken broth, 1 can (4 ounces) chiles, 2 coarsely chopped green onions, 1 tablespoon chopped fresh cilantro, 4 teaspoons lemon juice, 1 teaspoon grated lemon peel, 3/4 teaspoon garlic salt, and 1/2 teaspoon pepper. Bring to a boil. Reduce heat and simmer until slightly thickened. Transfer to a food processor. Add 1 large ripe avocado (peeled, seeded and cut into chunks). Process until almost smooth. Return to the saucepan, add 2 tablespoons sour cream, and stir over low temperature until heated through.

*To roast a pepper, place it under the broiler or over a gas flame, turning until it is charred on all sides. Cool. With knife point, remove stem, seeds, and skin.

Per Serving (approx):
Calories 225
Carbohydrate 8 gm

Protein 11 gm
Sodium 741 mg

Fat 16 gm
Cholesterol 33 mg

144

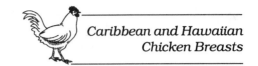

Gingered Jamaican Jerk Chicken

This is a slightly subdued version of the famous jerk chicken of Jamaica.

1 tablespoon chili powder
1 1/2 teaspoons curry powder
1 1/2 teaspoons dried thyme
1 teaspoon paprika
1 teaspoon pepper
1/2 teaspoon ground cumin
1/2 teaspoon garlic granules
1/2 teaspoon salt
1/4 teaspoon ground allspice
1/4 teaspoon cayenne
3 tablespoons olive oil

4 skinless, boneless chicken
   breast halves
1/3 cup diced ginger
6 large slices red onion
2 tablespoons butter
3 tablespoons lemon juice
3 Granny Smith apples, peeled,
   cored, and thinly sliced
1/4 cup light brown sugar
Parsley sprigs, for garnish

In a small bowl, make jerk seasoning by combining chili powder, curry, thyme, paprika, pepper, cumin, garlic, salt, allspice, and cayenne. Sprinkle on chicken, coating both sides.

In a large frying pan, heat oil and add chicken and ginger; cook about 10 minutes or until a fork pierces the chicken easily. Remove chicken from pan and keep warm. In the same pan, cook red onion slices, turning once, about 3 minutes or until tender. Remove and set aside.

In a frying pan, melt butter and add lemon juice and apples. Sauté until apples begin to soften. Add brown sugar and cook until liquid is reduced and thickens. Arrange onion slices on serving plate, top with chicken and apple mixture. Garnish with parsley.   Makes 4 servings.

Per Serving (approx):
Calories 607	*Protein 35 gm*	*Fat 22 gm*
Carbohydrate 67 gm	*Sodium 450 mg*	*Cholesterol 96 mg*

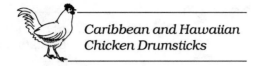

Caribbean Chicken Drums

The American Broiler Council picked this winner in a national competition.

2 tablespoons vegetable oil
8 chicken drumsticks
1 can (14 1/2 ounces) whole peeled
   tomatoes, cut in chunks
1 can (4 ounces) diced green chiles
1 tablespoon brown sugar

1/4 teaspoon ground allspice
1/4 cup mango chutney
1 tablespoon lemon juice
1/4 cup raisins
1 banana, sliced
1 mango, sliced, for garnish

In a frying pan, heat oil and add chicken. Cook, turning, about 10 minutes until chicken is brown on all sides. Add tomatoes, chiles, brown sugar, and allspice. Cover and simmer for 20 minutes. Add mango chutney, lemon juice, and raisins. Cover and cook about 15 minutes or until a fork pierces the chicken easily. Remove chicken to serving platter. Skim fat from sauce and discard. Add the banana to the pan. Heat thoroughly. Spoon fruit and some sauce over chicken. Garnish with mango slices. Serve remaining sauce at table.   **Makes 4 servings.**

Per Serving (approx):
Calories 619   *Protein 46 gm*   *Fat 30 gm*
Carbohydrate 41 gm   *Sodium 385 mg*   *Cholesterol 156 mg*

Sweet Chicken Drumsticks

1/4 (1/2 stick) cup light margarine
1 1/4 pounds skinless chicken
   drumsticks
1/2 cup orange juice

2 tablespoons honey
2 teaspoons grated, peeled
   ginger
1/2 teaspoon ground cinnamon

In a large skillet, melt the margarine. Add the chicken and fry for 6 to 8 minutes until brown on all sides, turning often. In a small bowl, combine orange juice, honey, ginger, and cinnamon. Add mixture to skillet. Simmer 25 to 35 minutes until chicken is fork-tender, glazed, and brown. Serve chicken with pan sauce.   **Makes 3 to 4 servings.**

Per Serving (approx):
Calories 226   *Protein 30 gm*   *Fat 6 gm*
Carbohydrate 12 gm   *Sodium 103 mg*   *Cholesterol 99 mg*

146

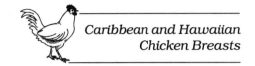

Caribbean Chicken Fajitas

The four types of peppers and two types of onions make this a very colorful dish.

4 skinless, boneless chicken breast
  halves, cut in strips
1 teaspoon garlic salt
1/2 teaspoon pepper
2 tablespoons vegetable oil
2 garlic cloves, minced
1 green bell pepper, red bell pepper,
  yellow bell pepper, roasted*, cut
  in strips

1/3 cup julienned jicama
1/3 cup chopped green onion
1/3 cup sliced red onion
10 flour tortillas
Orange Picante Salsa
Green onions, cut into daisies,
  for garnish
Cilantro, for garnish

In a bowl, sprinkle chicken with garlic salt and pepper. Stir to coat. In a frying pan, heat the oil. Add garlic; sauté 1 minute. Add chicken and cook, stirring, about 10 minutes until tender. Remove from the heat.

In a large bowl, combine bell peppers, jicama, green onion, and red onion. On warm serving platter, arrange chicken, pepper mixture, and tortillas with bowl of Orange Picante Salsa in center. Garnish with green onion daisies and cilantro. To serve, place some chicken strips and pepper mixture in center of each tortilla. Top with salsa and fold both sides of tortilla over filling. Makes 5 servings of 2 tortillas each.

ORANGE PICANTE SALSA:
Combine 1 cup bottled picante sauce, 2 tablespoons orange marmalade, and 1/4 cup fresh cilantro.

*To roast bell peppers, place under broiler, turning until charred. Cool. With knife point, remove stem, seeds, and skin.

Per Serving (approx):
Calories 426
Carbohydrate 45 gm

Protein 33 gm
Sodium 405 mg

Fat 13 gm
Cholesterol 64 mg

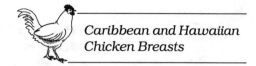

Chili Citrus Chicken

The Cayman Islands are the birthplace of this delightful recipe.

1 1/2 teaspoons chili powder
1/2 teaspoon ground cumin
1/2 teaspoon garlic salt
1/4 teaspoon cayenne
4 skinless, boneless chicken
    breast halves
1 tablespoon vegetable oil

1/4 cup lemon juice
1/4 cup lime juice
3 tablespoons jalapeño pepper
    jelly
Cilantro sprigs, for garnish
Red chile peppers, for garnish
Lemon slices, for garnish

In a small dish, combine chili powder, cumin, garlic salt, and cayenne. Rub mixture on each chicken breast half. In a frying pan, heat oil. Add chicken and fry, turning, about 12 minutes until chicken is brown and fork pierces chicken easily. Remove chicken to warm platter and keep warm.

In the same frying pan, bring lemon juice, lime juice, and jalapeño pepper jelly to a boil. Cook, stirring constantly, about 1 minute until mixture thickens. Spoon sauce over chicken. Garnish with cilantro sprigs, red chile peppers, and lemon slices.   Makes 4 servings.

Per Serving (approx):
Calories 238
Carbohydrate 14 gm

Protein 30 gm
Sodium 91 mg

Fat 7 gm
Cholesterol 80 mg

Ginger Chicken
with Carrots and Fruit

2 skinless, boneless chicken
  breast pieces cut into
  1 1/2-inch strips
1 teaspoon ground ginger, divided
3 tablespoons low-sodium soy sauce
1 1/2 cups sliced carrots,
  cooked

1/2 cup pineapple tidbits,
  drained
1/2 cup frozen red tart cherries,
  unsweetened
1 tablespoon lemon juice
1/4 teaspoon pepper

Preheat oven to 400 degrees. In a small bowl, sprinkle chicken strips with 1/2 teaspoon of the ginger. Stir in soy sauce and let sit about 10 minutes. In another bowl, combine carrots, pineapple, cherries, lemon juice, remaining 1/2 teaspoon ginger and pepper. Add chicken strips with sauce, mixing well. Place in shallow 1-quart baking dish and bake about 30 minutes. Serve on bed of boiled rice.   Makes 2 servings.

Per Serving (approx):
Calories 276   *Protein 33 gm*   *Fat 4 gm*
Carbohydrate 27 gm   *Sodium 817 mg*   *Cholesterol 80 mg*

Ginger Chicken and Carrots

6 carrots, cut in 1/4-inch slices
4 skinless chicken breast halves
1/2 cup chopped red bell pepper
4 tablespoons lemon juice
1/2 teaspoon salt

1/2 teaspoon ground ginger
2 tablespoons grated crystallized
  ginger
2 tablespoons butter-flavored
  vegetable oil spread

Preheat oven to 350 degrees. Place carrots in a 2-quart, greased casserole. Top with chicken breasts and sprinkle with bell pepper. In a small bowl, combine lemon juice, salt, and ground ginger; pour over chicken. In a small saucepan, combine crystallized ginger and oil spread. Cook, stirring, until the spread is melted; pour over the chicken. Cover the casserole and bake about 1 hour or until carrots are tender and a fork pierces the chicken easily.   Makes 4 servings.

Per Serving (approx):
Calories 286   *Protein 31 gm*   *Fat 10 gm*
Carbohydrate 18 gm   *Sodium 403 mg*   *Cholesterol 80 mg*

149

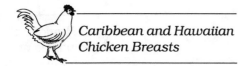

Chicken with Pineapple Salsa

2 tablespoons chopped cilantro
2 teaspoons minced ginger
3/8 teaspoon salt, divided
1 cup, seeded, diced Roma tomatoes
3/4 cup diced fresh pineapple
1/2 cup sliced green onion

1 can (4 ounces) diced green
   chiles, drained
1 tablespoon lemon juice
2 tablespoons butter
6 skinless, boneless chicken
   breast halves
Cilantro sprigs, for garnish

To make the pineapple salsa, in a small bowl, combine cilantro, ginger, 1/8 teaspoon salt, tomatoes, pineapple, onion, chiles, and lemon juice.

In a frying pan, melt the butter. Add the chicken and sprinkle with remaining salt. Sauté, turning, about 6 minutes until light brown on all sides. Cover and reduce heat to medium-low. Cook about 5 minutes until a fork pierces the chicken easily.

Arrange chicken on a serving platter and spoon pineapple salsa over. Garnish with cilantro sprigs.   Makes 6 servings.

Per Serving (approx):
Calories 209
Carbohydrate 5 gm

Protein 30 gm
Sodium 304 mg

Fat 7 gm
Cholesterol 91 mg

Raspberry Chicken Cutlets Supreme

4 skinless, boneless chicken breast halves

1/4 cup plus 1 tablespoon sweet vermouth

1 tablespoon lemon juice

3 1/2 tablespoons butter

1/4 cup chicken broth

4 1/2 tablespoons seedless red raspberry preserves

2 1/2 tablespoons Dijon mustard

1 1/4 teaspoons dried basil

2 kiwis, peeled, cut in slices

Red raspberries, for garnish

Basil sprigs, for garnish

Cut each chicken breast horizontally into 2 cutlets. Place chicken between sheets of wax paper and gently pound to uniform thickness. In a shallow dish, mix 1/4 cup vermouth and lemon juice. Add chicken, turning to coat. Cover and refrigerate for 30 minutes.

Remove chicken from marinade. In a large frying pan, melt the butter. Add chicken and cook about 3 minutes on each side until done. Remove chicken to a heated platter. To same pan, add chicken broth, stirring. Reduce liquid to half.

In a small bowl, combine preserves, mustard, and basil; add to frying pan and bring to boil. Reduce heat and boil, stirring constantly, for 2 minutes. Remove frying pan from heat and stir in remaining 1 tablespoon vermouth. Drain any juices from chicken on platter and add to sauce. Spoon some sauce over chicken and place a slice of kiwi on top of each cutlet.

Garnish with remaining slices of kiwi, red raspberries, and basil sprigs. Serve remaining sauce on the side.   Makes 4 servings.

Per Serving (approx):
Calories 364

Protein 33 gm

Fat 15 gm

Carbohydrate 23 gm

Sodium 419 mg

Cholesterol 113 mg

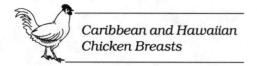
Chicken Fruiteria

4 skinless, boneless chicken
  breast halves
1 tablespoon vegetable oil
2 garlic cloves, minced
1/2 cup hot pepper jelly
2 teaspoons honey
1 tablespoon lime juice

1/2 cup orange juice
1 banana, quartered and
  quarters cut in half
  lengthwise
1 cup halved red seedless grapes
Strips lime peel, for garnish
Strips orange peel, for garnish

With palm of your hand, flatten chicken slightly. Heat oil in a large skillet. Add chicken and garlic to frying pan; sauté 10 minutes, turning the chicken once.

In a small bowl, combine pepper jelly, honey, and lime juice. Spoon mixture over chicken and continue cooking, turning once, about 5 minutes until chicken is glazed and fork can be inserted easily. Remove chicken to a serving dish. To the same frying pan, add orange juice, stirring. Place banana sections and grapes in the pan; spoon glaze mixture over the top of the fruit and cook about 1 minute until fruit is well coated. Arrange fruit on serving dish with chicken. Garnish with strips of lime and orange peel.   Makes 4 servings.

Per Serving (approx):
Calories 368
Carbohydrate 46 gm

Protein 30 gm
Sodium 78 mg

Fat 7 gm
Cholesterol 80 mg

MEXICAN & SOUTHWESTERN

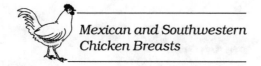
Chicken Picante

This recipe has all the flavor of Mexico, but you can control the heat by choosing a mild taco sauce.

1/2 cup medium chunky taco sauce
1/4 cup Dijon mustard
2 tablespoons lime juice
6 skinless, boneless chicken
   breast halves

2 tablespoons butter
6 tablespoons yogurt
1 lime, peeled, membrane
   removed, and sliced into 6
   segments
Chopped cilantro, for garnish

In a large bowl, mix taco sauce, mustard, and lime juice. Add chicken, turning to coat. Marinate for at least 30 minutes. In a large frying pan, heat the butter.

Remove chicken from marinade and place in the frying pan. Cook, turning, about 10 minutes or until brown on all sides. Add marinade and cook about 5 minutes more, until a fork pierces the chicken easily and the marinade is slightly reduced and beginning to glaze the chicken. Remove the chicken to a warmed serving platter.

Boil the marinade 1 minute; pour over chicken. Place 1 tablespoon yogurt on each breast half and top with lime segment. Garnish with chopped cilantro. Makes 6 servings.

Per Serving (approx):
Calories 220
Carbohydrate 4 gm

Protein 31 gm
Sodium 453 mg

Fat 9 gm
Cholesterol 92 mg

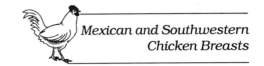
Chicken Avocado Melt

This recipe won first prize in the National Broiler Council competition a few years ago for its originality. It's also very easy to make.

4 skinless, boneless chicken breast
   halves
2 tablespoons cornstarch
1 teaspoon ground cumin
1 teaspoon garlic salt
1 egg, slightly beaten
1 tablespoon water
1/3 cup cornmeal
3 tablespoons vegetable oil

1 firm, ripe avocado, sliced
1 1/2 cups shredded Monterey
   jack cheese
1/2 cup sour cream
1/4 cup sliced green onion,
   tops only
1/4 cup chopped red bell
   pepper
Cherry tomatoes, for garnish
Parsley sprigs, for garnish

Preheat oven to 350 degrees.

Pound chicken to 1/4-inch thickness. In a shallow dish, combine cornstarch, cumin, and garlic salt; dredge chicken, one piece at a time. In a small bowl, mix egg and water. Place cornmeal in another small bowl. Dip chicken, first in egg and then in cornmeal.

In a large frying pan, heat oil; add chicken and cook 2 minutes on each side. Remove chicken to a shallow baking pan; place avocado slices over the chicken and sprinkle with cheese.

Bake about 15 minutes or until fork pierces chicken easily and cheese melts. Top chicken with sour cream, dividing equally; sprinkle with green onion and bell pepper. Garnish with cherry tomatoes and parsley sprigs.

                                     Makes 4 servings.

Per Serving (approx):
Calories 633
Carbohydrate 19 gm

Protein 44 gm
Sodium 353 mg

Fat 42 gm
Cholesterol 183 mg

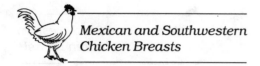

Caliente Fiesta Chicken

4 skinless, boneless chicken
    breast halves
4 flour tortillas
1 1/3 cup shredded reduced fat
    Monterey jack cheese
1 can (4 ounces) diced green
    chiles, drained
1 tablespoon minced green onion

1 tablespoon olive oil
1 tablespoon salt-free herb and
    spice seasoning, divided
Caliente Fiesta Sauce
1/2 cup chopped cilantro
Avocado Butter
Cilantro sprigs, for garnish
Green onion, cut into daisies,
    for garnish

Preheat oven to 350 degrees.

Place chicken between two pieces of plastic wrap and gently pound to 1/4-inch thickness. Arrange tortillas on a large baking sheet. In a bowl, combine cheese, chiles, and onion. Divide mixture and spread on tortillas. Bake about 10 minutes or until cheese is bubbly and light brown around edges.

In a large frying pan, heat oil and add chicken; sprinkle with half of herb seasoning and cook about 3 minutes or until brown. Turn and sprinkle remaining herb seasoning on chicken; cook 3 more minutes, or until chicken is brown and fork can be inserted into chicken easily.

Place 1 piece of chicken on each tortilla. In the same frying pan, heat Caliente Fiesta Sauce and spoon sauce over chicken; sprinkle with cilantro. Pipe or spoon Avocado Butter in the center of sauce. Garnish each serving with cilantro sprigs and onion daisies.   Makes 4 servings.

CALIENTE FIESTA SAUCE:
In a food processor or blender container, combine 1/2 cup drained bottled red peppers and 2 tablespoons mild bottled red taco sauce. Process until pureed. Pour into a small bowl and stir in 2 teaspoons olive oil.

AVOCADO BUTTER:
In a small bowl, mash 1 small peeled, seeded ripe avocado. Add 1 teaspoon lemon juice. Stir.

Per Serving (approx):		
Calories 54	*Protein 47 gm*	*Fat 25 gm*
Carbohydrate 27 gm	*Sodium 608 mg*	*Cholesterol 107 mg*

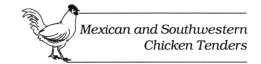

Mexican Chicken Stir-Fry

It takes only about 15 minutes to prepare this South-of-the-Border dish using cooking methods from the Far East.

1 pound skinless, boneless
  chicken tenders
1 teaspoon chili powder
1/2 teaspoon ground cumin
1/4 teaspoon dried oregano
2 tablespoons olive oil, divided

2 green onions, chopped
1 garlic clove, minced
1 can (4 ounces) chopped mild
  green chiles
1 can (19 ounces) black beans,
  drained

In a bowl, combine chicken, chili powder, cumin, oregano, and 1 tablespoon olive oil; toss well.

Heat a wok or a large skillet. Add the remaining oil. Add the tenders; stir-fry 4 to 5 minutes until barely cooked through. Add green onions, garlic, chiles, and beans. Stir-fry 2 to 3 minutes longer until heated through. Makes 4 servings.

Per Serving (approx):
Calories 534   *Protein 43 gm*   *Fat 12 gm*
Carbohydrate 63 gm   *Sodium 461 mg*   *Cholesterol 77 mg*

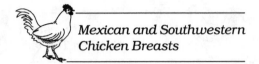

Corn, Cabbage, and Chicken

1 1/2 tablespoons flour
1 1/2 teaspoons salt, divided
3/8 teaspoon pepper, divided
1/8 teaspoon cayenne
4 skinless, boneless chicken breast
   halves
3 tablespoons olive oil, divided
1 1/2 pounds red cabbage,
   coarsely chopped

1 tablespoon vinegar
1/2 teaspoon hot pepper
   sauce
1 can (16 1/2 ounces)
   cream-style corn
1 green bell pepper, cut in strips
1 red bell pepper, cut in strips
Parsley sprigs, for garnish

In a dish, combine flour, 3/4 teaspoon of the salt, 1/8 teaspoon of the pepper and cayenne. Add chicken one piece at a time, dredging to coat. In a frying pan, heat 2 tablespoons oil. Add chicken and cook, turning, about 8 minutes on each side or until lightly browned, Remove chicken to small dish and cover to keep warm.

In the same frying pan, heat the remaining 1 tablespoon oil. Add cabbage and sauté about 10 minutes. Add remaining 1/4 teaspoon salt, vinegar, hot pepper sauce, corn, green and red bell peppers, stirring to mix. Simmer 10 minutes. Place chicken on top of mixture, cover, and simmer about 5 minutes or until a fork pierces the chicken easily. Garnish with parsley sprigs.   Makes 4 servings.

Per Serving (approx):

Calories 407	*Protein 33 gm*	*Fat 16 gm*
Carbohydrate 32 gm	*Sodium 1279 mg*	*Cholesterol 80 mg*

> Chicken feed consists of corn, corn gluten, and soybean meal, along with natural vitamins, ground oyster shells, and limestone.

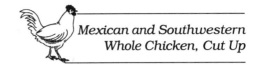

Crunchy Mexicali Chicken

1 teaspoon chili powder, divided
1/2 teaspoon salt
1/2 teaspoon garlic salt
1 whole chicken, cut up
1/2 cup ketchup

1/2 cup grape jelly
1 tablespoon tarragon vinegar
1/2 cup nacho-flavored
   tortilla chip crumbs
1/2 cup chicken broth

Preheat oven to 350 degrees. In a small bowl, combine 1/2 teaspoon chili powder, salt, and garlic salt. Rub on chicken pieces. Place the chicken in a baking pan and bake about 50 minutes. In a small saucepan, combine ketchup, grape jelly, vinegar, and remaining 1/2 teaspoon chili powder. Bring to a boil, reduce heat, and simmer about 5 minutes. Remove chicken from oven and save the pan drippings.

Baste the chicken with half of sauce and sprinkle with 1/4 cup tortilla crumbs. Turn chicken and repeat with remaining sauce and crumbs. Return the chicken to the oven and bake about 10 minutes until tender. Remove chicken to warm serving platter. Add broth to pan drippings and heat to boiling; serve on the side with the chicken.   Makes 4 servings.

Per Serving (approx):
Calories 574
Carbohydrate 27 gm

Protein 53 gm
Sodium 1084 mg

Fat 28 gm
Cholesterol 210 mg

Southwest Chicken

1 whole chicken, cut up
1 package (16 ounces) frozen corn
   and red and green pepper mixture
1 cup rice
1 3/4 cups water

1 tablespoon chili powder
1 can (11 ounces) condensed
   cheddar cheese soup
Salt and pepper to taste

Preheat oven to 350 degrees. Coat a skillet with vegetable spray. Brown the chicken on all sides. In a roasting pan lightly coated with vegetable spray, mix frozen corn mixture, rice, water, chili powder, and soup.

Place chicken skin side down on corn mixture. Cover and bake for 50 to 55 minutes, or until chicken is no longer pink inside. Season with salt and pepper to taste.   Makes 4 to 6 servings.

Per Serving (approx):
Calories 644
Carbohydrate 46 gm

Protein 52 gm
Sodium 572 mg

Fat 28 gm
Cholesterol 195 mg

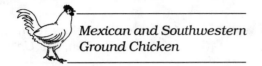

Pizza-Flavored Chicken Tacos

Italy comes to Mexico, or maybe Mexico goes to Italy with this unique recipe that marries the cuisine of two regions.

1 tablespoon vegetable oil	1/2 teaspoon dried oregano
1 pound ground chicken	1/4 teaspoon pepper
1 onion, chopped	1 can (8 ounces) tomato sauce
1 green bell pepper, chopped	1/2 cup water
1/4 pound mushrooms, sliced	12 taco shells, heated
1 clove garlic, minced	*Toppings:* chopped tomatoes,
1 tablespoon flour	chopped onion, shredded
1/2 teaspoon salt	lettuce, sliced black olives,
1/2 teaspoon dried basil	shredded mozzarella cheese,
	grated Parmesan cheese

In a frying pan, heat oil. Sauté ground chicken, stirring, until brown, about 5 minutes. Add onion, bell pepper, mushrooms, and garlic; cook until tender, about 5 minutes more. Sprinkle with flour, salt, basil, oregano, and pepper. Stir in tomato sauce and water; bring to a boil. Reduce heat to low and simmer about 15 minutes.

To serve, spoon sauce into warm taco shells, sprinkle with cheeses; and top with tomato, onion, lettuce, and olives.

Makes 6 servings (2 tacos each).

Per Serving (approx), excluding toppings:
Calories 227   *Protein 12 gm*   *Fat 10 gm*
Carbohydrate 22 gm   *Sodium 615 mg*   *Cholesterol 47 mg*

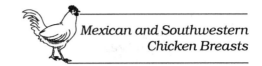

Margarita Chicken

You might guess that tequila and lemon juice are the key to the name of this recipe.

8 skinless, boneless chicken breast breast halves
1/2 teaspoon salt
1/4 teaspoon pepper
1/2 cup dry white wine
3 tablespoons olive oil, divided
1 tablespoon dried oregano
2 teaspoons ground cumin
1/4 teaspoon cayenne
1/4 teaspoon dried onion flakes
1/8 teaspoon red pepper flakes
1/4 cup chopped cilantro

5 garlic cloves, minced
1 jalapeño, chopped
1 cup white rice, cooked in chicken broth
1/4 cup gold tequila
1/4 cup lime juice
14 ounces canned Mexican style stewed tomatoes with chile peppers
Lime slices, for garnish
Avocado slices, for garnish
Cilantro sprigs, for garnish

Put chicken in a glass or ceramic bowl. Sprinkle it with salt and pepper. In a small bowl, combine wine, 1 tablespoon olive oil, oregano, cumin, cayenne, onion flakes, red pepper flakes, cilantro, 3 cloves garlic, and jalapeño. Pour marinade over chicken, cover, and refrigerate at least 1 hour.

Remove chicken from marinade and drain. In a large frying pan, heat remaining oil. Add remaining garlic and the chicken. Sauté chicken about 3 minutes on each side, or until brown; remove from pan. Reduce heat, add tequila and lime juice to deglaze the pan. Stir in tomatoes and return chicken to pan. Cover and simmer, turning once, about 6 minutes, or until a fork pierces the chicken easily. Remove chicken to a platter. Simmer sauce, uncovered, until reduced by one-third. Pour over chicken. Garnish with lime and avocado slices and cilantro sprigs.

Makes 8 servings.

Per Serving (approx):
Calories 340
Carbohydrate 25 gm

Protein 32 gm
Sodium 419 mg

Fat 10 gm
Cholesterol 80 mg

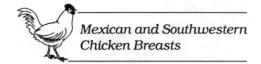

Taos Chicken Molé

1 cup white bread crumbs
4 teaspoons taco seasoning mix,
   divided
2 teaspoons cocoa, divided
1 1/2 tablespoons minced sage,
   divided

4 skinless, boneless chicken
   breast halves
2 tablespoons olive oil
2/3 cup prepared tomato-
   pepper salsa
1 teaspoon brown sugar
Sautéed red, green and yellow
   bell pepper strips, for garnish

In a paper bag, mix bread crumbs, 1 tablespoon taco seasoning mix, 1 teaspoon cocoa and 1 tablespoon sage. Add chicken pieces and shake until well coated. In a large frying pan, heat oil. Add chicken and sauté turning, about 6 minutes, or until brown on both sides. Cover and cook about 25 minutes or until the chicken is tender.

In a small saucepan, simmer salsa, sugar, remaining taco seasoning, cocoa, and sage for 2 minutes. Cover and reduce heat as low as possible. Serve the chicken topped with salsa and garnished with bell pepper strips.

Makes 4 servings.

Per Serving (approx):
Calories 334
Carbohydrate 23 gm

Protein 33 gm
Sodium 456 mg

Fat 12 gm
Cholesterol 81 mg

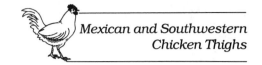

Herb-Rubbed Chicken with Jalapeño-Lime Glaze

1 teaspoon dried rosemary
1 teaspoon dried sage
1 teaspoon dried thyme
1/2 teaspoon ground cumin
1/2 teaspoon salt
8 skinless, boneless chicken
   thighs

4 teaspoons cream cheese,
   softened
2 tablespoons jalapeño jelly,
   divided
2 teaspoons vegetable oil
1 lime, peel grated and juiced
Lime slices, for garnish

In a small bowl, combine rosemary, sage, thyme, cumin, and salt. Sprinkle chicken with herb mixture and rub in, coating both sides; set aside. In another small bowl, mix cream cheese and 1 tablespoon of the jalapeño jelly until well blended. Refrigerate until ready to use.

Heat oil in a frying pan. Add the chicken and sauté about 6 minutes or until browned on both sides. Cover and simmer about 10 minutes until chicken is done. Stir in 1 tablespoon jalapeño jelly, lime juice, and grated peel. Cook, basting, 2 minutes longer.

To serve, place chicken on plate and pour pan juices over. The cream cheese mixture should be served on the side. Garnish with lime slices.

Makes 4 servings.

Per Serving (approx):
Calories 277
Carbohydrate 7 gm

Protein 27 gm
Sodium 398 mg

Fat 15 gm
Cholesterol 103 mg

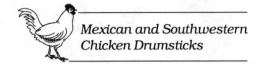
Easy Enchilada Chicken Skillet

*This is one of those meals that becomes a family favorite, not only because
it tastes good, but also because it is so easy to prepare.*

1 tablespoon vegetable oil
1 1/2 pounds chicken legs
2 cans (15 ounces each) black
   beans, drained
1 can (8 ounces) tomato sauce
1 1/2 teaspoons chili powder

1 teaspoon ground cumin
1/2 teaspoon garlic powder
1/4 cup diced green chiles
1 tomato, chopped
1/2 cup shredded cheddar
   cheese

Heat the oil in a skillet. Brown the chicken on all sides. Remove it. Add
the beans, tomato sauce, chili powder, cumin, and garlic powder.

Top with the chicken, cover, and cook, stirring occasionally, about 35
minutes until the chicken is no longer pink when cut into. Sprinkle with
chiles, tomato, and cheese. Makes 3 to 4 servings.

Per Serving (approx):
Calories 667   *Protein 57 gm*   *Fat 23 gm*
Carbohydrate 57 gm   *Sodium 1059 mg*   *Cholesterol 132 mg*

> " Ever since Eve started it all by offering
> Adam the apple, woman's punishment
> has been to have to supply man with
> food and then suffer the consequences
> when it disagrees with him."
>
> Helen Rowland,
> *A Guide to Men*

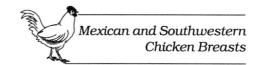

Chicken Santa Fe

4 skinless, boneless chicken breast
  halves
Sante Fe Marinade

4 tablespoons jalapeño jelly,
  melted
2 red bell peppers, roasted*

Place chicken between pieces of wax paper and pound to 1/4-inch thickness. In large zip-lock bag, arrange the chicken. Add marinade, seal bag, refrigerate, and let stand on the counter, turning once, for 1 hour.

Preheat broiler.

Remove the chicken from the marinade. Place on a broiler pan, and brush liberally with the marinade. Arrange rack so the chicken is about 6 inches from the heat and broil 8 minutes until chicken is brown and fork can be inserted easily. Brush chicken with melted jelly. Place 2 roasted bell pepper strips to form an X on each breast half; spoon on remaining jelly. Return to oven and broil until chicken is glazed.   Makes 4 servings.

SANTA FE MARINADE:
In a medium bowl, combine 1/4 cup olive oil, juice and grated peel of 1 small lime, 1 clove garlic, crushed, 3 tablespoons tequila, 1/4 teaspoon hot pepper sauce, 1/8 teaspoon liquid smoke, and 1/4 teaspoon salt.

*To roast bell peppers, place under broiler, turning often until charred. Cool. With point of sharp knife, remove stem, seeds, and charred skin. Cut into 8 strips each.

Per Serving (approx):
Calories 382
Carbohydrate 19 gm

Protein 30 gm
Sodium 220 mg

Fat 19 gm
Cholesterol 80 mg

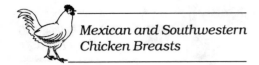

Mexican Chicken Rolls

3 tablespoons butter
6 skinless, boneless chicken breast
   halves, cut into strips
1/2 teaspoon garlic salt
1/4 teaspoon pepper
1/4 teaspoon dried thyme
Juice of 1 lemon
2 tomatoes, chopped
2 cups spinach leaves, torn
1 cup peeled, diced jicama

2 green onions, chopped
1 cup shredded Monterey jack
   cheese
1 can (16 ounces) dark red
   kidney beans, drained
1 can (6 ounces) ripe olives,
   drained, sliced
2 cups picante sauce, divided
18 large red lettuce leaves
1 pint sour cream

In a frying pan, heat the butter. Add chicken; sprinkle with garlic salt, pepper, thyme, and lemon juice. Cook, stirring, about 10 minutes. Remove from heat and set aside.

In a large salad bowl, combine tomatoes, spinach, jicama, onion, cheese, beans, olives, 1 cup picante sauce and chicken. Toss to mix.

To serve, place a portion of the chicken mixture in the center of each lettuce leaf; top with 1 tablespoon remaining picante sauce and 1 tablespoon sour cream. Fold over edges of lettuce leaf and roll up.

Makes 6 servings.

Per Serving (approx):
Calories 558
Carbohydrate 31 gm

Protein 43 gm
Sodium 1892 mg

Fat 29 gm
Cholesterol 127 mg

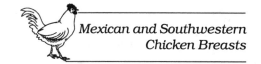

Chicken Fajitas

The Mexican fajita is now a favorite in the United States.

2 tablespoons lime juice
2 tablespoons lemon juice
4 tablespoons orange juice
1 clove garlic, minced
4 skinless, boneless chicken
   breast halves
1 teaspoon chili powder
1/2 teaspoon salt

2 tablespoons canola oil
1 each yellow, red, and green
   bell pepper, cut into strips
1 onion, sliced into rings
10 flour tortillas, heated
1 cup sour cream
1 cup prepared salsa
1/2 cup sliced black olives

In a small bowl, combine juices and garlic. Sprinkle chicken with chili powder and salt. Place chicken in a shallow bowl, add half the juice mixture, and turn to coat well. Cover and refrigerate chicken for at least 30 minutes.

Preheat the broiler. Put the chicken in a baking pan and broil it about 6 inches from the heat. Turn and baste the chicken with the reserved juice mixture about 10 minutes or until a fork pierces the chicken easily.

In a frying pan, heat oil and add bell peppers and onion. Fry, stirring, until onion is translucent but still crisp, about 5 minutes. Slice chicken breasts into strips and add to pepper mixture in frying pan.

Divide chicken mixture evenly and place in center of tortillas; top with dollop of sour cream, salsa, and olives; fold tortillas.

Makes 5 servings of 2 tortillas each.

Per Serving (approx):
Calories 581
Carbohydrate 55 gm

Protein 35 gm
Sodium 907 mg

Fat 24 gm
Cholesterol 83 mg

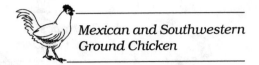

Enchiladas Santa Fe Style

2 tablespoons vegetable oil
1/2 to 3/4 cup chopped onion
1 1/4 pounds ground chicken
1 teaspoon chili powder
1/2 teaspoon ground cumin
1/2 teaspoon salt

2 cans (10 ounces each)
   enchilada sauce (mild or hot)
12 tortillas
1 cup shredded Monterey jack
   cheese
Sour cream or guacamole
   (optional)

Preheat oven to 375 degrees. In a large skillet, heat oil. Add onion and sauté 5 minutes until translucent. Add chicken, chili powder, cumin, and salt; sauté about 5 minutes until meat is cooked through. Transfer meat mixture to a bowl and set aside.

In the same skillet, heat enchilada sauce. Dip 4 tortillas in sauce to soften; place on lightly oiled or nonstick 12- by 14-inch jellyroll pan and top evenly with half of meat mixture.

Dip 4 more tortillas into sauce and place on top of meat; add another layer of meat mixture and top with remaining tortillas dipped in sauce. Spoon some sauce over each enchilada stack and sprinkle with cheese. Bake enchiladas 20 minutes or until cheese is melted.

To serve, top each enchilada stack with dollop of sour cream or guacamole.

Makes 4 to 6 servings.

Per Serving (approx):
Calories 445
Carbohydrate 40 gm

Protein 22 gm
Sodium 809 mg

Fat 22 gm
Cholesterol 76 mg

REGIONAL AMERICAN DISHES

Chicken with Blue Cheese Pecan Sauce

A favorite southern recipe from the state of Georgia.

1/2 cup flour
1/2 teaspoon salt
4 skinless, boneless chicken
   breast halves
1/4 cup olive oil

Blue Cheese Pecan Sauce
1 tablespoon chopped parsley
1/8 teaspoon white pepper
Parsley sprigs, for garnish

In a dish, mix flour and salt. Pound chicken to 1/4-inch thickness. Dredge chicken in flour mixture, coating evenly. In a large frying pan, heat oil. Add chicken and sauté about 6 minutes until light brown on each side and tender. Remove chicken to platter.

Prepare Blue Cheese Pecan Sauce. Spoon 2 tablespoons sauce over each chicken breast and sprinkle with a little crumbled blue cheese. Top with chopped parsley and white pepper. Garnish with parsley sprigs. Serve remaining sauce in sauceboat.   Makes 4 servings.

BLUE CHEESE PECAN SAUCE:
In a saucepan, melt 3 tablespoons margarine; add 3 tablespoons flour and stir until smooth. Stirring constantly, add 1 1/2 cups milk, 1 teaspoon dry sherry, 1/4 teaspoon minced garlic, and 1/2 cup chopped pecans. Cook until sauce thickens. From a 4-ounce package of blue cheese, reserve 2 teaspoons for topping on chicken. Add remaining cheese to sauce and remove from heat.

Per Serving (approx):
Calories 734
Carbohydrate 32 gm

Protein 43 gm
Sodium 904 mg

Fat 48 gm
Cholesterol 114 mg

Maryland Style Chicken and Slippery Dumplings

This is the traditional Sunday dinner on the eastern shore of Maryland.

1 whole chicken (5 to 7 pounds)
1/2 lemon
1 onion
2 cloves
Salt and ground pepper to taste
6 cups low-sodium chicken broth
Water
1 bay leaf

1 pound small white onions,
  peeled
1 pound carrots, cut into
  1 1/2-inch lengths
2 cups flour
1 cup warm water
1 teaspoon salt

Rub chicken inside and out with lemon. Cut yellow onion in half and stick with cloves; place in cavity of chicken. Truss bird and season with salt and pepper to taste; place in an 8-quart Dutch oven or stewing pot. Pour in chicken broth and enough water to reach halfway up the chicken; add bay leaf. Cover and simmer 20 minutes per pound. (To keep meat tender, do not allow to boil.) During the last 45 minutes of cooking, add white onions and carrots. The chicken is done if juices run clear when thickest part of thigh is pierced with a fork. Remove chicken and vegetables to a serving platter and keep warm.

Add more broth or water if necessary to bring it half way up the side of a Dutch oven; continue simmering. Meanwhile, in a bowl, combine flour, water, and salt; mix well. Turn dough out onto well-floured surface and knead 4 to 5 minutes until it becomes elastic, reflouring board as necessary. With a lightly floured rolling pin, roll out the dough as thin as possible. With a sharp knife, cut into 1 1/2- to 2-inch squares. Add squares to boiling liquid and cook 5 to 7 minutes. Remove dumplings to a serving bowl.

Over high heat, cook poaching liquid until reduced and slightly thickened. For a thicker gravy, stir in a small amount of flour blended with cold water. Serve chicken with vegetables and dumplings. Pour some gravy over dumplings and pass the remaining gravy separately.

Makes 6 servings.

Per Serving (approx):
Calories 1030
Carbohydrate 51 gm

Protein 98 gm
Sodium 689 mg

Fat 46 gm
Cholesterol 365 mg

Ground Chicken Gumbo

Create a New Orleans dinner with this easy-to-make gumbo. If your market doesn't have a frozen gumbo vegetable mix, just add frozen okra to any vegetable mix.

1 pound ground chicken
1 teaspoon salt
1 teaspoon New Orleans
   gumbo seasoning*
1 onion, sliced in rings
2 cups chicken broth

1 can (28 ounces) crushed
   tomatoes with basil
1 package (16 ounces) frozen
   gumbo vegetable mixture
1 rib celery, chopped
1/2 cup chopped cabbage
Croutons

Heat a large Dutch oven. Add chicken, salt and gumbo seasoning; brown, stirring, about 5 minutes. Add onion and continue to cook, stirring, about 5 minutes more. Stir in broth and tomatoes; bring to boil.

Add vegetable mixture, celery, and cabbage. Simmer about 20 minutes, or until vegetables are tender. Serve in bowls with croutons.

Makes 6 servings.

*Creole seasoning may be substituted if gumbo seasoning is not available.

Per Serving (approx):
Calories 216
Carbohydrate 25 gm

Protein 14 gm
Sodium 1299 mg

Fat 7 gm
Cholesterol 47 mg

Spicy Cajun Hash

In this spicy recipe, you can control the amount of heat by choosing a mild pepper sauce.

2 tablespoons vegetable oil
1 1/4 pounds ground chicken
2 tablespoons butter or margarine
2 tablespoons flour
1 cup chopped onion
1/2 cup chopped green bell pepper
1 cup chicken broth

1 1/2 tablespoons
  Worcestershire sauce
1 package (10 ounces) frozen
  corn kernels
2 cups sliced, cooked potatoes
Salt and pepper to taste
Hot pepper sauce to taste

In a large skillet, heat oil. Add chicken; sauté 10 minutes or until cooked through. Remove meat and set aside. Add butter and flour to skillet. Cook 4 to 5 minutes until mixture is brown, stirring constantly. Add onion and bell pepper; cook 5 minutes or until tender, stirring often. Stir in chicken broth and Worcestershire sauce; cook until thickened, stirring constantly.

Add cooked meat, corn, and potatoes; cook 2 to 3 minutes longer until heated through. Season with salt, pepper, and hot pepper sauce to taste.

Makes 4 to 6 servings.

Per Serving (approx):
Calories 305
Carbohydrate 26 gm

Protein 14 gm
Sodium 355 mg

Fat 16 gm
Cholesterol 69 mg

Creole Chicken and Okra

I never cared for the taste of okra until I spent time in Louisiana and learned that it can add wonderful flavor to other foods and is especially tasty when combined with tomatoes and parsley.

4 skinless chicken leg quarters, cut into 4 thighs and 4 drumsticks
1 tablespoon vegetable oil
1 cup coarsely chopped onion
1 cup coarsely chopped green bell pepper
1/2 cup sliced celery
1 clove garlic, minced
2/3 pound okra, sliced

2 cups coarsely chopped tomatoes
1/4 cup chopped parsley
1/2 teaspoon paprika
1 bay leaf
1/2 teaspoon salt
1/2 cup chicken broth
1/4 cup white wine
1/4 teaspoon hot pepper sauce

In a Dutch oven, heat oil. Add chicken and cook, turning, about 10 minutes or until brown on all sides. Remove chicken to a warm bowl.

To the Dutch oven, add onion, bell pepper, celery, and garlic; stir and cook about 5 minutes. Add okra and cook, stirring, about 5 minutes more. Stir in tomatoes, parsley, paprika, bay leaf, and salt. Return the chicken to the Dutch oven and stir.

In a small bowl, combine chicken broth, wine, and hot pepper sauce; pour over chicken. Cover, reduce heat to low and cook about 30 minutes or until a fork pierces the chicken easily. Remove bay leaf.

Makes 4 servings.

Per Serving (approx):
Calories 435
Carbohydrate 17 gm

Protein 38 gm
Sodium 619 mg

Fat 23 gm
Cholesterol 123 mg

Easy Cajun Chicken Breast

While many people think that Creole and Cajun cooking are the same cuisine, it is not true. Creole cooking was developed by the French and Spanish people in New Orleans. Cajun cooking is from the Cajuns, the country folk of Louisiana, who emigrated from France to Acadia in Canada, and then to Louisiana.

2 cloves garlic, minced
1 tablespoon minced parsley
1/4 teaspoon salt
1/4 teaspoon cayenne

1/4 teaspoon dried mint
2 tablespoons white wine
4 skinless, boneless chicken
   breasts

In a dish with a cover, combine garlic, parsley, salt, cayenne, mint, and wine. Spread mixture on all sides of chicken breasts, cover, and refrigerate at least 3 hours or overnight.

Spray a frying pan with vegetable spray. Heat the pan. Add chicken and cook about 5 minutes. Turn and cook it about 5 minutes more until a fork can be inserted easily. Makes 4 servings.

Per Serving (approx):
Calories 304
Carbohydrate 1 gm

Protein 59 gm
Sodium 286 mg

Fat 7 gm
Cholesterol 160 mg

> "A chicken to a cook is like a canvas to a painter."
> Jean-Brillat-Savarin, 19th-century
> French writer and gourmet

175

Cajun Chicken with Orange Mustard Sauce

This is highly spiced—delicious, but highly spiced!

4 skinless, boneless chicken
  breast halves
1 teaspoon paprika
1 teaspoon white pepper
1 teaspoon onion powder
1 teaspoon garlic powder
1 teaspoon cayenne

1 teaspoon dried basil
1/2 teaspoon pepper
1/2 teaspoon dried thyme
1/4 teaspoon salt
2 tablespoons vegetable oil
Orange Mustard Sauce

Gently pound chicken to 1/2-inch thickness. In a small bowl, combine paprika, white pepper, onion powder, garlic powder, cayenne, basil, black pepper, thyme, and salt. Sprinkle chicken with this Cajun seasoning mix and refrigerate 30 minutes.

Prepare Orange Mustard Sauce. In a large frying pan, heat oil. Add chicken and sauté about 5 minutes until a fork can be inserted easily. Add Orange Mustard Sauce to frying pan and heat until sauce begins to boil.

Makes 4 servings.

ORANGE MUSTARD SAUCE:
In a small saucepan, combine 1 1/2 cups orange marmalade and 6 tablespoons Dijon mustard. Stir over low temperature until marmalade melts.

Per Serving (approx):
Calories 586
Carbohydrate 88 gm

Protein 32 gm
Sodium 799 mg

Fat 12 gm
Cholesterol 80 mg

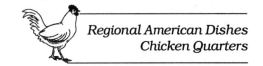

Creole Chicken and Zucchini

You can prepare this recipe a day or two in advance, refrigerate, and warm before serving.

4 chicken quarters
1/4 cup chopped green bell pepper
1 onion, diced
1 pound zucchini, diced
1 teaspoon celery salt
1/2 teaspoon pepper

1/2 teaspoon curry powder
1/4 teaspoon dried basil
1 bay leaf
2 cans (16 ounces each)
   tomatoes, undrained
1/4 cup dry sherry

Spray a Dutch oven with vegetable spray and heat. Add chicken and fry, turning, about 10 minutes until brown on all sides. Remove chicken from the pan. Add bell pepper and onion to the Dutch oven and cook, stirring, about 5 minutes.

Drain and discard any excess oil; add zucchini and sprinkle with celery salt, pepper, curry powder, and basil. Add bay leaf, tomatoes, and sherry. Return chicken to pan and simmer over medium-low heat about 30 minutes or until a fork pierces chicken easily and liquid is reduced. Remove bay leaf.   Makes 4 servings.

Per Serving (approx):
Calories 540
Carbohydrate 20 gm

Protein 63 gm
Sodium 164 mg

Fat 22 gm
Cholesterol 199 mg

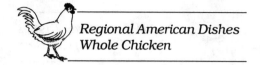

Southern Chicken Bog

This is a dish that you can prepare ahead for a buffet or a TV football game. Keep the Bog warm. Everyone will help themselves when they get hungry. No, we have no idea where the name came from.

3 tablespoons butter-flavored
  margarine
1 cup chopped onion
2 cups long-grain rice
1/2 cup chopped celery
1 teaspoon salt
1/2 teaspoon pepper

5 cups low-sodium chicken
  broth
1 pound smoked turkey sausage,
  cut in 1/2-inch slices
1 chicken, cooked, skinned,
  boned, and cut into
  small pieces

In a saucepan, melt margarine, add onion, and sauté about 5 minutes. Add rice and celery, stirring until rice is light brown, about 6 minutes. Sprinkle with salt and pepper. Add chicken broth and sausage and bring to boil. Cover, reduce heat to low. Cook until rice is done, about 30 minutes (do not remove cover during cooking time).

Slowly stir in cooked chicken, cover, and turn off heat, letting the Bog sit for about 5 minutes. Invite your guests to serve themselves.

Makes 8 servings.

Per Serving (approx):
Calories 458
Carbohydrate 30 gm

Protein 35 gm
Sodium 678 mg

Fat 22 gm
Cholesterol 107 mg

Chicken Smothered in Okra-Tomato Sauce

This recipe originated in Africa and was brought to the U.S. by black slaves.

1/2 cup flour	2 garlic cloves, minced
1/2 teaspoon Cajun seasoning	1 1/2 cup frozen sliced okra
1/4 teaspoon pepper	1 can (14 1/2 ounces) Cajun
4 chicken quarters	style stewed tomatoes
3 tablespoons olive oil	1 teaspoon dried thyme
1/2 cup minced onion	2 tablespoons minced parsley
1/2 cup minced green bell pepper	1 teaspoon hot pepper sauce
1/2 cup minced celery	

In a plate, combine flour and seasonings. Add chicken, turning to coat each piece. In a large frying pan, heat oil. Add the chicken and cook about 20 minutes, turning to brown on all sides. Remove chicken from frying pan and drain off all but 3 tablespoons of oil.

Add onion, bell pepper, celery; cook, stirring, about 4 minutes. Stir in garlic, okra, tomatoes, thyme, parsley, and hot pepper sauce. Return chicken to the frying pan. Cover and simmer about 15 minutes or until a fork pierces the chicken easily.   Makes 4 servings.

Per Serving (approx):
Calories 648
Carbohydrate 26 gm

Protein 63 gm
Sodium 473 mg

Fat 33 gm
Cholesterol 199 mg

Down-Home Smothered Chicken

1 tablespoon vegetable oil
4 skinless, boneless chicken breasts
1 1/2 teaspoons paprika
1/4 teaspoon salt
1/4 teaspoon pepper
1 cup baby carrots, peeled
1 cup sliced onions
1 cup sliced celery

1/2 cup dry white wine
1 can (14 ounces) low-sodium
  chicken broth
1 bay leaf
2 tablespoons flour
1/2 cup nonfat milk
1/4 teaspoon ground nutmeg
2 tablespoons chopped parsley

Heat oil in a skillet. Season chicken with paprika, salt, and pepper. Place in skillet and brown on both sides, about 10 minutes. Remove chicken.

Put carrots, onions, and celery in the skillet, adding a little water if necessary to prevent sticking. Cover and simmer for 15 minutes, stirring occasionally. Return chicken to the pan, add wine, broth, and bay leaf. Simmer for about 40 minutes, turning chicken several times, until tender. Remove bay leaf. Remove chicken and vegetables to serving platter.

In a small bowl, whisk together flour, milk, and nutmeg. Add to the skillet and stir until smooth. Simmer for 5 minutes. Pour over chicken. Sprinkle with fresh parsley.   Makes 4 servings.

Per Serving (approx):
Calories 681
Carbohydrate 31 gm

Protein 78 gm
Sodium 491 mg

Fat 25 gm
Cholesterol 176 mg

"You have to please men with cookery, or they will be worse than bears with sore heads."

Pullman Fried Chicken

You're probably too young to recall the wonderful fried chicken served in the Pullman dining cars of the railroads back in the forties. But you can recreate it with this recipe.

3 whole chickens, cut up
6 tablespoons cooking oil
1/4 cup flour
1/2 teaspoon salt
1/8 teaspoon pepper
3 slices salt pork, 1/2-inch
   thick, cut in square dice

3 pinches ground nutmeg
3/4 cup melted butter
3 cups light cream or
   evaporated milk, divided
Paprika
Parsley sprigs, for garnish

Brush the chicken pieces with oil and dredge in flour mixed with salt and pepper. In a large skillet, fry salt pork until brown. Add nutmeg. Place chicken on top of pork (without draining off fat) and baste with melted butter. Cover skillet and simmer about 30 minutes until tender.

Turn chicken pieces over. Add 1 cup cream, turn heat up, and cook uncovered to reduce sauce. When sauce is fairly thick, add another cup of cream, cook as before until thickened, and add the last cup cream. Cook until thick. To serve, spoon cream gravy over chicken pieces, sprinkle with paprika, and garnish with parsley sprigs.

Makes 12 servings.

Per Serving (approx):
Calories 669
Carbohydrate 5 gm

Protein 54 gm
Sodium 278 mg

Fat 48 gm
Cholesterol 262 mg

Chicken Maryland

Fried favorites like traditional Chicken Maryland are high in fat, but this version comes close to the real thing using a nonstick skillet and a little light margarine.

1/4 cup flour
Salt and pepper to taste
1/2 teaspoon paprika
1 1/4 pounds skinless,
   boneless chicken breasts

1 1/2 tablespoons light
   margarine (stick form)
1 can (8 1/2 ounces) creamed
   corn

On a plate, combine flour, salt and pepper to taste, and paprika; coat chicken on both sides with flour mixture. In large skillet, melt margarine. Add chicken; cook 2 to 3 minutes on each side or until browned, turning once. Simmer for about 10 minutes longer or until chicken is cooked through.

Remove chicken from skillet and set aside. To drippings in skillet, add corn; stir well to incorporate pan drippings. Season with salt, pepper and paprika to taste. Serve chicken with corn sauce on the side.

Makes 4 servings.

Per Serving (approx):
Calories 255	*Protein 37 gm*	*Fat 5 gm*
Carbohydrate 16 gm	*Sodium 250 mg*	*Cholesterol 97 mg*

"Three generations of Perdues have headed Perdue Farms, one of the largest poultry producers in the United States. The Perdue family (originally from Perdeaux) emigrated from France to the Maryland region more than 300 years ago."

Hot and Sour Chicken
on Saffron Rice

4 skinless, boneless chicken
  breast halves
2 tablespoons Cajun seasoning
1 tablespoon butter

1 tablespoon olive oil
2 cups cooked saffron rice*
Sweet and Sour Sauce

Sprinkle each chicken breast half with Cajun seasoning. In a frying pan, heat butter and olive oil. Add chicken and sauté, turning, until chicken is golden brown and a fork can be inserted easily. Remove chicken from frying pan and cut into 1/2-inch strips.

Prepare Sweet and Sour Sauce. To serve, place rice on plate, top with chicken strips and serve with warm Sweet and Sour Sauce on the side.

Makes 4 servings.

SWEET AND SOUR SAUCE:
In a small saucepan, combine 3/4 cup orange juice, 2 tablespoons lemon juice, 1 tablespoon sugar, 1/2 teaspoon ground allspice, and 1/2 teaspoon toasted sesame oil. Bring to a boil. In a small bowl, mix 1 tablespoon cornstarch and 2 tablespoons water. Add to saucepan and cook until mixture has slightly thickened.

*Packaged saffron rice mix is available in most markets. If not, you can substitute long-grain white rice seasoned with saffron or cumin.

Per Serving (approx):
Calories 395
Carbohydrate 41 gm

Protein 32 gm
Sodium 101 mg

Fat 11 gm
Cholesterol 88 mg

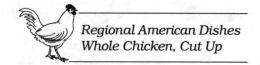

Fried Chicken and Onions

2 whole chickens, cut up
  (1 1/2 pounds each)
3 onions, sliced
1 teaspoon salt

1/4 teaspoon pepper
1/2 teaspoon poultry seasoning
3/4 cup water
Parsley, for garnish

In a large frying pan over low heat, place chicken, skin side up, topped with onion slices. Sprinkle with salt, pepper, and poultry seasoning. Cover; simmer for 40 minutes until chicken is tender. Remove chicken. Add water to onions and pan drippings. Cook until reduced by half. Serve over chicken. Garnish with parsley.   Makes 6 servings.

Per Serving (approx):
Calories 428	*Protein 47 gm*	*Fat 23 gm*
Carbohydrate 9 gm	*Sodium 525 mg*	*Cholesterol 182 mg*

Fried Chicken with Cream

5 tablespoons butter, softened,
 divided
1 whole chicken, cut up
1/4 cup flour
1/2 teaspoon dried marjoram

1/2 teaspoon salt
1/4 teaspoon lemon pepper
1/2 teaspoon poultry seasoning
1 tablespoon vegetable oil
1 cup whipping cream

Rub chicken with 2 1/2 tablespoons butter and refrigerate for 1 hour. On a large plate, mix flour, marjoram, salt, pepper, and poultry seasoning. Dredge cold chicken pieces in flour to coat well.

In a heavy skillet heat oil and remaining butter. Brown chicken pieces on both sides and add cream. Cover and simmer for 15 minutes; uncover and simmer for 15 minutes more. Remove chicken; add additional cream or milk to sauce if necessary. Serve sauce over chicken.
                    Makes 4 servings.

Per Serving (approx):
Calories 980	*Protein 71 gm*	*Fat 74 gm*
Carbohydrate 8 gm	*Sodium 714 mg*	*Cholesterol 394 mg*

Chicken Croquettes
with Cream Sauce

Vegetable oil for deep-fat frying
2 cups cooked, diced chicken
1 cup cooked rice
1/2 cup minced celery
2 tablespoons minced onion
1/4 cup diced pimento
1 teaspoon flour

1/4 teaspoon salt
1/4 teaspoon poultry seasoning
1 beaten egg
1/3 cup evaporated milk
3/4 cup fine, dry bread crumbs
Mustard Cream Sauce

Heat oil in a deep-fat fryer to 375 degrees. Combine chicken, rice, vegetables, pimento, flour, salt, and poultry seasoning. Stir in egg and milk. Shape into 12 croquettes. Coat with bread crumbs. Fry croquettes for 2 to 5 minutes until brown. Drain on absorbent paper. Serve with Mustard Cream Sauce.   Makes 6 servings.

MUSTARD CREAM SAUCE:
Blend 3 tablespoons melted butter, 1 tablespoon prepared mustard, 3 tablespoons flour, and 1/4 teaspoon salt. Heat, stirring constantly. Add 1 1/2 cups chicken broth (or 1 1/2 cups milk) and 1 chicken bouillon cube slowly. Cook over low heat, stirring constantly until thick.

Per Serving (approx):
Calories 335
Carbohydrate 23 gm

Protein 18 gm
Sodium 992 mg

Fat 19 gm
Cholesterol 87 mg

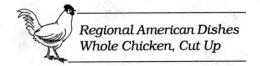

Southern Fried Chicken

This is our favorite recipe for fried chicken.

1 whole chicken, quartered
1 cup flour
1 teaspoon poultry seasoning
1/2 teaspoon dried basil
1/2 teaspoon pepper

2 cups cracker crumbs
2 eggs
1/3 cup milk
Vegetable oil
Salt to taste

Preheat oven to 350 degrees.

Combine flour, poultry seasoning, basil, and pepper. Mound on a plate or wax paper. Make another mound of cracker crumbs. Beat the eggs lightly with milk.

In a large skillet heat 1 inch of oil. Dredge chicken pieces in flour, shake off excess, and dip in egg mixture. Finish by rolling the chicken in cracker crumbs, thoroughly coating all surfaces. Fry pieces to rich, golden brown on both sides, turning once.

Transfer fried pieces to an ovenproof dish. Take care not to break the crust. Bake for 20 to 30 minutes or until chicken is cooked through. This tastes good with cream gravy. See the gravy described in the recipe for Herbed New Year's Roast Chicken (page 187). Use cream instead of chicken broth.   Makes 4 servings.

Per Serving (approx):
Calories 1323
Carbohydrate 83 gm

Protein 85 gm
Sodium 823 mg

Fat 72 gm
Cholesterol 437 mg

Herbed New Year's Roast Chicken

1 whole chicken (5 to 7 pounds)
4 green onions
3 tablespoons softened butter
  or margarine
1 tablespoon minced sage
  leaves, or 1 teaspoon dried sage

1 tablespoon minced thyme
  or 1 teaspoon dried thyme
2 tablespoons flour
2 cups chicken broth or 1 cup
  each chicken broth and
  half-and-half
Quick Hoppin' John

Preheat oven to 350 degrees. Remove giblets from chicken and set aside. Rinse chicken inside and out and pat dry. In a food processor, combine green onions, butter, sage, and thyme. Pulse on and off several times to form a paste. Rub mixture inside and outside of chicken, placing any remaining mixture in the cavity. Roast 2 to 2 1/2 hours (15 to 20 minutes per pound) until juices run clear, with no hint of pink when thigh is pierced. Remove chicken to a serving platter and keep warm.

To prepare gravy, pour pan juices into a heatproof measuring cup. Skim off 3 tablespoons clear yellow drippings from top of juices and return the drippings to roasting pan. Discard remaining drippings from measuring cup, reserving degreased juices for gravy; add enough chicken broth to make 2 1/2 cups total liquid. Stir flour into drippings in roasting pan. Cook over medium heat 4 to 5 minutes until well browned, stirring and scraping bottom of pan. Gradually stir in pan juice mixture; simmer 3 to 4 minutes until gravy is thickened, stirring occasionally. Serve with Quick Hoppin' John. Makes 6 to 8 servings.

QUICK HOPPIN' JOHN:
In a large skillet, fry 1/2 pound lean bacon until crisp. Remove bacon, drain on paper towels, crumble, and reserve. Pour off and discard all but 1 tablespoon bacon drippings from pan. Add 1 cup chopped onions and sauté about 5 minutes or until translucent. Stir in 1 cup long-grain rice, 1 can (16 ounces) undrained black-eyed peas, and 1–2/3 cups chicken broth or water. Cover and simmer 20 to 30 minutes until the rice is tender. Add the reserved crumbled bacon and toss to combine.

Per Serving (approx), including rice:

Calories 814	*Protein 75 gm*	*Fat 44 gm*
Carbohydrate 29 gm	*Sodium 1138 mg*	*Cholesterol 294 mg*

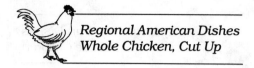
Little Italy Chicken and Rice

Every big city has its "Little Italy"; this recipe came from that neighborhood in New York City.

1 whole chicken, cut up
1 teaspoon dried Italian
   herb seasoning
Salt and pepper to taste
2 tablespoons olive oil
1 cup white rice

1 onion, coarsely chopped
1 green bell pepper, diced
1 can (14 1/2 ounces) Italian
   style stewed tomatoes
2 cups chicken broth

Preheat oven to 375 degrees.

Season chicken with Italian seasoning, and salt and pepper to taste. In a Dutch oven, heat oil. Add chicken; cook 6 to 8 minutes until brown on all sides, turning occasionally. Remove and set aside.

To the drippings in pan, add rice, onion, and bell pepper; sauté 2 to 3 minutes. Return chicken to the Dutch oven; stir in tomatoes and chicken broth. Cover and bake 45 to 50 minutes until rice is tender and chicken is cooked through.   **Makes 5 to 6 servings.**

Per Serving (approx):
Calories 618   *Protein 56 gm*   *Fat 32 gm*
Carbohydrate 26 gm   *Sodium 753 mg*   *Cholesterol 213 mg*

Between 1899 and 1909, poultry production in the United States increased by nearly 50 percent. Petaluma, California, which served the San Francisco market, and Vineland and Hunterdon County in New Jersey, which served the New York area, were almost totally responsible for this growth.

Chicken Biscuit Pie

Crusty biscuits topping a rich chicken pie is the ultimate in country cooking.

2 whole chickens, cut up
1 onion, sliced
2 carrots, cut into 2-inch pieces
3 cups water
2 tablespoons butter
2 tablespoons flour
1 cup light cream

1/2 teaspoon poultry seasoning
1/4 teaspoon dried basil
1 tablespoons minced chives
1 tablespoon chopped parsley
1/8 teaspoon pepper
1/2 teaspoon salt
Baking Powder Biscuits (from
    the refrigerator case)

Preheat oven to 425 degrees.

In a large saucepan, combine chicken, onion, carrots, and water and boil. Partially cover, lower heat, and simmer for about 35 minutes, turning chicken once and skimming any scum that rises to the surface. Continue to simmer the chicken until done.

In a skillet melt butter and stir in flour. Add the cream, and whisk carefully.

When chicken is done, pull meat from bones in large pieces and set aside. Stir 1 cup cooking liquid into the butter mixture and boil carefully, stirring constantly until sauce bubbles and thickens. In a baking dish combine sauce, chicken, and spices. Top with rounds of biscuit dough and bake 25 minutes.   Makes 6 servings.

Per Serving (approx):
Calories 1217
Carbohydrate 44 gm

Protein 98 gm
Sodium 1111 mg

Fat 72 gm
Cholesterol 415 mg

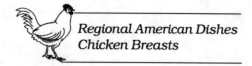

Chicken and Spinach Medley

If you like, you can call this Chicken Florentine, but it's called chicken and spinach in the Midwest where we got this recipe.

1 tablespoon vegetable oil	6 mushrooms, sliced
1 clove garlic, minced	2 bunches spinach
4 skinless, boneless chicken	(about 1 1/2 pounds)
breast halves	1/2 teaspoon salt
1/2 cup low-sodium chicken broth	1/4 teaspoon pepper
1/2 cup green bell pepper slivers	3 tablespoons grated Romano
1 onion, cut into thin rings	cheese
	1 cup fresh bread croutons

In a small frying pan, heat oil. Add garlic, stirring to spread it evenly in the frying pan. Arrange the chicken in a single layer over the garlic and cook about 5 minutes; turn and cook 5 minutes more. Set aside.

In a large frying pan, boil chicken broth. Add bell pepper, onion, and mushrooms; cook 3 minutes. Add spinach and cook, stirring with other vegetables, about 2 minutes more. Remove chicken from the small frying pan and cut into strips. Add chicken strips to vegetables in the large frying pan; stir to mix well. Sprinkle with salt and pepper. Remove to serving dish and top with cheese and croutons.   Makes 4 servings.

Per Serving (approx):
Calories 296

Carbohydrate 15 gm

Protein 35 gm

Sodium 580 mg

Fat 11 gm

Cholesterol 85 mg

CASSEROLES

Chicken and Onion-Potato Casserole

4 cups peeled, thinly sliced potatoes
4 to 5 onions, sliced
Salt and pepper to taste
Ground thyme to taste
1/2 cup hot water

1 can (13 ounces) evaporated milk
2 slices bacon
2 tablespoons butter
6 pounds cut-up chicken

Preheat oven to 400 degrees.

In a large roasting pan, combine potatoes and onions and sprinkle with salt, pepper, and thyme to taste. Add hot water. Reserve 1/4 cup milk and pour remainder over vegetables. Put in the roasting pan in the oven while preparing the chicken.

In a large skillet, cook bacon until browned; remove and drain on paper towels. Add butter to the skillet, then chicken, and brown on all sides, removing pieces as they brown. Put chicken in the roasting pan and sprinkle lightly with salt, pepper, and thyme to taste. Crumble bacon and sprinkle over top. Cover tightly with foil and bake for 1 hour. Uncover, pour reserved milk over top, and sprinkle with paprika. Bake 30 minutes longer.

Makes 8 servings.

Per Serving (approx):
Calories 782
Carbohydrate 32 gm

Protein 76 gm
Sodium 327 mg

Fat 39 gm
Cholesterol 285 mg

"What I say is that, if a man really likes potatoes, he must be a pretty decent sort of fellow."
A.A. Mine, *Not That It Matters*

Chicken Sour Cream Bake

6 skinless, boneless chicken
  breast halves
1 jar (4 ounces) chipped beef,
  rinsed in boiling water and drained

12 slices bacon
1 pint sour cream
1 can cream of asparagus or
  cream of mushroom soup
Paprika

Preheat oven to 325 degrees.

Wrap each breast section in a slice of chipped beef, then wrap with bacon. Mix sour cream and soup. Place the chicken rolls in a greased casserole dish and pour the soup mixture over it. Sprinkle with paprika. Bake uncovered for 2 hours.   Makes 6 to 8 servings.

Per Serving (approx):
Calories 353   Protein 31 gm   Fat 23 gm
Carbohydrate 6 gm   Sodium 746 mg   Cholesterol 101 mg

Chicken, Spinach, and Potato Casserole

4 medium potatoes, peeled,
  thinly sliced
1 package (10 ounces) frozen chopped
  spinach, thawed and well drained
1 cup sour cream
1/2 cup shredded Swiss cheese

1/2 teaspoon nutmeg
1 pound boneless chicken
  breasts
1/2 cup milk
Salt and pepper to taste
1/3 cup flavored bread crumbs

Preheat oven to 375 degrees.

Place the potatoes in a 1 1/2-quart glass casserole. Combine spinach, sour cream, cheese, and nutmeg. Spread mixture over potatoes.

Dip chicken breasts in milk; sprinkle with salt and pepper to taste. Coat with bread crumbs. Place on top of spinach mixture. Bake for 45 minutes or until chicken is thoroughly cooked.   Makes 4 servings.

Per Serving (approx):
Calories 645   Protein 42 gm   Fat 25 gm
Carbohydrate 62 gm   Sodium 270 mg   Cholesterol 117 mg

Baked Chicken Hungarian

1/4 cup butter
3 pounds cut up chicken
Paprika
1 small head cabbage, cored and
  cut 1/2-inch thick
2 red apples, cored and sliced

1 onion, thinly sliced
1 tablespoon grated lemon peel
2 teaspoons caraway seed
1 teaspoon sugar
1 1/2 cups shredded Swiss
  cheese

Preheat oven to 375 degrees.

In a large skillet, melt the butter. Dust the chicken with paprika. Brown the chicken on all sides. Cover, reduce heat, and simmer 30 minutes.

Place cabbage slices on the bottom of a buttered 9 x 13 baking dish. Cover with aluminum foil and bake 20 minutes, or until cabbage is almost tender.

Remove cabbage from oven. Uncover and arrange apples and onion over cabbage. Sprinkle with lemon peel, caraway seed, and sugar. Arrange chicken pieces on top. Cover and continue baking 25 to 30 minutes longer until cabbage and chicken are tender. Remove from oven. Uncover; sprinkle with cheese. Return to oven just until cheese is melted, about 5 minutes.   Makes 6 to 8 servings.

Per Serving (approx):
Calories 498
Carbohydrate 17 gm

Protein 42 gm
Sodium 236 mg

Fat 29 gm
Cholesterol 172 mg

Chicken and Noodles Almondine

This recipe freezes well and is perfect for making ahead when you'll need a special dinner in a hurry.

1/2 pound noodles
6 tablespoons butter
1/4 cup onion, chopped
1/4 cup celery, chopped
6 tablespoons flour
1 teaspoon salt
1/2 teaspoon celery salt
1/4 teaspoon pepper
1 1/2 cups chicken broth

1/2 cup sauterne or chablis
1 cup whipping cream
1 can (6 ounces) mushrooms
3 tablespoons minced parsley
1/2 cup grated cheddar cheese
1/2 cup slivered almonds
5 cups chicken, cooked, skinned
  and cut in pieces

Preheat oven to 375 degrees.

Cook noodles according to package directions.

In a saucepan, melt the butter; add onion and celery. Cook until onion is translucent. Blend in flour, salt, celery salt, and pepper. Heat until mixture bubbles. Remove from the heat and gradually stir in the chicken broth, wine, and cream. Stir constantly until sauce thickens. Stir in the mushrooms and parsley.

Combine cheddar cheese and almonds; set aside.

Into a greased 3-quart casserole, layer 1/3 each noodles, chicken, sauce, and almond cheese mixture. Repeat layers twice. Bake for 30 minutes.

Makes 10 servings.

Per Serving (approx):
Calories 439   *Protein 27 gm*   *Fat 25 gm*
Carbohydrate 24 gm   *Sodium 691 mg*   *Cholesterol 131 mg*

Chicken Rice Salad Casserole

2 cups diced cooked chicken
1 cup sliced celery
2 teaspoons minced onion
1/2 cup chopped walnuts
2 cups cooked rice
1 can cream of chicken soup
1/2 teaspoon salt

1/4 teaspoon pepper
1 tablespoon lemon juice
1/2 cup mayonnaise
1/2 cup water
3 hard-boiled eggs, sliced
2 cups crushed potato chips

Preheat oven to 450 degrees.

In a large bowl, combine first 9 ingredients. Mix mayonnaise with water until smooth and add to the chicken mixture. Gently fold in egg slices. Turn mixture into greased 9-inch square pan. Bake for 20 minutes. Remove and top with potato chips. Return to oven for another 5 minutes.

Makes 6 to 8 servings.

Per Serving (approx):
Calories 376
Carbohydrate 24 gm

Protein 16 gm
Sodium 616 mg

Fat 24 gm
Cholesterol 114 mg

Chicken Spinach Casserole

1 package (10 ounces) frozen
  spinach
1/4 cup minced onion
1/2 teaspoon garlic powder, divided
1/2 pound mushrooms, sliced

2 tablespoons diet margarine,
  melted
1 chicken, cooked, skinned,
  and chopped
1 cup grated low-fat mozzarella
  cheese

Preheat oven to 350 degrees.

Cook spinach according to package directions, eliminating any salt; drain. Mix onion with spinach. Arrange the spinach in a baking dish. Sprinkle with 1/4 teaspoon of the garlic powder. Arrange mushrooms on the spinach and drizzle with melted margarine. Place chicken on the mushrooms and sprinkle with remaining 1/4 teaspoon garlic powder. Top with cheese. Bake for 30 minutes.

Makes 6 servings.

Per Serving (approx):
Calories 79
Carbohydrate 5 gm

Protein 7 gm
Sodium 129 mg

Fat 3 gm
Cholesterol 11 mg

Chicken Noodle Casserole

1 pound egg noodles
1 cup cottage cheese
1 cup sour cream
6 tablespoons grated Parmesan
   cheese, divided

1 teaspoon salt
1/4 teaspoon hot pepper sauce
1/4 cup sliced pitted ripe olives
2 1/2 cups diced cooked chicken

Cook noodles according to package directions. Combine cottage cheese, sour cream, 4 tablespoons of the Parmesan, salt, and hot pepper sauce. Stir in olives, noodles, and chicken. Turn into greased 2-quart casserole and sprinkle with the remaining Parmesan. Cover and refrigerate. One hour before serving, place in 350 degree oven and bake, covered, for 35 minutes. Uncover and bake for 25 minutes longer.   Makes 6 servings.

Per Serving (approx):
Calories 314
Carbohydrate 17 gm

Protein 27 gm
Sodium 750 mg

Fat 16 gm
Cholesterol 87 mg

Hot Chicken Casserole

2 cups cubed cooked chicken
2 cups thinly sliced celery
1 cup mayonnaise
1/2 cup toasted, slivered almonds

2 teaspoons lemon juice
1/2 teaspoon salt
1/2 cup grated Parmesan cheese
1 cup toasted bread cubes
   or croutons

Preheat oven to 450 degrees.

Combine all ingredients except the cheese and bread cubes. Pile lightly into a greased baking dish. Sprinkle with bread cubes and cheese. Bake for 20 minutes, or until bubbly.   Makes 6 servings.

Per Serving (approx):
Calories 434
Carbohydrate 11 gm

Protein 18 gm
Sodium 714 mg

Fat 36 gm
Cholesterol 55 mg

Chicken Sweet Potato Bake

Some like yams better than sweet potatoes, so try both.

1 teaspoon ground ginger
1/2 teaspoon ground nutmeg
1/2 teaspoon pepper
1 skinless whole chicken, cut up

4 sweet potatoes, cooked,
   peeled, cut into 1/2-inch slices
2 teaspoons grated orange peel
3/4 cup apple juice

Preheat oven to 400 degrees.

Combine ginger, nutmeg, and pepper; sprinkle on all sides of the chicken. In a shallow 2-quart baking dish, arrange the chicken. Place sweet potatoes around the chicken. Sprinkle with orange peel and pour apple juice over all.

Bake, basting the chicken and sweet poatotes with liquid in dish several times. It should take about 1 hour until a fork pierces the chicken easily.   Makes 4 servings.

Per Serving (approx):
Calories 451
Carbohydrate 38 gm

Protein 47 gm
Sodium 224 mg

Fat 12 gm
Cholesterol 134 mg

Chicken and Potatoes au Gratin

Try Yukon Gold, a new variety of potatoes, for this recipe. Red or white potatoes also work well.

1 whole chicken, cooked, skinned,
  boned, cut into pieces
1/2 cup chicken broth
1 clove garlic, peeled and halved
3/4 cup nonfat sour cream
3/4 cup skim milk, divided
1 onion, minced
3 tablespoons chopped pimento
1 teaspoon prepared mustard

4 potatoes, sliced thin
1/4 teaspoon salt
1/4 teaspoon pepper
2 tablespoons lemon juice
2 tablespoons grated Romano
  cheese
2 tablespoons light butter-
  flavored margarine, melted
1 cup whole wheat bread crumbs

Preheat oven to 375 degrees.

Combine the cooked chicken with the broth. Spray a baking dish with vegetable spray. Rub dish with garlic halves. Mince garlic and place in small bowl. Add sour cream, 1/4 cup of the milk, onion, pimento, and mustard; stir to mix well.

Sprinkle the potatoes with salt and pepper.

In a prepared baking dish, layer 1/3 of potatoes, half of chicken mixture, and half of sour cream mixture. Repeat layers and top with remaining potatoes. Pour remaining 1/2 cup of milk over all; sprinkle with lemon juice and Romano cheese. Combine margarine and bread crumbs; spread over all. Bake about 1 hour until potatoes are tender.

Makes 6 servings.

Per Serving (approx):
Calories 243
Carbohydrate 48 gm

Protein 9 gm
Sodium 396 mg

Fat 1 gm
Cholesterol 3 mg

Casseroles
Chicken Breasts

Calico Chicken Skillet Casserole

The name comes from the "colorful as calico" look of this stove-top casserole.

1 package (5 ounces) yellow
long-grain rice
2 packages (5 ounces each) frozen
gumbo vegetables
1 pound chicken breast fillets,
cut in thick strips,
or 1 pound chicken tenders

1 1/2 teaspoons mesquite
flavored barbecue seasoning
1 tablespoon vegetable oil
1/3 cup minced onion

Cook rice and vegetables according to package directions. Keep hot and do not drain.

Sprinkle chicken with mesquite barbecue seasoning. In a skillet, heat oil. Add chicken, then onion, and sauté until chicken is brown and a fork can be inserted easily. Add cooked rice and gumbo vegetables, stirring well. Cover and simmer for about 5 minutes.   Makes 4 servings.

Per Serving (approx):
Calories 350
Carbohydrate 39 gm

Protein 33 gm
Sodium 109 mg

Fat 7 gm
Cholesterol 77 mg

Buffet Chicken Medley

2 tablespoons butter
4 boneless whole chicken breasts,
   quartered
1 onion, cut into 1/4-inch chunks
1 jar (16 ounces) marinated artichoke
   hearts, sliced, liquid reserved

4 tomatoes, cut into wedges
1 teaspoon salt
1/2 teaspoon pepper
1 avocado, cut into 1/2-inch
   wedges
1/4 pound feta cheese, crumbled

Preheat oven to 350 degrees.

In a frying pan, melt butter. Add chicken breast and sauté, turning, about 5 minutes until lightly browned. Remove the chicken to warm dish.

To pan drippings, add onion and fry about 3 minutes, stirring. Add artichoke hearts, reserved marinade, and tomato wedges; cook about 2 minutes and remove from heat.

In a baking dish, layer 8 pieces of chicken, 1/2 teaspoon of the salt, 1/4 teaspoon of the pepper, half vegetable mixture, half avocado wedges, and half feta cheese. Repeat layers. Bake about 25 minutes until thoroughly heated.
                                       Makes 8 servings.

Per Serving (approx):
Calories 398
Carbohydrate 14 gm

Protein 33 gm
Sodium 753 mg

Fat 23 gm
Cholesterol 100 mg

Cheese and Vegetables Chicken

1 1/2 cups coarsely chopped
  broccoli
1 1/2 cups coarsely chopped
  cauliflower
1 tablespoon lemon juice
2 tablespoons canola oil
4 skinless, boneless chicken breasts,
  cut into 1-inch chunks
2 tablespoons butter or margarine

3 tablespoons flour
1/2 teaspoon seasoned salt
2 cups milk
1 cup grated Monterey jack
  cheese
3/4 cup dry Italian seasoned
  bread crumbs
1 tablespoon butter or
  margarine, melted

Preheat oven to 350 degrees.

Cook broccoli and cauliflower until tender. Drain well and toss with lemon juice. Spread mixture evenly in a 9-inch baking dish. In large skillet, heat oil. Add chicken and stir-fry 5 to 8 minutes, until golden brown and cooked through. Cover pan and remove from heat.

In a saucepan, melt butter. Blend in flour and seasoned salt. Cook, stirring, until mixture is smooth and bubbly. Remove from heat and whisk in milk. Return to heat and cook, stirring constantly, for one minute. Fold 3/4 cup of the cheese and the cooked chicken into sauce. Spoon evenly over vegetable mixture. Sprinkle with remaining cheese. Toss bread crumbs with melted butter and spread evenly over cheese.

Bake for 20 to 25 minutes or until heated through.   Makes 4 servings.

Per Serving (approx):
Calories 613
Carbohydrate 28 gm

Protein 45 gm
Sodium 1077 mg

Fat 35 gm
Cholesterol 154 mg

Reuben Casserole

1 1/2 pounds chicken breast fillets
1 can (16 ounces) sauerkraut,
   drained
3/4 cup grated Swiss cheese
1/2 cup reduced calorie mayonnaise

1/4 cup reduced calorie
   Thousand Island dressing
1 tomato, thinly sliced
2 slices rye bread, cut into
   1/2-inch cubes

Preheat oven to 375 degrees. In an 8-inch square baking pan, spread sauerkraut. Top with chicken breasts and sprinkle with cheese. Mix mayonnaise and dressing; spread evenly over the cheese. Top with tomatoes and bread cubes. Bake, uncovered, 45 minutes until chicken is done. Let stand 5 minutes before serving. Makes 4 servings.

Per Serving (approx):
Calories 306
Carbohydrate 23 gm

Protein 50 gm
Sodium 1294 mg

Fat 24 gm
Cholesterol 143 mg

Chili Chicken Fiesta

2 tablespoons vegetable oil
2 skinless, boneless chicken breast
   halves, cut in 1-inch pieces
1/2 cup chopped celery
1/2 cup chopped onion
1 can (14 1/2 ounces) chicken broth
2 tablespoons chopped parsley
2 teaspoons chili powder

1 teaspoon dried oregano
1 clove garlic, minced
1/2 cup chopped tomato
1 cup quick-cooking long-grain
   rice and wild rice
1 can (15 ounces) red kidney
   beans
1 can (12 ounces) Mexican corn,
   undrained

Preheat oven to 350 degrees. In a frying pan, heat oil. Add chicken and sauté about 5 minutes until brown on all sides. Remove the chicken to a large baking dish. In the same pan, sauté celery and onion about 3 minutes until onion is translucent. Add broth, parsley, chili powder, oregano, garlic, tomato, rice, kidney beans, and corn. Stir to mix well. Add the mixture to chicken. Cover and bake for about 45 minutes.

Makes 6 servings.

Per Serving (approx):
Calories 444
Carbohydrate 63 gm

Protein 30 gm
Sodium 812 mg

Fat 8 gm
Cholesterol 30 mg

Easy Chicken Casserole

We like this recipe so much we make it a few days ahead and warm it up when we're ready to serve it.

4 tablespoons butter
1 whole chicken, cut up
3 teaspoons chopped green onions
   or chives
1 teaspoon curry powder
1/2 teaspoon salt

2 cans (10 3/4 ounces) cream of
   celery soup
1 can sliced mushrooms (3 or 4
   ounces), or 6 fresh
   mushrooms, sliced
1/2 cup sauvignon blanc

Preheat oven to 350 degrees.

In a large skillet, melt butter and brown the chicken. Place it in a casserole. Combine onions, curry powder, salt, soup, mushrooms, and wine. Pour over chicken. Cover and bake for 1 1/2 hours or until chicken is tender. Uncover for last 10 minutes of baking.   Makes 4 to 6 servings.

Per Serving (approx):
Calories 638
Carbohydrate 28 gm

Protein 49 gm
Sodium 1179 mg

Fat 35 gm
Cholesterol 214 mg

> "To a large extent we can let others do our cooking for us . . . but unless we too know how to cook, those who prepare our food will prepare it anyway they like and we must take what we get."
> John Erskine, *The Complete Life*

Sherry Chicken with Cheese

It's almost a shame to put cheese on this chicken, because it smells so good without it, but the cheese really adds a whole new taste.

6 chicken breasts
3 tablespoons flour
1 1/2 teaspoons paprika
1 1/2 teaspoons salt, divided
2 tablespoons vegetable oil
3 tablespoons butter

1/2 cup dry sherry
1 cup chicken broth
1 1/2 teaspoons cornstarch
1 cup light cream
1/2 cup white wine
1 cup grated Swiss cheese

Split and skin chicken breasts. Mix flour, paprika, and 3/4 teaspoon of the salt. Thoroughly dredge the chicken with this mixture. Heat the oil and butter. Brown the chicken. Add sherry and broth. Cover and simmer until tender. Set aside to an ovenware platter.

Mix cornstarch with cream and remaining salt. Stir into pan drippings. Add wine and cook until slightly thickened. Pour over chicken; sprinkle cheese over the top. Put in the oven until cheese is melted.

Makes 6 to 12 servings.

Per Serving (approx):
Calories 340
Carbohydrate 4 gm

Protein 32 gm
Sodium 542 mg

Fat 20 gm
Cholesterol 113 mg

*Casseroles
Precooked Chicken*

Good and Green Chicken Casserole

This is a very satisfying one-dish meal that can be prepared in less than 30 minutes.

1/2 pound spinach noodles
1/2 cup chicken broth
1 tomato, coarsely chopped
1 cup chopped green onion
1 avocado, cut into chunks
1/3 cup sliced ripe olives

1/2 teaspoon salt, divided
1/2 teaspoon pepper, divided
1 cup nonfat yogurt
1 chicken, cooked, skinned,
   boned, and cut in large pieces

Preheat oven to 350 degrees.

Cook spinach noodles according to package directions. Drain and place in large bowl; pour warm broth over the noodles.

In a medium bowl, combine tomato, onion, avocado, olives, 1/4 teaspoon of the salt and 1/4 teaspoon of the pepper. Sprinkle warm chicken with the remaining 1/4 teaspoon salt, and 1/4 teaspoon pepper; gently mix with yogurt. Add seasoned vegetables and chicken to the bowl of noodles, mixing well.

Pour into a baking dish and bake for about 15 minutes until heated through.   Makes 6 servings.

Per Serving (approx):
Calories 208
Carbohydrate 30 gm

Protein 7 gm
Sodium 435 mg

Fat 7 gm
Cholesterol 1 mg

Chicken and Rice Casserole

If you don't have champagne on hand for this recipe, a dry white wine is fine instead.

1 can (10 3/4 ounces) condensed
   cream of chicken soup
2 1/2 tablespoons grated onion
Salt and pepper to taste
1/2 teaspoon parsley flakes
1/2 teaspoon celery flakes
1/8 teaspoon dried thyme

1 cup champagne
2/3 cup chicken broth
1/4 cup chopped mushrooms
1/3 cup converted rice
1/2 cup cooked chicken, diced
1/2 teaspoon paprika

Preheat oven to 375 degrees.

In a saucepan, combine soup, onion, and seasonings. Gradually add champagne and broth; blend thoroughly. Add mushrooms; bring to a boil, stirring constantly. Pour half of the soup mixture into a casserole. Make 2 layers each of rice (right from the box) and chicken. Add remaining soup mixture.

Cover and bake for 20 minutes; stir after 10 minutes. Sprinkle with paprika.
                        Makes 4 servings.

Per Serving (approx):
Calories 134
Carbohydrate 13 gm

Protein 8 gm
Sodium 863 mg

Fat 5 gm
Cholesterol 19 mg

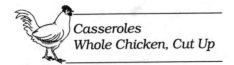

Casseroles
Whole Chicken, Cut Up

Chicken Curry Casserole

The tomato sauce and curry powder are responsible for the unusual flavor of this casserole.

2 whole chickens, cut up	2 cans (20 ounces each) tomatoes
2/3 cup flour	1 can (8 ounces) tomato sauce
1/2 cup vegetable oil	2/3 cup chablis
1 large onion, minced	2 teaspoons curry powder
1 large green bell pepper, minced	1 tablespoon chopped parsley
Salt and pepper to taste	

Preheat oven to 350 degrees.

Roll chicken in the flour. In a skillet, heat oil and brown the chicken. Remove to a large casserole.

In the same skillet, sauté the onion and bell pepper. Add salt and pepper to taste, tomatoes, tomato sauce, wine, curry powder, and parsley. Pour over chicken, cover, and bake for 45 minutes until chicken is tender.

Makes 8 to 10 servings.

Per Serving (approx):
Calories 453
Carbohydrate 18 gm

Protein 45 gm
Sodium 450 mg

Fat 21 gm
Cholesterol 168 mg

Chicken and Broccoli au Gratin

The recipe calls for Parmesan cheese, but you can use cheddar instead.

3 cups diced cooked chicken
2 packages frozen broccoli
1/3 cup butter or margarine
1/3 cup flour
1 1/2 cups chicken broth

1 cup evaporated milk
1 cup chardonnay
Salt and pepper to taste
Worcestershire sauce to taste
1/4 cup grated Parmesan cheese

Preheat oven to 400 degrees.

Cook broccoli according to the directions on the package; drain; arrange in a greased casserole. In a saucepan, melt butter or margarine and stir in flour; add broth, milk, and wine. Cook, stirring constantly until mixture is thickened and smooth; continue cooking and stirring for 2 or 3 minutes. Add salt, pepper, and Worcestershire sauce to taste.

Arrange the chicken over the broccoli in the casserole, cover with wine sauce, and sprinkle generously with grated cheese. Bake for about 20 minutes or until bubbly.   Makes 6 servings.

Per Serving (approx):
Calories 307   *Protein 25 gm*   *Fat 16 gm*
Carbohydrate 10 gm   *Sodium 631 mg*   *Cholesterol 85 mg*

A recent survey of American households ranked chicken as one of their two best food values (the other was turkey).

Chicken en Casserole

4 pounds cut-up chicken
Pinch of dried thyme
Pinch of dried marjoram
Salt and pepper to taste
4 tablespoons olive oil
1/2 pound raw, lean ham slices,
  cut into thin strips
1 large onion, sliced thin
3 carrots, cut in chunks

1 cup merlot or other red wine
1/2 cup chicken broth
3 tablespoons margarine or
  butter
1 clove garlic, mashed
1 teaspoon ground cloves
1 teaspoon dried tarragon
1 bay leaf

Season chicken with thyme, marjoram, and salt and pepper to taste. Heat oil to smoking in a wok or large saucepan. Add chicken pieces and brown evenly, turning frequently. Drain off oil and discard.

In a bowl, combine remaining ingredients. Mix thoroughly and add to the chicken.

Cover and simmer for 45 minutes, turning twice during the cooking. Remove bay leaf before serving.   Makes 6 to 8 servings.

Per Serving (approx):
Calories 589
Carbohydrate 9 gm

Protein 51 gm
Sodium 588 mg

Fat 32 gm
Cholesterol 194 mg

POT PIES,
PASTRIES, &
MEATLOAVES

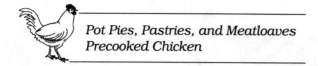

Chicken Pie

Although this recipe calls for a pie dough that is slightly thicker than one for a fruit pie, we've used the preformed ones that you can buy, and they work very well.

Pastry for a double crust pie
4 cups cooked and cubed chicken
Salt and pepper to taste
1/4 teaspoon ground nutmeg
1 tablespoon sugar

2 eggs, beaten
1 cup sauterne or chablis
1 cup chicken broth
4 artichoke bottoms, canned, drained, and diced
6 egg yolks, hard-cooked, sliced

Preheat oven to 450 degrees.

Line a a baking dish with pie pastry rolled a little thicker than for fruit pies. In a large bowl, toss the chicken with salt, pepper, nutmeg, and sugar. Add the remaining ingredients. Stir gently.

Place in the lined baking dish. Cover with a thinner pastry on top. Slit top to allow steam to escape. Bake for 15 minutes; reduce heat to 350 degrees; and bake for 30 minutes longer.

For a sharper taste, add 1/2 lemon sliced thin and use 3/4 cup white wine and 1/4 cup white vinegar.   Makes 4 to 6 servings.

Per Serving (approx):
Calories 405
Carbohydrate 16 gm

Protein 32 gm
Sodium 505 mg

Fat 21 gm
Cholesterol 346 mg

Chicken Pot Pie

This is a simple recipe for a traditional chicken pot pie.

1 whole chicken
1/2 stick butter
1 onion, chopped
1 cup chopped celery
1/2 cup chopped green bell pepper
8 mushrooms, sliced

1 package (12 ounces) frozen
  peas and carrots
1 cup chicken broth
1 tablespoon flour
Salt and pepper to taste
Biscuit mix

Preheat oven to 425 degrees.

Boil chicken until tender. Discard the skin and bones. Cut the meat into small pieces. In an ovenproof pan,* melt the butter. Add the onion, celery, bell pepper, and mushrooms. Cook over low heat for 15 minutes. Add peas and carrots. Simmer for 1 minute. Combine broth and flour and add to the vegetables. Add chicken and salt and pepper to taste. Top with biscuits and bake until brown.   Makes 4 to 6 servings.

*A glass or ceramic pie plate is good for this pie.

Per Serving (approx):
Calories 648
Carbohydrate 57 gm

Protein 43 gm
Sodium 1244 mg

Fat 27 gm
Cholesterol 142 mg

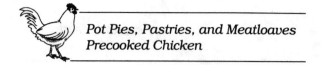

Fancy Puff Pie

Frozen puff pastry takes chicken pot pie uptown in this elegant presentation.

1/4 cup butter or margarine
1/4 cup chopped green onion
1/4 cup flour
1 cup chicken broth
1/4 cup dry sherry
Salt to taste
1/8 teaspoon white pepper
Pinch ground nutmeg
3 cups cooked chicken,
   cut into 1/4- by 2-inch strips

1/4 pound ham, cut into 1/4- by
   2-inch strips
1 1/2 cups asparagus,
   or 1 package (10 ounces)
   frozen asparagus, cut into
   2-inch pieces
1 cup whipping cream
1 sheet frozen puff pastry,
   thawed
1 egg, beaten

Preheat oven to 425 degrees. In a saucepan, melt the butter. Stir in the green onion and sauté 1 minute. Whisk in flour and cook 3 minutes. Add broth and sherry. Bring to a boil, whisking constantly. Season with salt to taste, pepper and nutmeg. Simmer 5 minutes. Stir in chicken, ham, asparagus, and cream. Pour chicken mixture into a 9-inch pie plate.

Using a dinner plate to trace the pattern, cut one 8-inch round crust from the pastry. Cut pastry shapes from extra pastry with a cookie cutter, if desired. Moisten cookie sheet with cold water. Place crust on a separate cookie sheet and prick with fork; brush with egg. Decorate with pastry shapes and brush shapes with egg.

Place crust and filled pie plate in oven. Bake 10 minutes. Reduce oven temperature to 350 degrees; bake 10 to 15 minutes longer until the crust is golden brown and the filling is hot and set. Remove crust and filled pie plate from oven. With a spatula, place the baked crust over the hot filling.
          Makes 4 servings.

Per Serving (approx):
Calories 618
Carbohydrate 15 gm

Protein 39 gm
Sodium 975 mg

Fat 43 gm
Cholesterol 256 mg

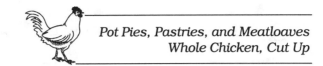
Chicken Pie Supreme

Chicken, mushrooms, and almonds in a cream sauce with a pie crust topping!

1/4 cup butter
1/4 cup flour
1 cup light cream
1/2 teaspoon salt (omit this if you use bouillon cube to make broth)
1/4 teaspoon pepper
1 cup chicken broth

1/4 teaspoon dried dill
1 teaspoon chopped parsley
3 to 4 cups diced cooked chicken
1 can (4 ounces) sliced mushrooms, drained
1/2 cup slivered almonds, toasted
Pastry for single-crust 9-inch pie

Preheat oven to 450 degrees.

Melt butter and blend in flour. Gradually stir in cream, and cook, stirring, until smooth and thick. Add salt, pepper, chicken broth, dill, and parsley, and cook until smooth and thick. Stir in chicken, mushrooms, and almonds.

Pour into 9-inch deep-dish pie plate* and cover with pastry. Slash top and bake for 10 minutes. Reduce heat to 350 degrees and bake 15 more minutes.   Makes 6 servings.

*We recommend a glass or ceramic pie plate.

Per Serving (approx):
Calories 442
Carbohydrate 22 gm

Protein 6 gm
Sodium 715 mg

Fat 36 gm
Cholesterol 65 mg

215

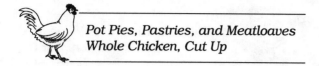

Two-Way Chicken Pie

Everybody likes chicken pie; whether you make it topped with biscuits or pastry, you can't go wrong. Here it is, both ways.

2 whole chickens, cut up
1 large onion, quartered
4 carrots, cut into pieces
Water to cook
1/4 teaspoon dried rosemary
1/2 teaspoon dried thyme
1/4 teaspoon dried marjoram
1 teaspoon salt

1 teaspoon pepper
1 package (10 ounces) frozen
  peas
1/3 cup butter
1/3 cup flour
1 cup light cream
Pastry or Baking Powder Biscuit
  topping*

Put chicken into pot with onion and carrots. Add water to cover, rosemary, thyme, marjoram, salt, and 1/2 teaspoon of the pepper. Simmer, covered, for about 45 minutes until chicken is cooked. Remove chicken and vegetables and reserve broth. Remove bones and skin from chicken and cut the meat into bite-sized chunks.

Remove 1 1/2 cups of the broth from the pot. In a saucepan, melt butter and blend in flour. Gradually add hot broth and cream, stirring constantly until thickened and smooth. Add remaining salt and pepper. Pour sauce over chicken and vegetables, adding more broth if necessary.

PASTRY:
Preheat oven to 350 degrees. Mix 3 cups flour with 1/2 teaspoon salt and cut in 1 cup shortening. Add 1/2 to 3/4 cup cold water. Mix well to form ball. Roll out top and bottom crusts.

Place bottom crust in 9-inch deep-dish pie plate. Pour in chicken mixture and cover with top crust. Brush with milk. Make three small holes in top crust to let steam escape. Bake for 35 to 40 minutes until brown.

Makes 6 to 8 servings.

*You can also use packaged prepared pie crust or biscuit mix.

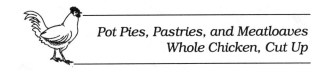

BAKING POWDER BISCUIT:

Preheat oven to 450 degrees. Sift 2 cups flour, 4 teaspoon baking powder, and 1 teaspoon salt together. Cut in 1/3 cup shortening. Add 3/4 cup milk to make soft dough. Knead few times on floured board. Lightly roll out to 1/2-inch thickness and cut with 2-inch cutter. Pour chicken mixture into 9 x 13 baking dish. Top with biscuits. Bake for 10 to 15 minutes until chicken mixture is hot and biscuits are well browned.

Makes 6 to 8 servings.

Per Serving (approx) with Pastry Crust:

Calories 937	*Protein 57 gm*	*Fat 70 gm*
Carbohydrate 20 gm	*Sodium 879 mg*	*Cholesterol 257 mg*

The United States produces more chicken than any other country—more than 6 billion chickens a year, about 25 billion pounds of chicken meat. Nice little business, considering it started in 1923 as a Delaware housewife's source of pin money.

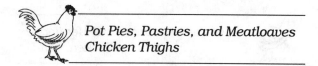

Cajun Skillet Pot Pie

2 cans (14 ounces each) beef broth
2 1/4 pounds chicken thighs
1 tablespoon Worcestershire sauce
1/2 teaspoon hot pepper sauce
3 tablespoons vegetable oil
5 tablespoons flour
2/3 cup chopped onion

1/2 cup chopped green bell pepper
1 package (10 ounces) frozen succotash
Worcestershire sauce (optional)
Pepper sauce (optional)
1 package refrigerated biscuits

In a saucepan, boil the beef broth. Add chicken, Worcestershire sauce, and hot pepper sauce. Simmer 30 minutes. Skim and discard foam from top. Remove chicken from the pan and discard skin and bones. Cut meat into pieces and reserve. Over high heat, boil broth until reduced to about 3 cups; reserve.

Preheat oven to 400 degrees.

In a 10-inch ovenproof skillet over medium heat, combine oil and flour. Cook 5 to 6 minutes, stirring constantly, until flour turns deep reddish brown. Stir in onion, bell pepper, and succotash; gradually add broth and cook 1 to 2 minutes, stirring constantly, until sauce thickens. Stir in chicken, adding Worcestershire and pepper sauce to taste, if desired.

Arrange biscuits on top of chicken mixture. Bake 10 minutes; reduce oven temperature to 350 degrees and bake 20 minutes longer until biscuit topping is browned and filling is bubbling.   Makes 4 to 6 servings.

Per Serving (approx):
Calories 622
Carbohydrate 39 gm

Protein 37 gm
Sodium 970 mg

Fat 35 gm
Cholesterol 115 mg

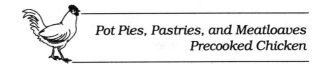

Easy Chicken à la King Pies

This is a good recipe for using leftover chicken or turkey.

1 cup sliced mushrooms
4 tablespoons butter
4 tablespoons flour
1/2 teaspoon salt
1/4 teaspoon pepper

2 cups milk or chicken broth
2 1/2 cups cooked, diced
  chicken
1 cup cooked peas
3 tablespoons pimento
Toast Cups

Melt the butter. Sauté the mushrooms. Blend in the flour, salt, and pepper. Gradually stir in the milk or broth. Cook, stirring, until the mixture is thickened. Add chicken, peas, and pimento. Heat well and serve in Toast Cups.*

Makes 8 servings.

TOAST CUPS:
Preheat the oven to 400 degrees. Cut crusts from 8 bread slices. Press slices into muffin tins so four points of bread stick up. Bake about 10 minutes or until toasted and brown. Allow to cool a few minutes in pan so cups will hold their shape. If making these ahead, warm them for a few minutes before using.

*You could also serve this in purchased patty shells.

Per Serving (approx):
Calories 186
Carbohydrate 9 gm

Protein 16 gm
Sodium 258 mg

Fat 10 gm
Cholesterol 57 mg

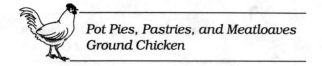
Cajun Quiche

This Louisiana version of the French cheese pie makes its own crust.

2 tablespoons vegetable oil
1 large onion, chopped
1 1/4 pounds ground chicken
1 tablespoon Cajun seasoning
2 cans (11 ounces each) Mexicorn,
  undrained

2 cups shredded Monterey
  jack cheese
1 cup buttermilk baking mix
2 eggs, or 1/2 cup egg substitute
3/4 cup water

Preheat oven to 375 degrees. Lightly grease a 10-inch pie plate.

In a large skillet, heat oil. Add onions and sauté about 5 minutes until translucent. Stir in chicken. Season with Cajun seasoning. Cook 3 to 5 minutes until chicken is browned, stirring often. Stir in Mexicorn and cheese.

In medium bowl, combine baking mix, eggs, and water; mix well. Transfer chicken mixture to prepared pie plate. Pour baking mix evenly on top. Bake 35 to 40 minutes until quiche is cooked through and golden.

Makes 6 servings.

Per Serving (approx):
Calories 556
Carbohydrate 45 gm

Protein 27 gm
Sodium 1068 mg

Fat 30 gm
Cholesterol 163 mg

Henry IV of France thought so highly of chicken that he wrote the first cookbook devoted entirely to chicken.

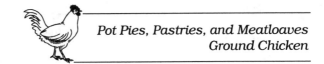

Italian Harvest Mini Loaves

This is a nice change from the usual meat sauce over pasta.

1 carrot, cut up in chunks
1 small zucchini
1 onion
1 1/4 pounds ground chicken
1/2 cup Italian bread crumbs

1 egg or 1/4 cup liquid egg
   substitute
1 tablespoon dried Italian herb
   seasoning
1 teaspoon salt
1/4 teaspoon pepper

Preheat oven to 375 degrees.

In a food processor, coarsely shred carrot and zucchini; chop the onion. In a bowl, combine chicken with vegetables and remaining ingredients. Divide mixture into 4 equal parts. Pat into lightly greased mini-loaf pans or form small, free-form loaves and place on greased baking sheet.

Bake loaves 35 to 40 minutes, or until loaves spring back to the touch and meat thermometer inserted in center registers 165 degrees. Serve loaves with marinara sauce. Makes 4 to 6 servings.

Per Serving (approx):
Calories 174
Carbohydrate 11 gm

Protein 14 gm
Sodium 523 mg

Fat 8 gm
Cholesterol 95 mg

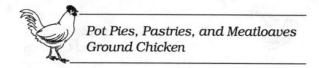

California Meatloaf

1 1/4 pounds ground chicken
1/2 cup bread crumbs
1/2 teaspoon salt
1/2 teaspoon dried oregano
1/2 teaspoon dried basil
1/2 teaspoon pepper
1 can (8 ounces) tomato sauce, divided

6 onion slices
6 bacon slices, cooked crisp
6 tomato slices
1/2 cup sliced black olives
1 cup shredded Monterey jack
  cheese, divided

Preheat oven to 375 degrees.

In a large bowl, combine chicken, bread crumbs, salt, oregano, basil, pepper, and 3/4 cup of the tomato sauce.

Divide meat mixture into thirds; pat one-third into bottom of 4 x 8 1/2 loaf pan. Arrange 3 slices each onion, bacon, and tomato over meat mixture; sprinkle with 1/4 cup of the olives and 1/3 cup of the cheese, and top with another third layer of the meat mixture. Repeat layering, ending with meat. Spread with remaining tomato sauce and top with remaining 2/3 cup cheese.

Bake 45 to 50 minutes. The meatloaf is cooked when it springs back to the touch and a meat thermometer inserted in the loaf registers 160 to 165 degrees.   Makes 4 to 6 servings.

Per Serving (approx):
Calories 397
Carbohydrate 33 gm

Protein 23 gm
Sodium 897 mg

Fat 19 gm
Cholesterol 83 mg

U.S. chickens are raised primarily in Arkansas, Georgia, Alabama, North Carolina, Mississippi, Maryland, Texas, Delaware, California, and Virginia. The most concentrated chicken-producing area is the Delmarva area—Delaware, Maryland, and Virginia.

Barbecue Meatloaf

6 tablespoons prepared
   barbecue sauce, divided
2 tablespoons water
2/3 cup rolled oats
1 large egg, lightly beaten
2 teaspoons chili powder
2 teaspoons Worcestershire sauce
1/2 teaspoon salt
1 1/4 pounds ground chicken

1/3 cup chopped red or
   green bell pepper
2/3 cup minced onion
1/2 cup corn kernels, fresh or
   frozen and thawed
2 tablespoons canned chopped
   green chiles, drained
   (optional)
Additional barbecue sauce or
   ketchup (optional)

Preheat oven to 375 degrees.

In a large bowl, combine 3 tablespoons barbecue sauce and water. Add oats, egg, chili powder, Worcestershire sauce, and salt; mix well. Add chicken, bell pepper, onion, corn, and chiles if using; mix well. Pat into 4 1/2 x 8 1/2 loaf pan.

Bake 45 to 50 minutes; spread top of loaf with remaining 3 tablespoons barbecue sauce during last 10 minutes of cooking. The meatloaf is cooked when it springs back to the touch and meat thermometer inserted in the loaf registers 160 to 165 degrees. Serve warm or cold, with additional barbecue sauce, if desired.   Makes 4 to 6 servings.

Per Serving (approx):

Calories 193	*Protein 14 gm*	*Fat 9 gm*
Carbohydrate 14 gm	*Sodium 402 mg*	*Cholesterol 94 mg*

223

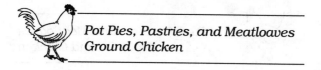
Russian Meatloaf

You need the real Russian rye bread for this, the one with all the seeds.

1 1/4 pounds ground chicken
1 cup rye bread crumbs (2 slices)
2/3 cup chopped onions
1/4 cup reduced calorie
   Russian dressing
1/4 cup nonfat sour cream
   substitute

2 tablespoons prepared
   horseradish
2 tablespoons minced parsley
1 teaspoon salt
1 teaspoon paprika
1/4 teaspoon pepper

Preheat oven to 375 degrees.

In a bowl, combine all ingredients. With lightly moistened hands, pat mixture into 4 1/2 x 8 1/2 loaf pan.

Cover and bake 35 minutes. Uncover and continue baking 10 to 15 minutes until loaf is cooked, springs back to the touch, and registers 170 degrees on a meat thermometer.

Remove from the oven and allow to stand 5 to 10 minutes before serving.

                                        Makes 4 to 5 servings.

Per Serving (approx):
Calories 212
Carbohydrate 17 gm
       Protein 15 gm
       Sodium 761 mg
              Fat 9 gm
              Cholesterol 72 mg

> If you've noticed how the price of chicken breasts is going down, you can thank Russia. They like dark meat, not white, so, since chicken is a perishable commodity, the producers lower the price of white meat here so they'll have enough dark meat to export to Russia.

POT ROASTS
& STEWS

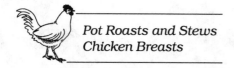

Chicken Breast and Goat Cheese in Grape Leaves with Bell Pepper Sauce

This California Cuisine recipe is simple and elegant.

4 skinless, boneless chicken
   breast halves
1/2 teaspoon salt
1/4 teaspoon pepper
6 ounces fresh goat cheese*
4 basil leaves

4 sage leaves
8 or 12 grape leaves in brine,
   drained
1 garlic clove
1 sprig rosemary
Bell Pepper Sauce

Sprinkle chicken with salt and pepper. Divide cheese into 4 portions and spread on top of each piece of chicken. Place 1 basil leaf and 1 sage leaf on each; wrap chicken with 2 or 3 grape leaves.

In a large saucepan with a steaming rack, place about 1 inch of water; add garlic and rosemary and bring to a boil. Arrange chicken on the rack, cover and steam on high heat for about 20 minutes, making sure the water doesn't totally evaporate. Serve the chicken on the Bell Pepper Sauce.

Makes 4 servings.

BELL PEPPER SAUCE:
Slice two green bell peppers and 1/4 small onion; put in a blender with 3 tablespoons olive oil, 1 teaspoon salt, and 1/8 teaspoon pepper; blend, strain, and bring just to a boil.

*You can substitute ricotta or cream cheese mixed with Parmesan.

Per Serving (approx):
Calories 468
Carbohydrate 6 gm

Protein 43 gm
Sodium 800 mg

Fat 30 gm
Cholesterol 125 mg

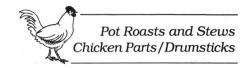

He-Man Stew

3 pounds skinless cut up chicken
Salt and ground pepper to taste
2 tablespoons olive oil
1 can (12 ounces) light beer
1 onion, sliced into rings

1 can (28 ounces) plum
  tomatoes, drained and
  chopped
1/4 cup spicy brown mustard

Season chicken with salt and pepper to taste. In a large skillet, heat oil. Add chicken; cook until brown, turning often (5 to 6 minutes on each side for larger pieces, 3 to 4 minutes on each side for smaller pieces). Combine the beer, onion, tomatoes, and mustard in a large saucepan. Add chicken. Cook, covered, 1 1/2 to 2 hours, or until a fork pierces the chicken easily.   Makes 3 to 4 servings.

Per Serving (approx):
Calories 953
Carbohydrate 55 gm

Protein 78 gm
Sodium 421 mg

Fat 44 gm
Cholesterol 273 mg

Drumstick Fricassee

1 1/4 pounds skinless chicken
  drumsticks
1 tablespoon spicy, salt-free
  seasoning
2 tablespoons olive oil
2 tablespoons flour

1 1/2 cups low-fat milk
1/2 cup dry vermouth or
  white wine
Salt to taste
1 package (16 ounces) mixed
  frozen vegetables of your
  choice

Sprinkle the chicken with half the spicy seasoning. In a Dutch oven, heat oil. Add chicken; cook 6 to 8 minutes until brown on all sides, turning often. Remove and set aside. Stir flour into drippings; cook about 1 minute until the chicken is golden, stirring often. Add milk and vermouth. Cook until the sauce is smooth, stirring constantly. Add remaining seasoning, salt to taste, and chicken. Cover and simmer 20 minutes, stirring occasionally. Add stew vegetables; simmer 10 minutes longer until chicken and vegetables are fork-tender. Serve chicken with generous portions of vegetables.   Makes 3 to 4 servings.

Per Serving (approx):
Calories 399
Carbohydrate 23 gm

Protein 37 gm
Sodium 261 mg

Fat 16 gm
Cholesterol 106 mg

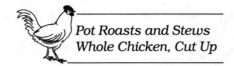

Sesame Chicken

1 whole chicken, cut up
3 cups water
1/4 teaspoon chili powder
1/4 cup soy sauce
2 tablespoons flour

1/2 cup chopped green onions
1 clove garlic, minced
3 tablespoons sesame seeds,
 whole or ground

In a Dutch oven, combine chicken, water, and chili powder. Cover and simmer for about 45 minutes. Remove chicken from pan and set aside. Boil stock for about 5 minutes until slightly reduced. In a small bowl, combine soy sauce and flour; add to stock, stirring. Cook over low heat until mixture boils and thickens. Return chicken to pan; add green onions, garlic, and sesame seeds. Cook about 10 minutes more until the chicken is done.   Makes 4 servings.

Per Serving (approx):
Calories 530
Carbohydrate 8 gm

Protein 57 gm
Sodium 1190 mg

Fat 30 gm
Cholesterol 210 mg

Heriseh

5 cups water
4 cups low-sodium chicken broth
1 whole chicken*
1 1/2 cups large pearl barley
Salt to taste

White pepper to taste
1/2 cube butter, melted
Paprika
Ground cumin (optional),
 for garnish

Preheat oven to 325 degrees. In a large pot, boil water and chicken broth. Add the chicken to the pot. Add barley and salt to taste. Cover the pot and cook in the oven until the water is absorbed. Stir every hour until it looks like mush. Chicken should be completely blended. Season with salt and white pepper to taste. Stir really hard and fast. Serve in bowls with melted butter and paprika on top. Cumin may also be used as a garnish.   Makes 6 servings.

*For a Heriseh less rich and easier to make, use 4 cups precooked, chopped chicken.

Per Serving (approx):
Calories 486
Carbohydrate 39 gm

Protein 40 gm
Sodium 118 mg

Fat 19 gm
Cholesterol 142 mg

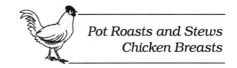

Chef's Chicken

1 gallon water
4 skinless, boneless chicken breasts
1 carrot, sliced
1/4 pound pearl onions
2 potatoes, diced

3 cups chicken broth
1/8 teaspoon saffron
Salt to taste
4 teaspoons chopped parsley

In a large saucepan, bring water to a boil over high heat. Drop chicken breasts into the water and stir gently. When water returns to strong boil, remove chicken and rinse in cold water; discard boiled water.

In another saucepan, combine chicken breasts, carrots, pearl onions, potatoes, chicken broth, and saffron; simmer gently until chicken is tender and vegetables are soft, about 15 minutes. Salt to taste.

To serve, place one chicken breast in each of 4 soup plates, spoon vegetables evenly over the chicken and ladle stock over all. Sprinkle with chopped parsley.   Makes 4 servings.

Per Serving (approx):
Calories 440
Carbohydrate 30 gm

Protein 63 gm
Sodium 1257 mg

Fat 8 gm
Cholesterol 160 mg

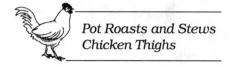

Irish Chicken Thighs

They cook many dishes with cabbage in Ireland. This is one of the best.

1 pound skinless, boneless chicken thighs	1 tablespoon vegetable oil
Salt and pepper to taste	1 medium head cabbage
2 teaspoons Dijon mustard	1/2 teaspoon caraway seed
	2 cups chicken broth

Preheat oven to 350 degrees.

Trim off and discard visible fat from thighs. Season chicken with salt and pepper to taste; spread with mustard.

In a Dutch oven, heat oil. Add thighs; cook about 3 minutes on each side until browned. Quarter cabbage and remove core. Add cabbage to pan with thighs; sprinkle with caraway seed and pour broth over all. Cover and place in oven.

Bake 1 hour or until cabbage is tender, basting occasionally. Season to taste with salt and pepper.   Makes 4 servings.

Per Serving (approx):
Calories 279   *Protein 26 gm*   *Fat 14 gm*
Carbohydrate 13 gm   *Sodium 908 mg*   *Cholesterol 81 mg*

The earliest authentic representation of a chicken appears on a Babylonian cylinder seal from between 3000 and 2500 B.C.

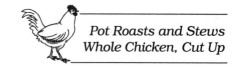

Autumn Chicken and Apple Stew

This is a great recipe for those cold, wet, dreary days when you want to make something different and you have a little extra time to cook.

1 whole chicken, cut up
1/2 teaspoon ground nutmeg
1/2 teaspoon salt
1/4 teaspoon pepper
2 teaspoons Dijon mustard
1 3/4 cups low-sodium chicken
   broth, warmed

1/4 cup apple cider vinegar
6 whole cloves
3 carrots, sliced
6 apples, peeled, cored, and
   and sliced
1 cup shredded cabbage
1 cup applesauce

Spray a large Dutch oven with vegetable spray and heat. Add chicken and cook, turning, to brown on all sides, about 10 minutes. Sprinkle with nutmeg, salt, and pepper. Spread mustard over chicken pieces; add broth, vinegar, cloves, and carrots; bring to a boil. Cover and simmer for 15 minutes.

Add apples and cook 5 minutes. Add cabbage, stirring it into the liquid. Simmer, covered, about 10 minutes more until a fork pierces the chicken easily. With a slotted spoon, remove chicken and vegetables to warm serving bowl.

Stir the applesauce into the Dutch oven holding the liquid. Boil for 5 minutes and pour over chicken and vegetables.   Makes 4 servings.

Per Serving (approx):
Calories 737
Carbohydrate 67 gm

Protein 54 gm
Sodium 537 mg

Fat 28 gm
Cholesterol 210 mg

> A whole chicken weighing 3 1/2 pounds will have 2 1/2 cups of edible meat.

African Bean and Chicken Stew

In North Africa, where this recipe originated, cooks use dried or fresh beans of many varieties. This adaptation using canned ingredients is very tasty and easy to make. One suggestion: Use the low-salt versions of canned beans and tomatoes.

1 or 2 tablespoons peanut oil
1 pound skinless, boneless chicken breast halves, cut into 1/2-inch chunks
2 or 3 green onions, chopped
1/2 cup fajita sauce
3 tablespoons creamy peanut butter
1 can (12 ounces) corn, drained
1 can (15 ounces) black beans, drained

1 can (15 ounces) red beans, drained
1 can (15 ounces) tomatoes
4 or 5 drops hot pepper sauce
1 cup cooked long-grain brown rice
Peanuts, roasted and minced (optional), for garnish
Green onion tops, julienned (optional), for garnish

Heat oil in a Dutch oven; add chicken and sauté over medium heat, stirring and turning frequently until almost all the pink color has disappeared. Add green onions; sauté 2 to 3 minutes longer, continuing to stir frequently; reduce heat to low.

Blend fajita sauce with peanut butter, drizzle over chicken and onions. Add corn, beans, tomatoes with their juice, and hot pepper sauce; stir well to combine ingredients. Simmer the mixture a few minutes longer to heat throughout, stirring occasionally.

Spoon over brown rice in individual serving bowls. Garnish with chopped peanuts and green onions, if desired.   Makes 4 to 6 servings.

Per Serving (approx):
Calories 805
Carbohydrate 126gm

Protein 51 gm
Sodium 2815 mg

Fat 11 gm
Cholesterol 51 mg

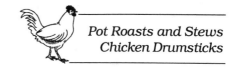

Chicken Sauerbraten

1/2 cup water
1/2 cup wine vinegar or
  cider vinegar
3 medium onions, sliced
Salt and pepper to taste
2 to 2 1/4 pounds skinless
  chicken drumsticks
3 or 4 tablespoons vegetable oil
1 can (14 ounces) beef broth

2 tablespoons tomato paste
4 teaspoons lemon juice
4 teaspoons Worcestershire
  sauce
1 tablespoon brown sugar
1 strip lemon peel
6 gingersnaps (2 inches each),
  crumbled
Mashed Potato Pancakes

In a ceramic bowl, combine water, vinegar, onions, and salt and pepper to taste. Add drumsticks, turning to coat well. Cover and refrigerate overnight, turning occasionally.

Remove the drumsticks from marinade and pat dry; reserve the marinade. In a Dutch oven, heat oil. Add drumsticks and cook 15 minutes until brown on all sides, turning occasionally. Remove the drumsticks from pot and reserve; discard the oil.

To a Dutch oven, add reserved marinade, broth, tomato paste, lemon juice, Worcestershire sauce, brown sugar, lemon peel, gingersnaps, and drumsticks. Simmer, partially covered, 50 to 60 minutes until chicken is tender, stirring occasionally. Remove drumsticks to a platter; remove and discard lemon peel. Spoon sauce over drumsticks. Serve with Mashed Potato Pancakes.

Makes 4 to 5 servings.

MASHED POTATO PANCAKES:
In a mixing bowl, combine 2 cups of firm, well-seasoned mashed potatoes with 1 egg; form into 8 round cakes. In another bowl, beat 1 egg. Dip potato cakes into beaten egg and roll in fresh bread crumbs. In a large skillet over medium heat, melt 2 tablespoons butter with 2 tablespoons oil. Fry pancakes in batches, about 2 minutes on each side, until golden brown; add more butter and oil as needed.

Per Serving (approx), excluding potato pancakes:
Calories 392   *Protein 41 gm*   *Fat 17 gm*
Carbohydrate 18 gm   *Sodium 418 mg*   *Cholesterol 129 mg*

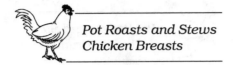

Oven-Easy Chicken Stew with Sesame-Sage Biscuits

1/4 cup vegetable oil
1/4 cup flour, divided
1/2 teaspoon salt
1/4 teaspoon pepper
4 skinless, boneless chicken
   breast halves, cut into chunks
6 carrots, thinly sliced
2 celery ribs, cut in 1-inch
   lengths
12 pearl onions

1/4 cup chopped parsley
1 teaspoon minced garlic
1/2 teaspoon dried thyme
1 bay leaf
1 can (14 1/2 ounces) fat-free,
   low-sodium chicken broth
1 package (10 ounces) frozen
   green peas
Parsley sprigs, for garnish
Sesame-Sage Biscuits

Preheat oven to 350 degrees.

In a large frying pan, heat oil. In a bag, combine 2 tablespoons of the flour, salt, and pepper. Add chicken and shake well to coat evenly. Add the chicken to the pan and fry, turning, about 6 minutes until brown. In a casserole dish, combine carrots, celery, onions, and parsley; add the chicken.

In the same frying pan, add remaining 2 tablespoons flour, garlic, thyme, and bay leaf. Scrape up brown bits from bottom of frying pan. Stir in chicken broth and heat to a boil; pour over chicken and vegetables. Cover and bake for 30 minutes. Add peas and continue baking about 30 minutes or until vegetables are tender and a fork pierces the chicken easily. Discard bay leaf. Garnish with parsley and serve with Sesame-Sage Biscuits.
Makes 4 servings.

SESAME-SAGE BISCUITS:
In a bowl, prepare biscuit dough for drop biscuits, by mixing together 2 1/4 cups buttermilk baking mix and 2/3 cup skim milk. Stir into the dough mixture 2 tablespoons toasted sesame seed and 1/2 teaspoon ground sage. Drop by spoonfuls onto ungreased cookie sheet. Sprinkle biscuits with 1 tablespoon toasted sesame seed. Bake in 450 degree oven about 8 minutes or until brown.

Per Serving (approx):
Calories 939
Carbohydrate 97 gm

Protein 53 gm
Sodium 1815 mg

Fat 38 gm
Cholesterol 81 mg

PASTAS & GRAINS

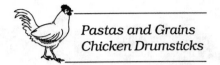
Spaghetti Chicken Drumsticks

The dark meat, favored in Italy, is the star of this spaghetti dish.

1/2 pound mushrooms, sliced
1 large onion, in rings
8 chicken drumsticks
1 large clove garlic, minced
1/2 teaspoon salt

1 teaspoon dried oregano
1 teaspoon dried basil
1 can (16 ounces) tomatoes
1 can (15 ounces) tomato sauce
1/2 pound thin spaghetti,
cooked

Preheat oven to 400 degrees.

In a baking dish, arrange sliced mushrooms. Arrange sliced onion rings over the mushrooms. Add the drumsticks aand sprinkle with minced garlic, salt, oregano, and basil. Drain juice from tomatoes and pour juice over chicken. Mash tomatoes with a fork or place in processor or blender container and process about 15 seconds; pour over drumsticks.

Pour tomato sauce over all. Bake about 1 hour until a fork pierces the chicken easily. Serve over cooked spaghetti.   Makes 4 servings.

Per Serving (approx):
Calories 565
Carbohydrate 36 gm

Protein 51 gm
Sodium 1329 mg

Fat 24 gm
Cholesterol 156 mg

"The best bill of fare I know of is a good appetite."

Josh Billings,
His Works Complete

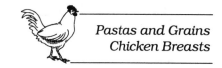

Chicken Breasts with Rotini, Pasta, Broccoli, and Garlic

1 head broccoli, broken into florets
4 boneless chicken breasts
Salt and pepper to taste
1/2 tablespoon vegetable oil
8 ounces rotini pasta
1 tablespoon olive oil

2 cloves garlic, minced
1 tablespoon butter
1/2 cup chopped Italian parsley
1/2 cup seasoned bread crumbs
1/4 teaspoon red pepper flakes

Preheat oven to 450 degrees.

Fill a saucepan half full of water. Season with salt to taste; bring to boil over high heat. Blanch broccoli about 4 minutes. Cool in ice water; set aside.

Season the chicken with salt and pepper to taste. In a Dutch oven, heat oil. Add chicken, skin side down, and fry 30 seconds.

Cover the Dutch oven and place in the oven. Bake 10 to 12 minutes or until chicken is no longer pink inside. Slice chicken into 1/4-inch slices. Cook rotini according to package directions.

Meanwhile, in a skillet, heat olive oil. Add the garlic; cook 1 minute, do not brown. Add blanched broccoli and butter; stir to melt butter. To serve: toss broccoli, chicken and rotini. Stir in parsley, bread crumbs, and pepper flakes. Season to taste with salt and pepper.

Makes 4 servings.

Per Serving (approx):
Calories 547
Carbohydrate 59 gm

Protein 42 gm
Sodium 258 mg

Fat 16 gm
Cholesterol 96 mg

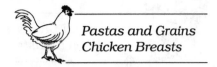
Chicken in Tomato Marsala Sauce

If you're not familiar with Marsala, it is a Sicilian wine, ranging from very sweet to very dry. If you don't have any on hand, substitute a sweet vermouth.

2 large skinless, boneless chicken breasts	1/4 teaspoon pepper
1/2 teaspoon dried oregano	1/4 pound mushrooms, sliced
1/4 teaspoon garlic powder	1 can (8 ounces) tomato sauce
1/4 teaspoon onion powder	1/4 cup Marsala

Cut chicken breasts into chunks. Combine oregano, garlic powder, onion powder, and pepper and sprinkle over all chicken pieces.

Spray a skillet with vegetable spray. Add chicken and sauté about 5 minutes more. Push chicken to the side and add mushrooms, tomato sauce, and wine, stirring to mix well. Stir chicken into sauce and simmer about 12 minutes or until a fork pierces the chicken easily.

Makes 2 servings.

Per Serving (approx):
Calories 257
Carbohydrate 15 gm

Protein 32 gm
Sodium 763 mg

Fat 4 gm
Cholesterol 80 mg

In 1801 when Napoleon returned to camp, fresh from a victory on the Italian battlefield, his cook discovered that only one chicken was available, along with some mushrooms, tomatoes, and garlic. The dish he created with these ingredients is now one of the most famous of all chicken recipes: Chicken Marengo, named for the battle.

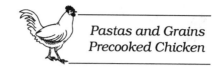
Chicken and Spinach Noodles

Leftovers? With this recipe no one will believe it..

1 1/2 cups thinly sliced carrots
2 cups chicken broth
12 ounces low-fat, small curd
   cottage cheese
2 tablespoons lemon juice

1 chicken, cooked, boned,
   skinned, cut into pieces
1/2 pound spinach noodles,
   cooked and drained
1/4 teaspoon pepper

In a Dutch oven, bring carrots and chicken broth to a boil over high heat. Reduce heat and simmer until carrots are just tender, about 5 minutes. Remove carrots from the broth.

In a blender, combine cottage cheese and lemon juice and blend until smooth, about 1 minute. Add the warm broth to the cottage cheese mixture. Blend 1 more minute.

Combine cheese mixture and carrots, stir in chicken and cooked noodles; sprinkle with pepper. Simmer, uncovered, about 20 minutes (keep temperature low so sauce does not separate).   Makes 4 servings.

Per Serving (approx):
Calories 716
Carbohydrate 50 gm

Protein 68 gm
Sodium 1242 mg

Fat 27 gm
Cholesterol 157 mg

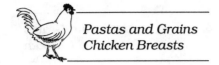
Chicken with Herb Bulgur

The Mideast is the source of this beautiful and flavorful recipe. If you're not familiar with bulgur, you may find it in the rice section and labeled bulgur (or bulghur) cracked wheat.

2 tablespoons butter
4 skinless, boneless chicken
   breast halves
1 cup sliced mushrooms
1 onion, cut in half and sliced
1/2 green bell pepper, julienned
1/2 red pepper, julienned
1/2 yellow bell pepper, julienned

1 1/3 cups chicken broth
3 tablespoons dry sherry
2 tablespoons chopped parsley
1/4 teaspoon dried crushed
   chervil
1/4 teaspoon dried chives
1/4 teaspoon dried tarragon
2/3 cup bulgur

In frying pan, melt the butter. Add the chicken and sauté 2 minutes on each side. Remove from pan. In the same pan, combine mushrooms, onion, and bell peppers; stir-fry for 2 minutes. Remove from pan and set aside. In the same pan, boil the broth. Add sherry, parsley, chervil, chives, and tarragon. Simmer and add bulgur.

Place the chicken on top of the bulgur, cover, and simmer about 10 minutes until a fork pierces the chicken easily. Remove pan from heat and place reserved vegetables on chicken. Replace cover and let stand 3 minutes.
                                            Makes 4 servings.

Per Serving (approx):
Calories 342
Carbohydrate 26 gm

Protein 34 gm
Sodium 626 mg

Fat 10 gm
Cholesterol 96 mg

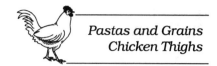

Chicken and Vegetables on Pasta

2 tablespoons olive oil
8 chicken thighs
3 tomatoes, cut in chunks
1 onion, cut in chunks
1 rib celery, cut in chunks
3 yellow squash, cut in chunks
3 zucchini, cut in chunks

4 tablespoons lemon juice
1 teaspoon dried basil
1 teaspoon curry powder
1/8 teaspoon salt
1/2 pound angel hair pasta,
  cooked

In a Dutch oven, heat oil. Add chicken and cook, turning to brown on all sides. Remove chicken to a platter and keep warm. To a Dutch oven, add tomatoes, onion, and celery; cook, stirring, about 2 minutes. Add both squashes, lemon juice, basil, and curry powder; sprinkle with salt. Stir and cook about 3 minutes more. Arrange chicken on top of vegetables, cover, reduce heat to low and cook, turning several times to coat with sauce, until a fork pierces the chicken easily, about 20 minutes. Serve on hot pasta.   Makes 4 servings.

Per Serving (approx):
Calories 577
Carbohydrate 69 gm

Protein 37 gm
Sodium 372 mg

Fat 17 gm
Cholesterol 90 mg

Garden Chicken on Noodles

1/4 cup olive oil
1/4 cup butter
1 1/2 pounds skinless,
  boneless chicken thighs,
  cut into bite-size pieces
1 onion, coarsely chopped
2 cloves garlic, minced
1 pound yellow squash, sliced
  into 1/4-inch rounds

1 teaspoon salt
1/2 teaspoon pepper
2 pounds Italian tomatoes,
  peeled and quartered, or
  2 cans (16 ounces each)
  Italian tomatoes
1 pound spinach noodles,
  cooked

In a Dutch oven, heat oil and butter. Add chicken, onion, and garlic. Cook, stirring, about 10 minutes until onion is translucent. Add squash and sprinkle with salt and pepper. Cook another 5 minutes. Add Italian tomatoes, cover, and continue cooking for about 15 minutes or until the chicken is done. Serve on spinach noodles.   Makes 6 servings.

Per Serving (approx):
Calories 405
Carbohydrate 13 gm

Protein 25 gm
Sodium 557 mg

Fat 28 gm
Cholesterol 102 mg

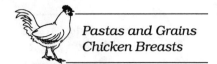

Ruby and Emerald Chicken Pasta

This recipe gets its name from the tomatoes and broccoli florets.

1/4 pound sun-dried tomatoes, packed in olive oil, cut in pieces, oil reserved
1 garlic clove, pressed
1 1/2 pounds boneless chicken breasts, cut in bite-size pieces
1 can (15 ounces) chicken broth
1/3 cup black olive pieces
2 tablespoons lemon juice

1/4 cup white wine
2 cups broccoli florets
1 teaspoon salt
1/4 teaspoon pepper
1 1/2 tablespoons cornstarch, dissolved in cold water
1 pound pasta, cooked
Grated Romano cheese

In a large frying pan, heat 2 tablespoons of reserved oil from tomatoes. Add garlic and cook about 1 minute until brown. Add chicken and stir-fry about 3 minutes or until light brown and a fork can be inserted easily.

Stir in broth, tomato pieces, olives, lemon juice, wine, broccoli, salt and pepper. Simmer for 3 minutes until broccoli is tender-crisp. Add dissolved cornstarch and cook until sauce thickens. Serve over cooked pasta; sprinkle with cheese. Makes 6 servings.

Per Serving (approx):
Calories 492
Carbohydrate 51 gm

Protein 39 gm
Sodium 1112 mg

Fat 14 gm
Cholesterol 136 mg

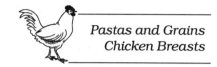
Chicken Tortellini with Salsa

1 tablespoon oil
4 skinless, boneless chicken
   breast halves
1 zucchini, sliced
1 red bell pepper, sliced

1 onion, sliced
1/2 teaspoon no-salt herb and
   spice seasoning
2 cups frozen cheese tortellini
1/2 cup prepared salsa

In a large frying pan, heat oil. Add chicken and sauté 6 minutes until light brown. Remove chicken from the frying pan and keep warm. Spray frying pan with cooking oil. Add zucchini, red pepper, and onion. Sprinkle with seasoning. Do not stir. Cook about 4 minutes, or until vegetables are tender crisp. Add frozen tortellini and place chicken on top. Spread salsa evenly over chicken. Cover and cook about 20 minutes or until a fork pierces chicken easily.   Makes 4 servings.

Per Serving (approx):
Calories 353	*Protein 37 gm*	*Fat 10 gm*
Carbohydrate 29 gm	*Sodium 346 mg*	*Cholesterol 100 mg*

Chicken and Vegetable Medley

4 skinless, boneless chicken
   breasts
2 teaspoons olive oil
2 cans (14 1/2 ounces each)
   low-sodium Italian style
   stewed tomatoes
1 zucchini, thinly sliced

1 cup sliced mushrooms
1 small onion, minced
1/2 teaspoon garlic powder
1/2 teaspoon pepper
2 cups brown rice, cooked
2 tablespoons chopped parsley

Cut each breast into 1-inch cubes. In a skillet, heat oil. Add chicken and stir for 5 minutes. When chicken is browned and no longer pink inside, add stewed tomatoes, zucchini, mushrooms, onion, garlic powder, and pepper. Cover and simmer until vegetables are almost tender, 10 to 15 minutes. Uncover pan, raise heat and cook off excess liquid, stirring frequently, until sauce thickens. Serve over brown rice; sprinkle with parsley.   Makes 4 servings.

Per Serving (approx):
Calories 360	*Protein 35 gm*	*Fat 7 gm*
Carbohydrate 38 gm	*Sodium 101 mg*	*Cholesterol 80 mg*

Capri Chicken Polenta

This recipe does take some extra effort, but it's worth it. You might want to make it a day ahead, refrigerate, and add the cheese after reheating.

8 chicken thighs
1 tablespoon lemon pepper
1 tablespoon olive oil
2 3/4 cups water
1 cup cornmeal
1 cup chicken broth
1 teaspoon salt
1/2 cup thinly sliced green bell
  pepper
1/2 cup minced celery
1/2 cup minced onion

1 jar (7 ounces) roasted red
  bell peppers, drained and
  sliced
1 jar (7 ounces) sliced
  mushrooms, drained
1/2 cup sliced water chestnuts,
  drained
1/2 cup grated Monterey jack
  cheese
1/2 cup minced parsley

Starting at top center of the chicken thigh, loosen skin, leaving outer sides of skin intact. Sprinkle lemon pepper on each thigh between skin and meat. In a frying pan, heat oil. Add chicken, skin side down, and cook, turning once, about 10 minutes on each side or until a fork pierces the chicken easily. Remove chicken and keep warm. Discard all but 1 tablespoon of pan drippings. Set the frying pan aside.

In a saucepan, bring water to a boil. In a small bowl, combine cornmeal, broth, and salt. Slowly add mixture to water, stirring constantly, until mixture comes to a boil. Reduce to low heat, cover, and simmer, stirring frequently, for 10 minutes.

In the frying pan used to cook the chicken, combine bell pepper, celery, and onion. Sauté about 5 minutes, but do not brown. With a slotted spoon, remove the vegetables and add to polenta. Add roasted pepper, mushrooms, and water chestnuts. Stir to mix. Place polenta mixture in 9-inch quiche dish. Remove skin and bones from chicken and discard. Place chicken meat on top of the polenta in a ring around outer edge. Sprinkle with cheese and place in oven; Broil just until cheese melts. Sprinkle with parsley. Makes 8 servings.

Per Serving (approx):
Calories 259
Carbohydrate 20 gm

Protein 17 gm
Sodium 743 mg

Fat 12 gm
Cholesterol 51 mg

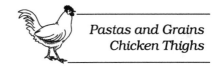

Far East Chicken Fettuccine

If the produce department doesn't have bok choy, Napa cabbage will work just fine.

1 pound fettuccine, divided
3 tablespoons butter
4 tablespoons vegetable oil, divided
6 chicken thighs
1 teaspoon minced ginger
2 garlic cloves, minced
6 cups coarsely chopped bok choy
1 cup chopped green onion

1 red bell pepper, cut in strips
1 package (10 ounces) frozen
  chopped broccoli, thawed
2 tomatoes, chopped
2/3 teaspoon salt
1/8 teaspoon cayenne
1 tablespoon honey

In a large frying pan, heat 1 tablespoon butter and 1 tablespoon oil. Add chicken and sauté, turning once, about 11 minutes. Remove chicken from frying pan and set aside.

In the same frying pan, heat remaining butter and oil. Add ginger, garlic, bok choy, green onion, bell pepper, and broccoli. Cook, stirring, about 2 minutes. Add tomatoes, salt, cayenne, and honey. Cook, stirring carefully, an additional 2 minutes.

To serve, spread fettuccine on a platter and spoon vegetable mixture on top, leaving several inches of pasta showing. Place chicken thighs in a row on top of vegetables.   Makes 6 servings.

Per Serving (approx):
Calories 314   *Protein 16 gm*   *Fat 23 gm*
Carbohydrate 11 gm   *Sodium 418 mg*   *Cholesterol 61 mg*

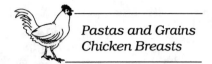

Chicken Florentine Over Linguini

This is about as Italian as you can get.

1/2 cup lemon juice
1/4 cup balsamic vinegar
1/4 cup olive oil
1/2 teaspoon salt
1/4 teaspoon pepper
2 pounds skinless, boneless chicken breasts, cubed
3 leeks, white part only, cut in thin slices

1/3 cup sun-dried tomatoes
1 cup boiling water
2 teaspoons green peppercorns
1 package (10 ounces) frozen chopped spinach, thawed and drained
1 pound linguini, cooked

In a small bowl, combine lemon juice, vinegar, olive oil, salt, and pepper. Pour mixture over chicken and leeks in medium bowl. Cover and marinate 1 hour in refrigerator.

In a small bowl, soak sun-dried tomatoes in boiling water for 30 minutes; drain and chop. In a hot frying pan, combine peppercorns and chicken mixture. Sauté about 7 minutes until leeks are soft. Add spinach and sun-dried tomatoes. Cook about 20 minutes until a fork pierces the chicken easily. Serve over linguini.   Makes 6 servings.

Per Serving (approx):
Calories 429
Carbohydrate 28 gm
Protein 43 gm
Sodium 340 mg
Fat 16 gm
Cholesterol 122 mg

On an average 3 1/2 pound chicken, each breast half weighs 10 1/2 ounces, of which nearly half is edible meat.

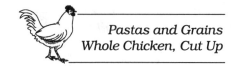

Balsamic Chicken on Fettuccine

Really good balsamic vinegar comes from Italy. It is made from a special variety of grapes and aged in wooden barrels. Get some for this recipe, and others, as well. It really is worth the effort.

1 teaspoon salt, divided
1 teaspoon pepper, divided
2 tablespoons olive oil, divided
1 whole chicken, cut up
1 Bermuda onion, diced
1 red bell pepper, diced
1 yellow bell pepper, diced
3 garlic cloves, minced

4 tomatoes, seeded and diced
2 teaspoon chopped basil
2 teaspoon chopped oregano
2 teaspoons chopped parsley
1/2 cup balsamic vinegar
3/4 pound spinach fettuccine, cooked
Grated Parmesan cheese

Sprinkle 1/2 teaspoon salt and 1/2 teaspoon pepper on the chicken. In a frying pan, heat 1 tablespoon oil. Add dark meat parts to the frying pan and cook, turning frequently, about 10 minutes. Add remaining chicken parts and cook 7 more minutes. Cover and cook 20 minutes until juices run clear when the chicken is pierced with a fork.

Remove the chicken from the pan and keep warm. Drain the frying pan and add remaining 1 tablespoon oil. Add onion, red and yellow bell peppers, and garlic. Sauté about 2 minutes on medium temperature. Add tomatoes, basil, oregano, parsley, and vinegar and cook 1 minute. Add remaining salt and pepper. Spoon vegetables around chicken and pasta and sprinkle with Parmesan cheese.   Makes 4 servings.

Per Serving (approx):
Calories 940
Carbohydrate 81 gm

Protein 69 gm
Sodium 899 mg

Fat 38 gm
Cholesterol 215 mg

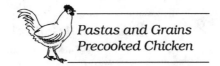

Hot or Cold Chicken and Pasta

Make this ahead and decide, at the last minute, if you want it hot or cold!

1 chicken, cooked, skinned,
  boned, and cut in pieces
1/2 cup chicken broth
1/4 teaspoon pepper
1 cup nonfat cottage cheese
2 tablespoons lemon juice
1/2 teaspoon bouquet garni*

1 clove garlic, minced
1/4 cup chopped pimento,
  drained
6 ounces tri-color rotelle pasta,
  cooked
2 tablespoons grated Romano
  cheese

In a Dutch oven, cook chicken, broth, and pepper about 2 minutes. While chicken is heating, place cottage cheese and lemon juice in a food processor or blender and process until smooth, about 1 minute. Add seasoning and garlic; process 30 seconds more. Remove chicken from heat and stir in cottage cheese mixture. Add chopped pimento and rotelle. Stir to mix well and return to low heat about 2 minutes until heated through.

Serve the chicken sprinkled with cheese. Serve hot or chill in refrigerator and serve as a salad.   Makes 4 servings.

*If bouquet garni seasoning is unavailable, use a mixture of 1/4 teaspoon parsley, 1/8 teaspoon dried thyme, and 1/8 teaspoon crumbled bay leaf.

Per Serving (approx):
Calories 181
Carbohydrate 27 gm

Protein 13 gm
Sodium 645 mg

Fat 2 gm
Cholesterol 35 mg

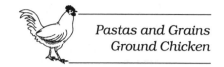

Lasagna Rolls

This is a company version of a family favorite. Each guest receives an individual portion of pasta.

2 tablespoons olive oil, divided
1/4 pound mushrooms, chopped
1/2 cup chopped onion
2 garlic cloves, minced
1 1/4 pounds ground chicken
2 tablespoons butter or margarine
1/4 cup flour
1 1/4 cups milk
Salt and pepper to taste

Dash grated nutmeg
16 curly lasagna noodles, cooked
2 packages (10 ounces) frozen chopped spinach, thawed, and well drained
1/4 cup shredded mozzarella cheese
2 cups prepared marinara sauce

Preheat oven to 350 degrees.

Grease a large, shallow baking dish. In a skillet, heat 1 tablespoon oil. Add mushrooms, onion, and garlic; sauté 2 to 3 minutes. Add chicken and sauté 5 minutes until cooked through. With a slotted spoon, remove chicken mixture from the skillet.

Add butter to the skillet. Melt and blend in the flour. Cook 2 to 3 minutes, stirring often. Whisk in the milk until thickened (sauce will be very thick). Return chicken mixture to the skillet and stir well. Season with salt and pepper, and nutmeg to taste.

Lay lasagna noodles out on a work surface. Spread the spinach thinly over the cooked lasagna. Spread the chicken mixture over the spinach in a thin layer. Sprinkle the noodles with mozzarella. Roll noodles up, jelly-roll style, enclosing filling. Place in a greased baking dish.. Spoon marinara sauce over and around rolls. Bake, loosely covered, for 20 to 30 minutes, until hot and bubbly.   Makes 8 servings.

Per Serving (approx):
Calories 275
Carbohydrate 17 gm

Protein 14 gm
Sodium 584 mg

Fat 17 gm
Cholesterol 60 mg

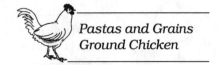

Do-Ahead
Ground Chicken Lasagna

Prepare this recipe the night before, pop it in the oven for a half hour when you get home, and dinner is ready.

1 pound ground chicken
1 can (16 ounces) tomatoes
1 can (6 ounces) tomato paste
1 1/2 tablespoons chopped parsley, divided
1/2 teaspoon salt, divided
1 teaspoon dried basil

1 carton (16 ounces) low-fat, small curd cottage cheese
1 egg, beaten
1/4 teaspoon pepper
1/3 pound lasagna noodles
1/3 pound skim milk mozzarella cheese, shredded
1/4 cup grated Parmesan cheese

Heat a frying pan. Add ground chicken and brown, stirring, for about 6 minutes. In a processor, combine tomatoes, tomato paste, 1/2 tablespoon parsley, 1/4 teaspoon salt, and basil; process about 1 minute. Stir tomato mixture into the chicken and simmer for about 20 minutes.

In a bowl, combine remaining parsley and salt, cottage cheese, egg, and pepper. In the bottom of a shallow baking dish, spread a small amount of the ground chicken mixture.

Layer half of noodles (uncooked), cottage cheese mixture, mozzarella cheese, Parmesan cheese, and ground chicken mixture. Repeat layers, but save Parmesan cheese for topping. Cover and let sit in refrigerator overnight.

Preheat oven to 375 degrees. Bake for 30 minutes. Let stand about 10 minutes and cut into squares.   Makes 6 servings.

Per Serving (approx):
Calories 416
Carbohydrate 34 gm

Protein 33 gm
Sodium 888 mg

Fat 17 gm
Cholesterol 114 mg

SAUTÉ,
STIR FRY, & FRY

Japanese Stir-Fry

If you can't find the Japanese noodles for this recipe, any thin noodle such as fettuccine will do nicely.

1 pound skinless, boneless
   chicken breast, cut in chunks
1/4 cup teriyaki sauce
1/2 teaspoon ground ginger
1 garlic clove, pressed
1/4 to 1/2 teaspoon red pepper
   flakes (optional)

2 teaspoons cornstarch
2 tablespoons vegetable oil
1 package (16 ounces) frozen
   Japanese style vegetables,
   thawed
2 to 3 tablespoons water
1 package or 1/2 pound
   fettuccine, cooked

In a medium bowl, combine chicken, teriyaki sauce, ginger, garlic, and red pepper flakes. Sprinkle cornstarch on top; mix thoroughly. Let marinate 15 minutes.

In a wok or skillet, heat the oil. Add chicken; stir-fry 4 minutes until just cooked through. Add vegetables and water; cook 3 to 4 minutes until vegetables are heated through. Serve over the cooked noodles.

Makes 3 to 4 servings.

Per Serving (approx):
Calories 336
Carbohydrate 25 gm

Protein 34 gm
Sodium 1230 mg

Fat 11 gm
Cholesterol 77 mg

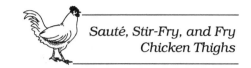

Stir-Fry Chicken and Vegetables

You can follow this recipe exactly, or you can substitute bite-size pieces of asparagus for the cauliflower and broccoli, as we often do.

1 1/2 pounds skinless, boneless chicken thighs, cut in thin slices
1 1/2 cups cauliflower florets
1 1/2 cups broccoli florets
1 cup thinly sliced carrots

1 cup sliced green onion
1 teaspoon salt
1/4 teaspoon pepper
1/2 cup chicken broth, heated

Heat a skillet; spray with vegetable oil. Add chicken slices and stir-fry about 3 minutes. Increase heat and add cauliflower, broccoli, and carrots; continue to stir-fry about 3 minutes. Add onion, salt, and pepper, continuing to stir-fry about 3 minutes more. Add warm chicken broth, scraping drippings from bottom of frying pan, and cook about 2 minutes more. Check the cauliflower and broccoli to see if they are tender-crisp.

Makes 4 servings.

Per Serving (approx):
Calories 306
Carbohydrate 8 gm

Protein 36 gm
Sodium 904 mg

Fat 14 gm
Cholesterol 121 mg

Ginger Hot Thighs

2 tablespoons olive oil
1 1/4 pounds skinless chicken thighs
1 onion, minced
4 garlic cloves, minced

1/4 cup red wine
1 tablespoon grated ginger
1 1/2 teaspoons ground cumin
1/2 teaspoon chili powder
1 tablespoon minced parsley

In a skillet, heat oil. Add chicken; cook 7 to 8 minutes on each side until browned. In a small bowl, combine onion, garlic, wine, ginger, cumin, and chili powder. Add mixture to skillet; partially cover and reduce heat. Cook about 20 to 30 minutes until chicken is fork-tender and liquid has been reduced to a glaze. Serve, sprinkled with parsley.

Makes 3 to 4 servings.

Per Serving (approx):
Calories 325
Carbohydrate 6 gm

Protein 29 gm
Sodium 101 mg

Fat 20 gm
Cholesterol 101 mg

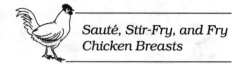

California Chicken Stir-Fry

Prunes and peas in a stir-fry? Why not! Try it; it's a great combination.

4 skinless, boneless chicken
  breast halves, cut in 2-inch
  strips
1 teaspoon grated lemon peel
1 1/2 tablespoons lemon juice
1/4 teaspoon salt
1/4 teaspoon pepper
1/2 cup coarsely chopped prunes

3/4 cup low-sodium chicken
  broth, heated
2 carrots, cut in 1-inch
  matchsticks
1 leek, sliced thin
2 cups sugar snap peas
1 tablespoon light butter-
  flavored margarine

In a bowl, sprinkle chicken with lemon peel, lemon juice, salt, and pepper, stirring to coat well. In another bowl, combine prunes and chicken broth and let sit for about 15 minutes, stirring occasionally.

Spray large frying pan with vegetable spray and heat. Add chicken and cook, stirring, about 4 minutes. Add carrots, then leek; cook about 1 minute more. Add sugar snap peas and margarine and continue to stir-fry until chicken is fork-tender and peas are tender-crisp, about 3 minutes. Stir in prunes and broth, separating pieces of prunes. Cook about 1 minute more or until heated through. Serve with saffron rice, if desired.

Makes 4 servings.

Per Serving (approx):
Calories 289
Carbohydrate 32 gm

Protein 30 gm
Sodium 279 mg

Fat 5 gm
Cholesterol 80 mg

It was not until 1892 that a poultryman in Petaluma, California, began shipping baby chicks by railway express to destinations up to 2000 miles away. The freight cars were staffed by young men who fed and watered the chicks en route.

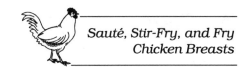

Orange Pineapple Chicken Stir-Fry

This is a favorite at our house because it is so tasty, and also because it is so easy and fast to prepare.

1 1/2 pounds skinless, boneless
    chicken breasts, cut in thin slices
1 clove garlic, minced
1 onion, sliced in rings
1 package (6 ounces) frozen
    snow peas
1 teaspoon salt

1/4 teaspoon pepper
1/2 teaspoon ground ginger
1 can (14 ounces) pineapple
    tidbits in juice, drained
2 tablespoons cornstarch
1/2 cup chicken broth, divided
1 can (11 ounces) mandarin
    orange slices, drained

Preheat a frying pan and spray with vegetable spray. Add chicken breast slices and minced garlic and stir-fry about 3 minutes. Add onion and snow pea pods, stir-frying about 3 minutes. Add salt, pepper, ginger, and pineapple, continuing to stir-fry about 3 minutes more.

In a small bowl, mix cornstarch with 2 tablespoons of the chicken broth, stirring until smooth. Slowly stir in remaining broth and add to mixture in frying pan. Incorporate the cornstarch mixture gently into the chicken and snow peas. Add mandarin oranges and heat through, about 2 minutes, stirring gently to keep orange sections from breaking.

Makes 4 servings.

Per Serving (approx):
Calories 334
Carbohydrate 36 gm

Protein 36 gm
Sodium 672 mg

Fat 5 gm
Cholesterol 92 mg

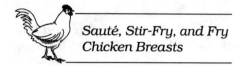
Simple Marinated Chicken Breasts

This basic recipe is a classic. Mark this page; you'll use it often.

2 teaspoons Dijon mustard
1/2 teaspoon salt
1/2 teaspoon pepper
1/8 teaspoon dried savory
1/8 teaspoon dried tarragon

2 tablespoons olive oil, divided
1/4 cup dry white wine
4 boneless chicken breast halves
1/2 cup warm water

In a small bowl, combine mustard, salt, pepper, savory, and tarragon. Stir in 1 tablespoon olive oil and white wine. Place chicken in a shallow dish; pour marinade mixture over chicken and turn to coat well. Cover and place in refrigerator to marinate overnight.

Heat remaining 1 tablespoon olive oil in a frying pan. Add the chicken breasts and cook, turning, about 15 minutes (about 7 minutes per side) until brown and done. Remove the chicken to a warm serving platter.

In the same frying pan, combine marinade with water. Boil and stir about 3 minutes; pour over chicken and serve.   Makes 4 servings.

Per Serving (approx):
Calories 441
Carbohydrate 1 gm

Protein 56 gm
Sodium 489 mg

Fat 23 gm
Cholesterol 159 mg

It was not until the 1960s that chickens were specifically bred for egg laying or meat. Up until then, the same breeds of chickens were used for both. "Egg birds" are bred for their egg-producing qualities, "meat birds" for meatiness, flavor, and rapid growth.

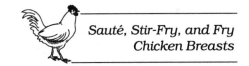

Smoky Chicken Breast Fillets and Apples

This is great for a chafing dish, from which everyone serves themselves.

6 skinless, boneless chicken
   breasts
1 1/2 teaspoons liquid smoke
1/2 teaspoon poultry seasoning
1/2 teaspoon salt
1/4 teaspoon ground mace

1/4 teaspoon nutmeg
1/4 teaspoon dry mustard
1/4 teaspoon pepper
3 tablespoons butter
3 apples, peeled, cored,
   and sliced

Rub each chicken breast with liquid smoke. In a small bowl, combine poultry seasoning, salt, mace, nutmeg, dry mustard, and pepper; sprinkle on both sides of chicken and let sit about 5 minutes.*

In a frying pan, melt the butter about 2 minutes. Add seasoned chicken and cook about 5 minutes. Turn chicken and add apples on top of the chicken; cover and cook 5 minutes more. Rearrange so that chicken is on top of apples; cook about 4 minutes more or until chicken and apples are tender. Makes 6 servings.

*Chicken may be seasoned and refrigerated for later cooking, if desired.

Per Serving (approx):
Calories 268
Carbohydrate 16 gm

Protein 30 gm
Sodium 322 mg

Fat 10 gm
Cholesterol 96 mg

Chafing Dish Chicken

2 1/2 pounds skinless, boneless, chicken breasts, cut in bite-size pieces
4 tablespoons flour
1 teaspoon salt
1/4 teaspoon pepper
4 tablespoons vegetable oil
1/2 cup chopped onion
3 1/2 cups chicken broth

1 package (10 ounces) frozen peas
1 can (8 ounces) water chestnuts, drained and sliced
1 jar (3 ounces) pimento, drained and chopped
12 ounces small curd cottage cheese
2 tablespoons lemon juice
1/4 cup white wine

Coat chicken with flour. Sprinkle with salt and pepper. In a Dutch oven, heat oil; add chicken and cook, stirring about 5 minutes or until lightly browned. Remove the chicken to a warm plate. Add onion to pan drippings, stir, and cook about 3 minutes.

Pour the chicken broth into the Dutch oven, scraping the bottom and stirring. Boil at high temperature about 5 minutes, reducing liquid by half. Add peas, chicken, water chestnuts, and pimento; simmer about 10 minutes.

In a food processor or blender, process cottage cheese and lemon juice about 30 seconds until smooth. After chicken mixture has simmered, slowly stir in cottage cheese, then wine. Heat through, but do not boil.

Makes 8 servings.

Per Serving (approx):
Calories 362   *Protein 44 gm*   *Fat 14 gm*
Carbohydrate 15 gm   *Sodium 1230 mg*   *Cholesterol 103 mg*

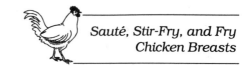

Golden Glow Chicken

The "glow" comes from the hot pepper sauce.

6 skinless, boneless chicken
   breast halves
1 tablespoon water
1 egg, slightly beaten
1 cup corn flake crumbs
3 tablespoons butter
2 teaspoons cornstarch
1/2 teaspoon ground ginger

1/4 teaspoon salt
3/4 cup apricot nectar
1/8 teaspoon hot pepper
   sauce
1 can (8 ounces) apricot halves,
   drained, for garnish
Minced parsley, for garnish

Place chicken between two pieces of waxed paper. Pound it to 1/4-inch thickness. In a small bowl, mix water and egg. Place corn flake crumbs in shallow dish. Dip chicken one piece at a time in the egg mixture, then in the corn flake crumbs, pressing lightly to make the crumbs adhere.

In a frying pan, melt butter. Add the chicken and cook, turning once, about 10 minutes, until chicken is golden brown and a fork can be inserted easily.

While chicken is cooking, in a small saucepan, combine cornstarch, ginger, salt, apricot nectar, and hot pepper sauce. Stir over low heat until the cornstarch dissolves and the mixture is thickened.

Place chicken on platter and top with apricot nectar sauce. Garnish with apricot halves and parsley.   Makes 6 servings.

Per Serving (approx):
Calories 276   *Protein 31 gm*   *Fat 10 gm*
Carbohydrate 15 gm   *Sodium 298 mg*   *Cholesterol 131 mg*

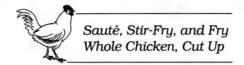

Carmelized Chicken

1 tablespoon garlic salt
1/2 tablespoon pepper
1 tablespoon onion powder
1 whole chicken, cut up
1 cup flour
2 tablespoons olive oil
2 pears, cored and sliced

1 apple, cored and sliced into
  rings
1/2 cup dry white wine
2 tablespoons butter
1/2 cup light corn syrup
1 teaspoon grated lemon peel
1/2 cup brandy

Mix together garlic salt, pepper, and onion powder; rub on chicken. Put flour in a paper bag; add chicken, and shake to coat. In a large frying pan, heat oil. Add chicken and cook for about 15 minutes until brown on all sides. Drain oil from pan and discard it. Reduce heat. Add pears, apples, and wine. Cover and simmer 15 minutes.

In a small saucepan, melt the butter. Add corn syrup; cook, stirring, about 3 minutes. Turn off heat. Add brandy and lemon peel to syrup.

Pour brandy mixture over chicken. Turn chicken skin side up, and pour brandy mixture over chicken. Simmer, uncovered, about 20 minutes or until a fork pierces the chicken easily.   Makes 4 servings.

Per Serving (approx):
Calories 992
Carbohydrate 77 gm

Protein 57 gm
Sodium 306 mg

Fat 41 gm
Cholesterol 225 mg

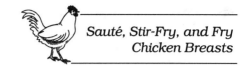

Chicken Claret

2 tablespoons olive oil
4 chicken breast halves
1/2 teaspoon salt
1/2 teaspoon pepper

1/4 teaspoon dried basil
1/2 cup warm water
1/2 cup claret
1 cup applesauce

In a frying pan, heat oil. Sprinkle the chicken with salt and pepper. Sauté the chicken about 5 minutes until brown on all sides. Drain off the oil. Sprinkle the chicken with basil and pour claret and water into the frying pan. Cover and simmer for about 30 minutes. Turn chicken pieces over, spread applesauce evenly over chicken and simmer about 10 minutes more until applesauce is warm and a fork pierces the chicken easily.

Makes 4 servings.

Per Serving (approx):
Calories 323
Carbohydrate 13 gm

Protein 28 gm
Sodium 362 mg

Fat 15 gm
Cholesterol 79 mg

"Now and then it is a joy to have one's table red with wine and roses."
Oscar Wilde, "De Profundis"

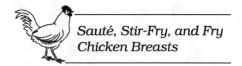
Sautéed Chicken with Pears

2 whole chicken breasts, skinned,
  boned, and cut into strips
4 tablespoons low-sodium soy sauce
2 teaspoons grated orange peel
4 bartlett pears, peeled, cored,
  and sliced in 8 pieces lengthwise
1/2 cup sliced celery
3 green onions, sliced

1/2 pound sugar snap peas,
  ends cut
1/2 cup orange juice
1/4 cup low-sodium chicken
  broth
1/2 teaspoon salt
1/4 teaspoon pepper

Sprinkle chicken with soy sauce and 1 teaspoon of the orange peel; let
sit 5 minutes. Spray large frying pan with vegetable spray and heat. Add
chicken and sauté, turning, about 2 minutes.

Sprinkle pears with remaining 1 teaspoon orange peel and add to pan;
cook 2 minutes. Add celery and onions; cook 2 minutes more. Add sugar
snap peas and sauté about 3 more minutes until just tender. Add orange
juice, broth, salt, and pepper; cook 1 minute.   Makes 6 servings.

Per Serving (approx):
Calories 247   *Protein 23 gm*   *Fat 3 gm*
Carbohydrate 32 gm   *Sodium 940 mg*   *Cholesterol 53 mg*

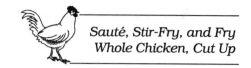

Royal Chicken

4 pounds chicken, split or quartered
1/4 pound butter
3 carrots, diced
3 onions, chopped

1 cup diced celery
1 cup white wine
1/4 cup dry sherry

In a skillet combine all ingredients except the wines. Simmer 20 or 25 minutes. Add white wine and continue simmering until chicken is done.

Just before serving, add the sherry.   Makes 4 to 6 servings.

> *Per Serving (approx):*
> *Calories 754*
> *Carbohydrate 14 gm*
>
> *Protein 63 gm*
> *Sodium 372 mg*
>
> *Fat 46 gm*
> *Cholesterol 285 mg*

Deviled Chicken

Mustard and Worcestershire can really enhance a chicken.

1 whole chicken, cut up
Paprika to taste
Salt and pepper to taste
1/2 cup vegetable oil
2 tablespoons flour
1 1/2 teaspoons dry mustard

1 cup chicken broth (canned or
    made with bouillon cube)
2 teaspoons Worcestershire
    sauce
2 tablespoons ketchup
1/2 cup dry sherry

Sprinkle chicken with paprika, salt, and pepper to taste. Brown in heated oil; remove from pan. Stir flour and mustard into the fat remaining in the pan. Slowly stir in stock. Cook, stirring constantly, until thick. Add remaining ingredients. Return chicken to pan. Simmer for 1 hour, covered.   Makes 4 servings.

> *Per Serving (approx):*
> *Calories 599*
> *Carbohydrate 5 gm*
>
> *Protein 47 gm*
> *Sodium 443 mg*
>
> *Fat 41 gm*
> *Cholesterol 182 mg*

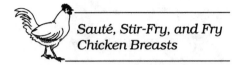

Chicken Breasts with Brandied Mushrooms

2 skinless, boneless chicken
  breasts, split
Salt and white pepper
3 tablespoons unsalted butter
Brandied Mushrooms
1/2 cup whipping cream

1 cup chicken broth
1 tablespoon brandy or cognac
1 egg yolk
2 tablespoons minced parsley

Pound breast pieces between sheets of waxed paper to about 1/2-inch thickness. Season with salt and pepper to taste. In a large frying pan, heat butter until it bubbles. Add chicken and cook, turning occasionally, about 5 minutes until tender.

Remove to a serving platter. Spoon Brandied Mushrooms over breasts. Drain the butter from the chicken pan and discard it, leaving brown (not burned) drippings. Add cream and broth to pan and cook over high heat, stirring, until reduced to 1 cup liquid. Remove from heat.

Whisk cognac with egg yolk; whisk in a little of the cream sauce. Gradually whisk yolk mixture into cream sauce. Heat and stir over low heat until sauce thickens slightly (do not allow to bubble). Stir in parsley. Season with salt and pepper to taste. Pour over breasts. Sprinkle with parsley.   Makes 4 servings.

BRANDIED MUSHROOMS:
In a frying pan, heat 4 tablespoons unsalted butter. Add 3/4 pound thinly sliced mushrooms. Cook and turn occasionally until liquid disappears and mushrooms begin to sizzle. Add 1/4 cup brandy or cognac and continue cooking until the liquid disappears and mushrooms are slightly browned. Season with salt to taste.

Per Serving (approx):
Calories 478
Carbohydrate 6 gm

Protein 34 gm
Sodium 254 mg

Fat 34 gm
Cholesterol 219 mg

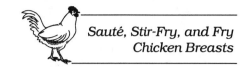

Quick Coriander Chicken Breasts

If you're not familiar with the flavor of coriander seed, you have a real treat coming. It's a distinctive, mild, lemonlike flavor. This dish is excellent cold or hot. You may want to double the recipe.

3 tablespoons light soy sauce
1 tablespoon crushed coriander
  seeds
1 tablespoon red wine vinegar
1 teaspoon brown sugar
2 cloves garlic, minced

1/4 teaspoon poultry seasoning
4 skinless, boneless chicken
  breast halves
1/2 teaspoon pepper
1 tablespoon olive oil

In a food processor container, blend soy sauce, crushed coriander seeds, vinegar, brown sugar, garlic, and poultry seasoning. Place chicken breasts in a shallow bowl; pour the sauce over chicken and turn to coat well. Sprinkle with pepper. If it's more convenient for you, you can let the chicken marinate overnight in the refrigerator.

In a frying pan, heat olive oil. Add chicken and cook, turning, about 7 minutes per side or until a fork can be inserted easily. Serve the chicken with its sauce.   Makes 4 servings.

Per Serving (approx):
Calories 204
Carbohydrate 3 gm

Protein 31 gm
Sodium 699 mg

Fat 8 gm
Cholesterol 80 mg

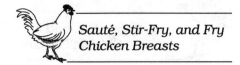
Chicken Breast Chardonnay

4 skinless, boneless chicken
  breast halves
2 tablespoons flour
Salt and pepper to taste
2 tablespoons olive oil
1/2 pound sliced mushrooms
1/2 cup sliced green onions

2 tablespoons minced shallots
2 tablespoons minced sun-dried
  tomatoes, drained
1 teaspoon dried tarragon
1/2 cup chardonnay
1/2 cup chicken broth
1/2 cup whipping cream

Shake the chicken in a bag with the flour, salt, and pepper. In a skillet, heat oil. Remove the coated chicken from the bag. Retain any extra seasoned flour. Brown the chicken on all sides for approximately 10 minutes.

Add mushrooms, onions, shallots, tomatoes, and tarragon and cook 2 minutes longer. Add chardonnay and broth (reserving 2 tablespoons) and heat. Add 1 tablespoon remaining seasoned flour, mixed with 2 tablespoons reserved chicken broth. Stir until smooth. Add cream and simmer to desired consistency.   Makes 4 servings.

Per Serving (approx):
Calories 360   *Protein 33 gm*   *Fat 18 gm*
Carbohydrate 11 gm   *Sodium 146 mg*   *Cholesterol 121 mg*

The expression "spring chicken" applied to a person refers to the boisterous, energetic bustling about of chickens first released outdoors in the spring.

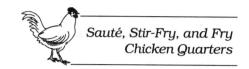

Tarragon Chicken

1/4 cup flour
1 teaspoon salt
1/2 teaspoon dried tarragon
1/2 teaspoon pepper

4 tablespoons tarragon vinegar
4 chicken quarters
3 tablespoons olive oil

On wax paper, combine flour, salt, tarragon, and pepper. Place the vinegar in a shallow dish. Roll each piece of chicken in vinegar, then dust lightly with the flour mixture. In a frying pan, heat olive oil. Add chicken and cook, turning, about 10 minutes until brown on all sides. Pour any remaining vinegar over chicken. Reduce heat and continue to cook, turning, until chicken is done (about 20 minutes) and a fork can be inserted easily.   Makes 4 servings.

Per Serving (approx):
Calories 643
Carbohydrate 7 gm

Protein 59 gm
Sodium 778 mg

Fat 42 gm
Cholesterol 207 mg

Raspberry-Caraway Chicken

2 tablespoons vegetable oil
2 tablespoons flour
6 boneless chicken legs and thighs
Salt and pepper to taste
1/2 cup red raspberry vinegar

1/2 cup water
1 chicken bouillon cube
1/2 teaspoon caraway seeds
1/4 cup whipping cream
Raspberries, for garnish

In a frying pan, heat oil. Flour chicken on both sides, sprinkle lightly with salt and pepper to taste. Brown in hot oil. When golden brown, drain oil and fat from pan. Return chicken to heat. Add raspberry vinegar, water, and bouillon cube. Sprinkle with caraway seed. Cover and simmer for 40 minutes. Remove chicken to a plate and keep warm. Reduce sauce to a syrupy consistency. Pour sauce over chicken and garnish with raspberries.   Makes 6 servings.

Per Serving (approx):
Calories 609
Carbohydrate 3 gm

Protein 59 gm
Sodium 387 mg

Fat 39 gm
Cholesterol 221 mg

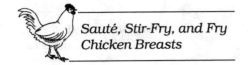

Creole Chicken

1 1/2 pounds chicken breast halves
1/2 cup chopped onion
1/2 cup chopped green bell pepper
1/2 cup chopped celery
1 can (8 ounces) tomato sauce

1/2 teaspoon dried basil
1/2 to 1 teaspoon hot pepper
  sauce
1/2 teaspoon dried thyme

In a large skillet coated with vegetable spray, cook chicken until browned on all sides. Remove chicken; drain off any grease. Add the remaining ingredients. Cover and simmer about 25 minutes, stirring occasionally, until chicken is no longer pink inside. Remove. This is tasty over white rice.   Makes 3 servings.

Per Serving (approx):
Calories 565
Carbohydrate 49 gm

Protein 59 gm
Sodium 607 mg

Fat 15 gm
Cholesterol 153 mg

Herbed Chicken Breasts

6 chicken breast halves
1 tablespoon each minced basil,
  oregano, and rosemary
1/4 cup flour
1 teaspoon salt
1/4 teaspoon pepper

1 tablespoon butter
2 tablespoons olive oil
1/2 cup chopped green onions
1/2 cup sliced mushrooms
1/2 cup fumé blanc or other
  dry white wine

Bone chicken breasts; sprinkle with the fresh minced basil, oregano, and rosemary. Dredge in flour, salt, and pepper. Lightly sauté until brown in butter and olive oil, about 7 minutes. Turn once. Add onions and mushrooms and sauté three minutes. Add wine and simmer, covered, for 10 minutes.   Makes 6 servings.

Per Serving (approx):
Calories 280
Carbohydrate 5 gm

Protein 29 gm
Sodium 477 mg

Fat 15 gm
Cholesterol 84 mg

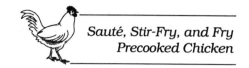

Chicken à la King

This is a good recipe for leftover chicken or turkey.

1/4 pound mushrooms
1/4 cup butter, melted
1/2 green bell pepper,
   chopped
2 pimentos, chopped
3 tablespoons flour
1/2 teaspoon salt
1 cup chicken broth

1/4 cup milk
1/4 cup chablis or other white
   wine
1/2 teaspoon white pepper
1 teaspoon sugar
1/2 cup whipping cream
2 egg yolks, slightly beaten
2 cups cooked chicken, cubed

Sauté mushrooms in butter; add bell pepper and pimentos. Simmer about 5 minutes. Stir in flour and salt until smooth. Blend in broth, milk, and wine. Cook, stirring constantly, until mixture thickens. Stir in pepper and sugar. Mix cream with egg yolks; stir into sauce. Add chicken and stir until all is combined and hot. Serve over hot rice or noodles.

Makes 4 to 6 servings.

Per Serving (approx):
Calories 267
Carbohydrate 7 gm

Protein 15 gm
Sodium 555 mg

Fat 19 gm
Cholesterol 153 mg

> "A good meal makes a man feel more charitable toward the whole world than any sermon."
>
> Arthur Pendenys,
> *New York Times*

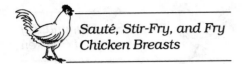

Rosemary with Mushroom Chicken

1 tablespoon butter
1 tablespoon olive oil
2 or 3 cloves fresh garlic,
    minced
2 cups sliced fresh mushrooms
2 teaspoons minced rosemary

6 skinless, boneless chicken
    breast halves pounded to 1/4-
    inch thickness
1/2 cup lemon juice
1/2 cup white wine
Parsley or rosemary, for garnish

In a heavy skillet, melt butter and oil. Sauté garlic, mushrooms, and rosemary then cover pan and simmer about 2 to 3 minutes, until mushrooms are tender.

Remove the mushrooms with a slotted spoon. Set aside. In the same skillet, brown the chicken breasts approximately 2 to 3 minutes on each side.

Return mushrooms to the pan, add lemon juice and wine and simmer, covered, for 5 to 7 minutes. Remove lid and continue cooking 2 minutes longer to reduce liquid.

To serve, top chicken breasts with mushroom mixture, garnish with parsley or rosemary.   Makes 6 servings.

Per Serving (approx):
Calories 218
Carbohydrate 3 gm

Protein 30 gm
Sodium 92 mg

Fat 8 gm
Cholesterol 85 mg

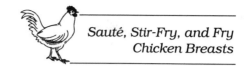

Lively Lemon Caper Chicken

Sounds like a nightclub act, doesn't it? But it describes the recipe perfectly.

4 skinless, boneless chicken
   breast halves
1/8 teaspoon salt
2 tablespoons minced mint
1 tablespoon minced basil
2 teaspoon minced thyme
1/4 cup minced sun-dried
   tomatoes
2 tablespoons olive oil

1/2 cup chicken broth
2 tablespoons lemon juice
1 tablespoon dehydrated
   minced onion
2 teaspoons cornstarch
1/4 cup dry vermouth
1 tablespoon capers
Lemon slices, for garnish
Mint sprigs, for garnish

Gently pound chicken between sheets of wax paper to 1/4-inch thickness; sprinkle with salt. In a bowl, combine mint, basil, thyme, and tomatoes; sprinkle over chicken. Roll up each chicken breast and fasten with toothpicks.

In a frying pan, heat olive oil. Add chicken and cook, turning, about 10 minutes or until brown on all sides. Stir in broth and lemon juice, scraping any brown bits from bottom of pan. Add onion, cover and simmer about 10 minutes until the chicken juices run clear. Remove chicken rolls from frying pan, set aside and keep warm.

In a small dish, blend cornstarch and vermouth. Add to the frying pan and cook, stirring, until mixture is clear and thickened; stir in capers.

To serve, slice the chicken breasts and cover with sauce. Garnish with lemon slices and mint sprigs.   Makes 4 servings.

Per Serving (approx):
Calories 260
Carbohydrate 5 gm

Protein 30 gm
Sodium 363 mg

Fat 12 gm
Cholesterol 80 mg

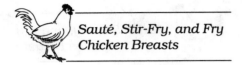
Skillet Chicken for Two

1 tablespoon butter
2 chicken breast halves
1/2 cup chopped onion
1 cup chopped tomato

1 tablespoon Worcestershire
  sauce
1/2 teaspoon dry mustard
1/2 teaspoon salt
1/4 teaspoon pepper

In a frying pan, melt butter. Add chicken and cook, turning, about 5 minutes or until brown on all sides. Add onion and cook about 2 minutes more. Add tomato, Worcestershire sauce, mustard, salt, and pepper. Bring to boil. Reduce heat to low, cover, and simmer about 20 minutes more until a fork pierces the chicken easily. Serve with rice.

Makes 2 servings.

Per Serving (approx):
Calories 257
Carbohydrate 8 gm

Protein 30 gm
Sodium 733 mg

Fat 14 gm
Cholesterol 95 mg

"Strange to see how a good dinner and feasting reconciles everybody."
Samuel Pepys,
Diary of Samuel Pepys

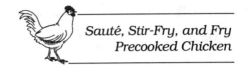

Easy Chicken Shrimp Surprise

4 tablespoons butter
1/2 pound sliced mushrooms
2 tablespoons sliced green onions
4 tablespoons flour
1 cup sour cream
1 can (10 1/2 ounces) chicken broth
1/2 cup dry sherry

1 cup shredded cheddar cheese
1/4 cup grated Parmesan cheese
2 cups cooked chicken,
   cut in pieces
2 cups cooked shrimp
2 tablespoons chopped parsley

In a saucepan, melt the butter. Add mushrooms and onions. Sauté 5 minutes. Blend in flour. Add sour cream and broth. Gradually stir in sherry. Add cheeses and heat over low heat, stirring occasionally until cheese is melted. Add chicken and shrimp and heat. Sprinkle with parsley and serve.   Makes 8 servings.

Per Serving (approx):
Calories 382
Carbohydrate 22 gm

Protein 25 gm
Sodium 549 mg

Fat 20 gm
Cholesterol 139 mg

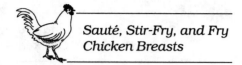

Chicken Dijon with Capers

3 tablespoons margarine
4 boneless, skinless chicken
   breast halves
2 tablespoons flour

1 cup chicken broth
1/2 cup milk
2 tablespoons Dijon mustard
2 tablespoons capers, drained

In a frying pan, melt margarine. Add chicken and sauté until browned on all sides. Remove chicken to a warm serving platter.

To the same frying pan, add flour and cook 1 minute, stirring. Slowly add chicken broth and milk. Cook, stirring, until sauce thickens. Stir in mustard. Return chicken to frying pan, cover, and simmer for 10 minutes until a fork pierces the chicken easily. Serve the chicken with its sauce sprinkled with capers.   Makes 4 servings.

Per Serving (approx):
Calories 421
Carbohydrate 6 gm

Protein 61 gm
Sodium 869 mg

Fat 17 gm
Cholesterol 165 mg

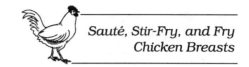

Light and Lean Chicken

Look at the nutritional analysis to see how this recipe got its name.

4 skinless chicken breast halves	2/3 cup skim milk
1/2 teaspoon pepper, divided	2 teaspoons arrowroot or
2 cloves garlic, peeled and cut in half	2 tablespoons instant potatoes
1 cup low-sodium chicken broth	1 teaspoon minced chives
1/2 cup dry white wine	

Coat a frying pan with vegetable spray. Heat the pan; add chicken and sprinkle with 1/4 teaspoon of the pepper. Cook, turning, until brown on all sides. Reduce temperature to low, add garlic halves, and continue cooking until a fork pierces the chicken easily, about 10 minutes more.

Remove the chicken, leaving the garlic in the pan; add chicken broth and wine. Boil about 5 minutes; reduce temperature to low. Mix in skim milk with arrowroot until smooth and slowly add mixture to pan liquids. Sprinkle with remaining 1/4 teaspoon of the pepper and cook, stirring, until thickened, about 2 minutes. Return the chicken to the pan and sprinkle with chives. Heat the chicken through, about 5 minutes more.

Makes 4 servings.

Per Serving (approx):
Calories 338
Carbohydrate 4 gm

Protein 60 gm
Sodium 163 mg

Fat 7 gm
Cholesterol 161 mg

"We are all dietetic sinners; only a small portion of what we eat nourishes us, the balance goes to waste and loss of energy."
Sir William Ostler, Aphroisms from His Bedside Teachings and Writings

275

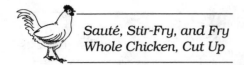

Coffee Paprika Chicken

1/2 cup flour
1/2 teaspoon salt
3 tablespoons paprika, divided
3 tablespoons margarine
1 whole chicken, cut up

1 small onion, chopped
1/2 cup water
1 teaspoon instant coffee powder
1 cup chicken broth
1/2 cup light cream

In a shallow dish, combine flour, salt, and 2 tablespoons of the paprika. Dredge the chicken in this mixture. Reserve remaining flour mixture. In a frying pan, melt the margarine. Add chicken and cook, turning, until brown on all sides.

Remove the chicken from the pan. Add onion and cook, stirring frequently, until it's translucent. Return the chicken to the pan, add water, cover, and simmer about 35 minutes until chicken is done.

Remove chicken, cover, and keep warm. To liquid in frying pan, add, stirring, 2 tablespoons of reserved flour, remaining 2 teaspoons paprika, and coffee powder. Add broth and cream, bring to boil, stirring constantly, and simmer about 5 minutes. Return chicken to pan and heat thoroughly.   Makes 4 servings.

Per Serving (approx):
Calories 840
Carbohydrate 49 gm

Protein 59 gm
Sodium 925 mg

Fat 45 gm
Cholesterol 243 mg

BAKE & ROAST

Roast Chicken Stuffed
with Mushrooms

3 cups day-old bread crumbs	2 tablespoons lemon juice
2 tablespoons chopped parsley	2 whole chickens
1/2 cup minced onion	3 tablespoons flour
Salt and pepper to taste	2 cups chicken broth
1/2 pound mushrooms, chopped	1 teaspoon ground mace
1/2 teaspoon dried thyme	1/2 teaspoon salt
1/2 cup melted butter, divided	1/2 teaspoon pepper

Preheat oven to 375 degrees.

Combine crumbs, parsley, onion, salt and pepper to taste, mushrooms, thyme, and 1/4 cup of the butter. Stuff chickens. Skewer openings; tie legs securely. Place the chickens in a baking pan. Combine remaining 1/4 cup butter and lemon juice; brush over the skin of both chickens.

Roast for 1 hour and 15 minutes until tender. Remove the chickens to a hot platter. Remove ties and skewers.

In a saucepan combine 3 tablespoons of the pan drippings, flour, broth, mace, salt, and pepper. Cook until thick. Serve on the side with the chicken.   Makes 6 servings.

Per Serving (approx):
Calories 880
Carbohydrate 44 gm   *Protein 84 gm*   *Fat 41 gm*
                              Sodium 1471 mg   *Cholesterol 306 mg*

Southwestern Oven-Fried Chicken

This was a winner in the National Broiler Council Cookoff, and when you make it you'll understand why. The pine nuts and cornmeal in the breading make all the difference.

3 slices white bread, torn in
   small pieces
3 tablespoons cilantro
2 tablespoons yellow cornmeal
2 tablespoons pine nuts
2 garlic cloves
1 1/2 teaspoons ground cumin
1/2 teaspoon dried oregano
Salt to taste

1/4 teaspoon cayenne
1/8 teaspoon ground cloves
2 teaspoons egg white
2 tablespoons Dijon mustard
1 tablespoon water
1 teaspoon honey
4 skinless chicken drumsticks
4 skinless chicken thighs
1/4 teaspoon pepper

Preheat oven to 400 degrees.

In a food processor, combine bread, cilantro, cornmeal, pine nuts, garlic, cumin, oregano, salt to taste, cayenne, and cloves. Process to form fine crumbs. Add egg white and mix until moist. Place mixture on a large shallow plate and set aside.

In a small bowl, combine mustard, water, and honey; brush evenly over the chicken. Sprinkle with pepper and salt to taste. Dip chicken, one piece at a time, in bread crumb mixture and press gently to adhere thin coating. Place the chicken on a rack in a greased pan.

Bake about 40 minutes until chicken is crisp and brown and a fork can be inserted easily.   Makes 4 servings.

Per Serving (approx):
Calories 369   *Protein 41 gm*   *Fat 14 gm*
Carbohydrate 18 gm   *Sodium 723 mg*   *Cholesterol 129 mg*

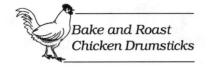
Oven-Fried Cornmeal Drumsticks

There is nothing quite as satisfying as fried chicken particularly when it is oven fried—it requires less fat and much less work, and attendant mess.

3/4 cup buttermilk
1/4 cup minced onion
1 1/4 pounds skinless chicken
  drumsticks
1/2 cup yellow cornmeal
1/2 cup bread crumbs,
  lightly toasted

1/4 cup grated Parmesan cheese
1 tablespoon chopped thyme
  or 1 1/2 teaspoons dried
  thyme
Dash cayenne
Salt and pepper to taste
1 to 2 tablespoons vegetable oil

In a bowl, combine buttermilk and onion. Add chicken; cover and marinate in the refrigerator 2 to 3 hours.

Preheat oven to 425 degrees.

On a plate, combine cornmeal, bread crumbs, cheese, thyme, cayenne, and salt and pepper to taste. Dredge chicken in crumbs, coating all sides. Place chicken on baking sheet; drizzle with oil.

Bake 20 to 30 minutes until chicken is crisp and cooked through.

Makes 2 to 3 servings.

Per Serving (approx):
Calories 489
Carbohydrate 35 gm

Protein 50 gm
Sodium 478 mg

Fat 17 gm
Cholesterol 142 mg

In 1910, poultry, most of which consisted of chicken, passed corn as the number 1 revenue-producing crop in America.

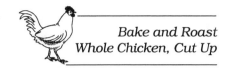

Oven-Fried Chicken

1 whole chicken, cut up in 8 pieces
1/4 pound melted butter
1/8 teaspoon garlic powder
1/8 teaspoon paprika

1/8 teaspoon dried thyme
1 teaspoon salt
1 1/2 cups dry bread crumbs
    or finely crushed corn flakes

Preheat oven to 350 degrees. Dip chicken pieces in butter, then shake in a paper bag containing seasonings and crumbs. Place skin side up in a lightly greased 9 x 13 baking dish and bake for 50 minutes or until done.

Makes 6 to 8 servings.

Per Serving (approx):
Calories 399
Carbohydrate 14 gm

Protein 29 gm
Sodium 624 mg

Fat 25 gm
Cholesterol 137 mg

Chicken Baked in Red Wine

The success of this dish depends on the wine, so use a good red, like a cabernet sauvignon, a chianti, or a merlot.

2 whole chickens, quartered*
1/2 teaspoon salt
1/8 teaspoon pepper

1 cup flour
1/4 cup vegetable oil
1 to 1 1/2 cups red wine
1 onion

Preheat oven to 400 degrees. Sprinkle salt and pepper generously on both sides of the chicken. Toss two pieces at a time in a bag with the flour. Lightly brown chicken in a skillet, using only enough oil to prevent burning. Add more oil as needed. Remove the chicken pieces as they brown, adding more until all are brown. Place chicken, skin side up, in a baking pan; pour 1 cup red wine over all. Peel onion and slice into rings on top of the chickens. Bake for approximately 30 to 45 minutes or until done.* Baste occasionally; add more wine if necessary. Remove from oven, baste, and serve.

Makes 4 to 6 servings.

*Adjust your baking time according to the size of the chicken.

Per Serving (approx):
Calories 793
Carbohydrate 20 gm

Protein 73 gm
Sodium 404 mg

Fat 44 gm
Cholesterol 280 mg

*Bake and Roast
Whole Chicken*

Roast Chicken, Mashed Potatoes and Sherry Gravy

1 whole chicken
2 teaspoons vegetable oil
3/4 teaspoon poultry seasoning
Salt and pepper to taste
2 tablespoons flour
1 1/2 cups reduced-sodium
   chicken broth

1/2 cup low-fat milk
1 tablespoon dry sherry
   (optional)
Salt and pepper to taste
Light and Fluffy Mashed
   Potatoes

Preheat oven to 375 degrees.

Remove giblet packet from chicken cavity; refrigerate for another use. Rinse chicken and pat dry. Rub the skin with vegetable oil; sprinkle with poultry seasoning and salt and pepper to taste. Place the chicken on a rack in a roasting pan. Roast it (about 20 minutes per pound) until the juices run clear with no hint of pink when a thigh is pierced with a fork. Remove the chicken to a serving platter and keep warm.

Pour off and discard all but 1 tablespoon drippings from the roasting pan and place the pan over medium heat; stir in flour. Cook about 5 minutes until flour is lightly browned, stirring constantly. Gradually stir in broth, milk, and sherry, if using. Cook 2 to 3 minutes longer, stirring constantly, until gravy is smooth and thickened. Season gravy with salt and pepper to taste. Serve the chicken with Light and Fluffy Mashed Potatoes and the sherry gravy.   Makes about 6 servings.

LIGHT AND FLUFFY MASHED POTATOES:
Peel and dice 3 large baking potatoes. In a saucepan, combine potatoes and enough lightly salted water to cover; bring to a boil. Cook potatoes 10 to 15 minutes until tender. Pour into a colander and drain well. Put drained potatoes through a ricer or mash well. In a saucepan, bring 2/3 cup low-fat milk to a simmer. Whisk in potatoes, 2 tablespoons light margarine, and salt, pepper, and ground nutmeg to taste.

Per Serving (approx):
Calories 541
Carbohydrate 30 gm

Protein 50 gm
Sodium 167 mg

Fat 24 gm
Cholesterol 183 mg

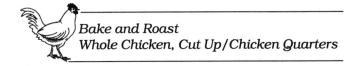

Baked Chicken Parmesan

1 cup uncooked oatmeal
1/3 cup grated Parmesan cheese
1/2 teaspoon salt
1/2 teaspoon paprika
1/8 teaspoon pepper
2 cloves garlic, minced

1/3 cup milk
1/4 cup margarine, melted
1 skinned whole chicken, cut up
Parsley, for garnish
Cherry tomatoes, for garnish

Preheat oven to 375 degrees. In a blender, combine oatmeal, Parmesan cheese, salt, paprika, and pepper. Blend about 1 minute. Place the mixture in a shallow dish. In another dish, mix the garlic and milk. Place chicken one piece at a time in the oatmeal mixture, then dip in milk mixture and again in the oatmeal mixture. In a baking pan, arrange the chicken and drizzle it with margarine. Bake for about 1 hour until tender. Garnish with parsley and cherry tomatoes.   Makes 4 servings.

Per Serving (approx):
Calories 681
Carbohydrate 16 gm

Protein 60 gm
Sodium 746 mg

Fat 42 gm
Cholesterol 219 mg

Harvest Fruit Chicken

1 1/2 pounds chicken quarters
1 can (17 ounces) apricot halves,
    drained, juice reserved
1 large apple, cored and chopped
1/3 cup raisins

1/4 cup chopped walnuts
1/4 cup brown sugar
1 teaspoon cinnamon
1/4 teaspoon ground cloves

Preheat oven to 375 degrees. Spray a baking pan with vegetable spray. Arrange the chicken in the pan. Top with apricots, apple, raisins, walnuts, and 1/3 cup reserved apricot juice. Sprinkle with brown sugar, cinnamon, and cloves. Cover and bake for 40 to 50 minutes until chicken is no longer pink inside. Serve with the baked spiced fruit.

Makes 3 servings.

Per Serving (approx):
Calories 648
Carbohydrate 45 gm

Protein 49 gm
Sodium 205 mg

Fat 30 gm
Cholesterol 157 mg

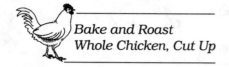
Sweet and Sour Chicken

There's a hint of the Orient in this dish.

1 whole chicken, cut up
1 cup sugar
1/4 cup white vinegar
1 tablespoon ketchup
1 teaspoon soy sauce
1/4 cup rosé
1 tablespoon chopped green bell
  pepper

1 tablespoon chopped canned
  pimento
1/2 cup water
1/2 teaspoon salt
2 teaspoons cornstarch
1 tablespoon cold water
1 teaspoon paprika
1 teaspoon dried parsley flakes

Preheat oven to 375 degrees.

Place the chicken in a casserole dish and set aside.

In a small saucepan, mix sugar, vinegar, ketchup, soy sauce, wine, bell pepper, and pimento. Add water and salt; simmer for 5 minutes. Combine cornstarch with cold water; add to hot mixture. Cook and stir until bubbling. Cool. Add paprika and stir well.

Pour sauce over the chicken and sprinkle with parsley flakes. Cover and bake for 1 1/2 hours. Uncover and bake 10 more minutes or until golden brown.   Makes 4 servings.

Per Serving (approx):
Calories 613
Carbohydrate 54 gm

Protein 46 gm
Sodium 558 mg

Fat 23 gm
Cholesterol 182 mg

The poultry industry is one of the very few agricultural fields that does not receive any government subsidies.

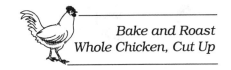

Chicken Marmalade

This recipe is so simple, it is hard to believe that it tastes so good.

1/3 cup orange marmalade
1/3 cup hot barbecue sauce
2 tablespoons Worcestershire sauce

2 tablespoons lemon juice
1 whole chicken, cut up
Salt and pepper to taste

Preheat oven to 350 degrees. Combine marmalade, barbecue sauce, Worcestershire sauce, and lemon juice, mixing well. Place chicken, skin side up, in a 9 x 13 pan lined with aluminum foil. Sprinkle with salt and pepper to taste. Pour sauce over chicken and bake 1 hour, basting occasionally. Increase temperature to 400 degrees and bake 15 minutes longer.

Makes 4 servings.

Per Serving (approx):
Calories 539
Carbohydrate 22 gm

Protein 53 gm
Sodium 346 mg

Fat 26 gm
Cholesterol 210 mg

Honey-Mustard Chicken

3/4 cup flour
1/2 teaspoon pepper
1 whole chicken, cut up
1/3 cup honey

2 tablespoons sliced green
 onions
1 tablespoon Dijon mustard
1/4 teaspoon onion powder

Preheat oven to 375 degrees.

Line a jellyroll pan with aluminum foil. In a paper bag, combine flour and pepper. Shake the chicken in the flour mixture. Arrange in a baking pan. Bake for 45 to 55 minutes until chicken is no longer pink inside.

In a small saucepan over medium heat, heat honey, onions, mustard, and onion powder. Place the chicken on a serving platter and drizzle sauce over it.   Makes 6 servings.

Per Serving (approx):
Calories 505
Carbohydrate 28 gm

Protein 48 gm
Sodium 199 mg

Fat 23 gm
Cholesterol 182 mg

Chicken in Lemon-Mint Sauce

1 1/2 tablespoons olive oil
1 1/2 pounds skinless,
  boneless chicken breasts,
  sliced into 1/2-inch fillets
1/4 cup lemon juice
1 teaspoon grated lemon peel
1/2 cup low-sodium chicken broth

1/2 cup dry white wine
1 clove garlic, minced
2 tablespoons minced green
  onions
1 tablespoon chopped parsley
1 tablespoon chopped mint

Preheat oven to 350 degrees.

Grease a baking dish with oil. Slice each chicken breast in half, horizontally. Place individual half-fillets between two pieces of waxed paper. Pound with a mallet to flatten slightly. Place fillets in a baking dish.

Whisk together lemon juice, lemon peel, chicken broth, white wine, garlic, green onion, parsley, and mint. Pour over chicken, cover loosely with foil, and bake 25 to 30 minutes until chicken is no longer pink inside. Remove chicken and place on a platter in the warm oven.

Pour sauce from the casserole into a small pan and boil, stirring, until it is reduced by half. Ladle over chicken fillets.   Makes 4 servings.

Per Serving (approx):
Calories 294
Carbohydrate 2 gm

Protein 42 gm
Sodium 104 mg

Fat 11 gm
Cholesterol 116 mg

Gold Coin Chicken

2 tablespoons butter
8 skinless, boneless chicken thighs
1 teaspoon seasoned salt
1/4 teaspoon garlic powder
1/4 teaspoon pepper
1/4 cup golden molasses
1/4 cup frozen orange juice
  concentrate, thawed

2 tablespoons minced onion
1 tablespoon grated ginger
2 cups carrots, cut in 1/4-inch
  rounds
1 tablespoon chopped parsley
Parsley sprigs, for garnish

Preheat oven to 375 degrees.

In a frying pan, melt butter and add the chicken. Sprinkle with salt,
garlic powder, and pepper and cook about 8 minutes until chicken is
brown on all sides. Remove chicken to a 7 x 10 baking pan. To the frying
pan, add molasses, orange juice, onion, and ginger. Stir until heated
through and well blended. Brush mixture generously over chicken. Cover
and bake for 30 minutes.

In a saucepan, steam carrots in a bit of water about 5 minutes until
tender-crisp. Drain. Baste chicken again with molasses-orange glaze and
bake about 10 minutes more until fork can be inserted in chicken with
ease. Add drained carrots to frying pan and stir gently until carrots are
well coated with glaze.

To serve, arrange chicken on serving platter and place carrot "coins" as
a border around chicken. Sprinkle with chopped parsley and garnish
with parsley sprigs.   Makes 4 servings.

Per Serving (approx):
Calories 367
Carbohydrate 25 gm

Protein 28 gm
Sodium 1241 mg

Fat 17 gm
Cholesterol 114 mg

Autumn Garden Chicken Bake

2 tablespoons seasoned rice vinegar
1 tablespoon light soy sauce
2 tablespoons olive oil
1 teaspoon chopped rosemary
1 teaspoon chopped marjoram
1 tablespoon chopped green onion
1 1/2 pounds skinless chicken
   breast halves
2 medium acorn squash,
   halved and seeded

Boiling water
2 Jonathan apples, cored and
   sliced
1 tablespoon margarine
1 tablespoon orange juice
   concentrate, thawed
6 tablespoons brown sugar
1/2 teaspoon cinnamon
1 teaspoon olive oil

Blend vinegar, soy sauce, olive oil, rosemary, marjoram, and green onion in medium bowl. Add chicken; stir to coat. Cover and refrigerate 2 to 4 hours, stirring several times.

Preheat oven to 400 degrees.

Place squash halves, cut side down, in a baking pan. Pour in boiling water to 1/2-inch depth. Bake for 30 minutes. Reduce oven temperature to 350 degrees; remove from oven. Fill squash centers with apple slices.

In a small saucepan, melt the margarine. Add the orange juice, brown sugar, and cinnamon and bring to a boil, stirring. Drizzle sugar mixture over apple slices. Return to the oven and bake, uncovered for 30 minutes until tender.

Coat an 8 x 8 baking pan with vegetable spray. Remove the chicken from the refrigerator, drain the chicken and reserve the marinade. In a skillet, heat the oil and sauté the chicken until golden brown. Remove the chicken to the prepared pan and pour marinade over. Cover the chicken and bake 30 minutes at 350 degrees until it is no longer pink inside. Serve each breast half with a squash half.   Makes 4 servings.

Per Serving (approx):
Calories 599
Carbohydrate 51 gm

Protein 45 gm
Sodium 354 mg

Fat 24 gm
Cholesterol 116 mg

Citrus-Mint Chicken

4 skinless, boneless chicken
   breast halves
1 lemon, peel grated and juiced
1/2 cup flour
1 tablespoon lemon pepper
1/8 cup vegetable oil
1/8 cup margarine
1/4 teaspoon chicken bouillon

1/4 cup hot water
1/4 cup orange juice
1/4 cup white wine
Worcestershire sauce
2 tablespoons brown sugar
1 tablespoon chopped mint
Mint sprigs, for garnish

Preheat oven to 375 degrees.

Place chicken in a bowl, pour lemon juice over it and turn to coat. In a paper bag, mix flour and lemon pepper. Add chicken, one piece at a time, shaking to coat. In a frying pan, heat the oil and margarine. Add the chicken and fry about 10 minutes until the chicken is brown on both sides.

Remove the chicken from the frying pan and place in a casserole dish. In the same pan, combine bouillon, water, orange juice, and Worcestershire sauce to taste with the pan drippings; pour over chicken. Sprinkle brown sugar, mint, and lemon peel over chicken. Bake for 45 minutes or until a fork can be inserted in the chicken easily. Garnish with mint sprigs.

Makes 4 servings.

Per Serving (approx):
Calories 350
Carbohydrate 20 gm

Protein 31 gm
Sodium 852 mg

Fat 16 gm
Cholesterol 80 mg

For really tender boiled chicken, put in a couple of slices or half of a lemon.

Honey-Baked Chicken
with Fruit Sauce

*Despite the honey, this dish is not too sweet, as the mustard, lemon juice,
and spices balance the flavors.*

2 pounds skinless chicken
    breast halves
1 3/4 pounds skinless chicken
    thighs
Salt and pepper to taste
1 cup honey, divided
2 tablespoons lemon juice
2 tablespoons Dijon mustard

2 or 3 large apples, peeled,
    cored, and thickly sliced
1 cup dried apricot halves
1 cup prunes
1 cup white wine
1 teaspoon ground allspice
1/2 teaspoon ground ginger

Preheat oven to 350 degrees.

In a roasting pan, arrange chicken, bone side up. Season chicken with
salt and pepper to taste. In a small bowl, combine 1/2 cup of the honey,
lemon juice, and mustard; mix well. Pour mixture over chicken and bake
30 minutes, basting occasionally with honey mixture and turning chicken
over halfway through cooking time.

Meanwhile, in a saucepan place apples, apricots, prunes, wine, allspice,
ginger, and remaining 1/2 cup honey; bring to a boil. Cover and simmer
10 minutes. Pour fruit sauce over chicken; bake 15 to 25 minutes longer,
basting occasionally, until chicken is cooked through with no trace of
pink remaining. (Breasts may be done before thighs.) Makes 8 servings.

Per Serving (approx):
Calories 510
Carbohydrate 81 gm

Protein 22 gm
Sodium 166 mg

Fat 9 gm
Cholesterol 71 mg

Honey-Glazed Rosemary Chicken

12 small new red potatoes, halved
4 skinless, boneless chicken
   breast halves
1 cup honey
1/8 cup hot water
1 teaspoon dried rosemary
2 tablespoons olive oil

1 teaspoon grated orange peel
1 teaspoon salt
1 teaspoon coarse white pepper
1/2 teaspoon garlic powder
1/2 teaspoon onion powder
4 sprigs rosemary
Tomato wedges, for garnish

Preheat oven to 375 degrees.

Steam potatoes in a little water about 10 minutes until slightly tender; drain. Place chicken in a baking pan and arrange potatoes around chicken. In a jar with a lid, combine honey, water, dried rosemary, olive oil, orange peel, salt, pepper, garlic powder, and the onion powder. Cover and shake vigorously; pour over the chicken and potatoes.

Place 1 sprig of rosemary on each chicken breast. Cover and bake about 30 minutes until a fork pierces the chicken easily and potatoes are tender. Spoon hot honey glaze over chicken and potatoes and place under broiler about 2 minutes to brown. Garnish with tomato wedges.

Makes 4 servings.

Per Serving (approx):
Calories 1157
Carbohydrate 218gm

Protein 45 gm
Sodium 705 mg

Fat 12 gm
Cholesterol 80 mg

Chicken Drumsticks Supreme

1 cup yogurt
3 tablespoons seeded, minced
  cucumber
2 tablespoons chopped cilantro
1 tablespoon prepared mustard
1 tablespoon lime juice
1 tablespoon grated ginger
1 1/4 teaspoons pepper, divided
1 1/4 teaspoons ground cumin,
divided

1/2 teaspoon salt
8 skinless chicken drumsticks
1 cup pecan pieces
1 cup corn flakes
3/4 teaspoon cayenne
1/4 cup minced chives
Red leaf lettuce, for garnish
Cherry tomatoes, for garnish

Preheat oven to 375 degrees.

In a bowl, combine yogurt with cucumber, cilantro, mustard, lime juice, ginger, 1/2 teaspoon of the pepper, 1/2 teaspoon of the cumin, and the salt; stir to mix well. Add chicken to the mixture and turn to coat evenly. In a food processor or blender, process pecans and corn flakes to form fine crumbs; add cayenne, remaining 3/4 teaspoon cumin, and remaining 3/4 teaspoon pepper. Stir in chives, mix well and remove crumb mixture to shallow dish. Remove chicken from yogurt mixture and roll in crumbs, turning to coat evenly.

Place the chicken on a rack in a baking pan and bake for about 45 minutes, until chicken is brown and a fork can be inserted easily. Arrange lettuce on platter, add chicken, and garnish with cherry tomatoes.

Makes 4 servings.

Per Serving (approx):
Calories 558
Carbohydrate 17 gm

Protein 54 gm
Sodium 618 mg

Fat 31 gm
Cholesterol 166 mg

Yam Chicken with Wild Pecan Rice

2 tablespoons olive oil
8 skinless chicken thighs
1 yam, peeled and coarsely
  shredded
Ice water
1 tablespoon minced ginger
1/2 cup flaked coconut

1/4 cup minced pecans
2 tablespoons orange marmalade
1/2 cup melted butter
1/2 teaspoon paprika
1 tablespoon minced cilantro
7 ounces Wild Pecan Rice,
  cooked

Preheat oven to 400 degrees.

Line a 9 x 12 baking dish with foil and spread with olive oil. Add chicken, bone side down. In a bowl, cover shredded yam with ice water. Let stand 5 minutes, drain, and pat dry. In the same bowl with the shredded yam, combine yam, ginger, coconut, pecans, and marmalade. Form a coating of the yam mixture around each chicken thigh. Brush the butter over the yam-coated chicken and sprinkle with paprika.

Bake for about 35 minutes or until potato crust is golden and a fork pierces the chicken easily. Sprinkle chopped cilantro on top. Serve the chicken over Wild Pecan Rice.   Makes 4 servings.

Per Serving (approx):
Calories 675
Carbohydrate 24 gm

Protein 29 gm
Sodium 598 mg

Fat 51 gm
Cholesterol 165 mg

Quick-as-a-Wink Chicken

2 1/4 pounds skinless chicken
   breasts
Salt and pepper to taste

1/2 cup prepared Italian salad
   dressing
2 tablespoons minced parsley
Lemon wedges (optional), for
   garnish

Preheat oven to 350 degrees. Season chicken with salt and pepper to taste. Pour salad dressing into an 8 x 12 baking dish. Add chicken, turning it to coat it with dressing. Bake, uncovered, 10 minutes. Turn chicken and bake 15 minutes longer or until cooked through. Sprinkle with parsley and garnish with lemon wedges, if using. This dish is good over rice or parsley.   Makes 4 servings.

Per Serving (approx):
Calories 280
Carbohydrate 34 gm

Protein 3 gm
Sodium 237 mg

Fat 15 gm
Cholesterol 0 mg

Chicken Breasts in Sour Cream

4 boneless chicken breasts, boned
1 can (3 ounces) mushrooms,
   drained and sliced

1 can (10 1/2 ounces) cream of
   mushroom soup
1/2 cup dry sherry
1 cup sour cream
Paprika

Preheat oven to 350 degrees. Arrange chicken in a baking pan so pieces do not overlap. Cover with mushrooms. Combine soup, sherry, and sour cream. Stir until blended. Pour over chicken, completely covering it. Sprinkle with paprika. Bake for 1 1/2 hours.   Makes 4 servings.

Per Serving (approx):
Calories 613
Carbohydrate 11 gm

Protein 60 gm
Sodium 780 mg

Fat 33 gm
Cholesterol 182 mg

Chicken Supreme

1 cup fine dry bread crumbs
1/4 teaspoon ground cardamom
1/4 teaspoon dried chervil
1 teaspoon salt
1/4 teaspoon pepper
1 egg
1/4 cup milk

4 whole skinless, boneless
   chicken breast halves
6 tablespoons butter
2 cups chicken broth
1/4 cup brandy
1/2 cup burgundy
Chopped roasted peanuts

Preheat oven to 350 degrees.

Combine bread crumbs, cardamom, chervil, salt, and pepper. In another bowl, beat egg with milk. Cut chicken breasts in half and dip each piece in egg mixture and then in bread crumbs. In a frying pan, melt butter. Add chicken and brown on both sides. Remove chicken to a baking dish.

To the same frying pan, add chicken broth and deglaze, scraping up bits from the bottom of the pan. Turn off heat and add brandy and burgundy; stir. Pour over chicken in the baking dish and bake for about 30 minutes until chicken is fork tender. Sprinkle with chopped roasted peanuts.
Makes 6 to 8 servings.

Per Serving (approx):
Calories 353
Carbohydrate 11 gm

Protein 34 gm
Sodium 943 mg

Fat 17 gm
Cholesterol 132 mg

If you want really tender, moist chicken breasts, soak them in buttermilk for a couple of hours before cooking.

Lemon Mustard Chicken

5 tablespoons lemon juice
3 tablespoons lime juice
4 tablespoons prepared mustard
6 chicken thighs
3/4 teaspoon salt
1/2 teaspoon white pepper
1/4 teaspoon curry powder

1/4 teaspoon ground oregano
1 tablespoon grated lemon peel
1 cup fine dry bread crumbs
6 tablespoons margarine
Lemon wedges, for garnish
Lime wedges, for garnish
Parsley, for garnish

Preheat oven to 350 degrees.

In small bowl, combine lemon juice, lime juice, and mustard. Brush over chicken and set aside. In a dish, combine salt, pepper, curry powder, oregano, lemon peel, and bread crumbs. Roll the chicken in this mixture, turning to coat it on all sides.

In an iron skillet, melt margarine. Add chicken, skin-side down, and bake, uncovered, for 20 minutes. Turn chicken and bake 30 minutes longer until a fork can be inserted easily. Place chicken on a serving platter and garnish with lemon, lime, and parsley.   Makes 4 servings.

Per Serving (approx):
Calories 452
Carbohydrate 23 gm

Protein 22 gm
Sodium 1070 mg

Fat 30 gm
Cholesterol 69 mg

If possible, chill chicken pieces after flouring or breading. The coating will adhere better during the cooking process.

Dilled Chicken in Foil

8 skinless chicken thighs
1 teaspoon salt
1/2 teaspoon pepper
1/2 cup butter-flavored
  margarine, melted
2 tablespoons lemon juice
1/2 teaspoon dried dill

8 teaspoons sliced green onion,
  divided
1 cup thinly sliced carrots,
  divided
1/2 pound Swiss cheese,
  cut into 8 slices

Preheat oven to 400 degrees.

Sprinkle chicken thighs with salt and pepper. In a small bowl, combine margarine, lemon juice, and dill. Cut eight 12-inch squares of heavy duty aluminum foil. Spray each with vegetable spray. Place 1 teaspoon dill-margarine sauce on the center of each foil square. Place 1 chicken thigh on sauce. On each chicken thigh, sprinkle 1 teaspoon of the green onion and 2 tablespoons carrot slices. Top each with 1 additional teaspoon of the sauce and 1 slice of cheese.

Fold foil into packets, sealing securely. Place foil packets in a baking pan and bake for about 35 minutes or until a fork pierces the chicken easily.
                                                       Makes 4 servings.

Per Serving (approx):
Calories 594
Carbohydrate 6 gm

Protein 40 gm
Sodium 1062 mg

Fat 46 gm
Cholesterol 137 mg

Pizza Chicken

4 chicken quarters
1 teaspoon garlic salt
1/2 teaspoon pepper
1 jar (15 1/2 ounces) pizza sauce
1/4 cup sour cream

1 can (4 ounces) mushroom
  stems and pieces, drained
1/2 teaspoon dried oregano
1/2 cup shredded mozzarella
  cheese

Preheat broiler to 450 degrees.

Line a baking pan with foil and spray it with vegetable spray. (Pan should be large enough for all pieces of chicken to fit in one layer.) Arrange chicken in the pan and sprinkle with garlic salt and pepper.

Broil chicken about 15 minutes about 6 inches from the heat until very brown on skin side (don't turn the chicken).

While chicken is broiling, in a bowl, mix pizza sauce, sour cream, mushrooms, and oregano. When the chicken is brown, remove from the oven and lower temperature to 350 degrees. Pour sauce over the chicken and return to the oven for about 30 minutes until a fork pierces the chicken easily. Remove the pan from the oven and sprinkle cheese over each piece. Return the pan to the oven for about 5 minutes more until cheese is melted.   Makes 4 servings.

Per Serving (approx):
Calories 739
Carbohydrate 13 gm

Protein 68 gm
Sodium 1025 mg

Fat 46 gm
Cholesterol 246 mg

Wine-Baked Chicken

3 pounds chicken parts
1/4 cup salad oil
1 cup chablis
1 1/2 teaspoons salt
1 tablespoon dried thyme
2 tablespoons chopped parsley, divided

1/4 pound mushrooms, sliced
3 tablespoons butter
1 can (10 1/2 ounces) chicken broth
2 tablespoons flour

Marinate chicken in oil and wine for at least 3 hours, turning frequently. Preheat oven to 370 degrees. Remove chicken from the marinade. In a baking pan, sprinkle chicken with salt, thyme, and 1 tablespoon of the parsley. Bake for 1 hour until tender. Meanwhile, in a frying pan sauté mushrooms in butter. Add chicken broth and remaining chopped parsley. When chicken is done, remove it from the pan. Add mushrooms, butter, chicken broth, and parsley sauce to the pan and thicken with flour.

Makes 6 servings.

Per Serving (approx):
Calories 570
Carbohydrate 4 gm

Protein 47 gm
Sodium 1089 mg

Fat 38 gm
Cholesterol 198 mg

Herbed and Spiced Chicken

1/2 cup nonfat yogurt
1/2 teaspoon curry powder
1 cup herb-seasoned stuffing mix

8 chicken parts
1 teaspoon salt
1/2 teaspoon pepper

Preheat oven to 350 degrees. Grease a 9 x 13 baking pan. Combine yogurt and curry powder. Pour dry stuffing mix into a food processor and process into crumbs. Sprinkle chicken with salt and pepper, brush with yogurt and curry mix and roll in stuffing crumbs. Place chicken skin side up in a baking pan. Bake for about 55 minutes until chicken is tender. (It is not necessary to turn the chicken.) Serve hot or cold.

Makes 4 to 6 servings.

Per Serving (approx):
Calories 185
Carbohydrate 5 gm

Protein 18 gm
Sodium 523 mg

Fat 10 gm
Cholesterol 60 mg

*Bake and Roast
Chicken Breasts*

Chicken Breasts with Wine Sauce

You can use a chardonnay, fumé blanc, or sauvignon blanc instead of the chablis, if you like, but use a good wine.

1 teaspoon salt
1/2 teaspoon ground allspice
1/4 teaspoon ground cinnamon
12 skinless, boneless chicken
  breast halves
1/4 cup butter

3 minced green onions
2/3 cup whipping cream
1/2 cup chablis
1/2 cup unstuffed green olives,
  cut in quarters lengthwise
1/4 cup chopped parsley

Preheat oven to 300 degrees.

Combine salt, allspice, and cinnamon and sprinkle mixture on both sides of chicken breasts. Set aside for 1/2 hour.

Melt butter in a skillet. Sauté chicken breasts for 1 minute, then turn, and sauté other side for 1 minute.

Transfer chicken breasts to a baking dish, cover, and bake for approximately 10 minutes. Add green onions to the skillet. Sauté until they are soft, then stir in cream and wine.

Simmer until the liquid is reduced by half and sauce is slightly thickened. Stir in olives. Arrange chicken on serving dish, cover with sauce and sprinkle with chopped parsley.   Makes 6 servings.

Per Serving (approx):
Calories 489
Carbohydrate 2 gm

Protein 60 gm
Sodium 890 mg

Fat 26 gm
Cholesterol 218 mg

Chicken Sauterne

If speed of preparation is your thing, this recipe is for you.

6 skinless, boneless chicken breasts
Salt and pepper to taste
4 tablespoons butter
1 can (8 ounces) water chestnuts,
    drained and sliced

1 can (10 3/4 ounces) cream of
    chicken soup
1 1/2 cups sauterne or
    chablis

Preheat oven to 350 degrees.

Lightly salt and pepper chicken. Melt butter in a skillet. Sauté breasts quickly on both sides until browned; remove to a casserole. Sprinkle with water chestnuts. Combine soup and wine; pour over chicken. Bake, covered, for 30 minutes; uncover; bake 30 minutes longer, basting several times.   Makes 6 servings.

Per Serving (approx):
Calories 325
Carbohydrate 9 gm

Protein 31 gm
Sodium 554 mg

Fat 14 gm
Cholesterol 105 mg

"All cooking is a matter of time. In general, the more time the better."
John Erskine, *The Complete Life*

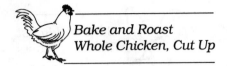

Glazed Chicken

1/2 cup flour
1 teaspoon salt
1/4 teaspoon pepper
8 tablespoons butter, divided
1 whole chicken, cut up
2 tablespoons julienned orange peel

1/4 cup lemon juice
1/4 cup orange-flavored liqueur
1 tablespoon soy sauce
1/4 cup honey
8 baby carrots, cooked

Preheat oven to 350 degrees.

In a paper bag, combine flour, salt, and pepper; add chicken a few pieces at a time and shake to coat all sides. In a baking pan, melt 4 tablespoons of the butter. Roll chicken in butter to coat all sides and arrange skin-side down in a single layer. Bake for 30 minutes.

In a small saucepan, melt remaining 4 tablespoons butter; stir in orange peel, lemon juice, liqueur, soy sauce, and honey. Set aside 2 tablespoons of the mixture.

Remove the chicken from the oven, turn and pour the orange-honey mixture over it. Return to the oven and bake, basting occasionally, 30 minutes longer or until chicken is glazed and a fork can be inserted easily. Add reserved glaze to the carrots and serve on the side.

Makes 4 servings.

Per Serving (approx):
Calories 849
Carbohydrate 41 gm

Protein 55 gm
Sodium 1245 mg

Fat 49 gm
Cholesterol 272 mg

ROLLED & STUFFED BREASTS

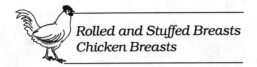

Curried Chicken Rolls

This is so good, it defies description. We strongly recommend that you double the recipe and freeze the extra four rolls for reheating later.

4 skinless, boneless chicken
   breast halves
1/2 teaspoon salt
1/8 teaspoon pepper
1 tablespoon margarine
1/2 onion, minced
3/4 cup cooked rice
1/4 cup raisins
1 tablespoon chopped parsley

1 teaspoon curry powder
1/2 teaspoon poultry seasoning
1 teaspoon brown sugar
1/16 teaspoon garlic powder
1 tablespoon vegetable oil
1/2 cup white wine
1 teaspoon chicken bouillon
   granules

Pound chicken between sheets of wax paper to 3/8-inch thickness. Sprinkle pieces with salt and pepper. In a frying pan, melt margarine. Add onion and sauté about 3 minutes or until soft. Add rice, raisins, parsley, curry powder, poultry seasoning, brown sugar, and garlic powder. Stir until well mixed. Divide stuffing into 4 portions. Place one portion on each piece of chicken. Roll, jellyroll fashion. Fasten with toothpicks.

In another frying pan, heat oil. Add chicken rolls and cook, turning, about 15 minutes until brown on all sides. Add wine and bouillon granules. Cover and simmer about 30 minutes until chicken is tender.

Makes 4 servings.

Per Serving (approx):
Calories 322
Carbohydrate 22 gm

Protein 31 gm
Sodium 461 mg

Fat 10 gm
Cholesterol 80 mg

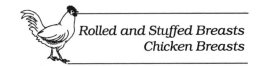

Basil-Stuffed Chicken Breasts

2 1/4 pounds split chicken breasts
Salt and pepper to taste
1/2 cup minced basil
2 tablespoons olive oil

2 tablespoons dried bread
  crumbs
2 garlic cloves, minced
Basil leaves, for garnish

Preheat oven to 375 degrees. Season chicken with salt and pepper to taste. In a bowl, combine basil, oil, crumbs, and garlic. Gently separate skin from chicken breast along one side to form a pocket. Gently place stuffing under the skin of the breast pieces. Rub the stuffing over the outside of each breast piece. Place the chicken in a 9-inch square baking dish. Bake 35 to 40 minutes until cooked through and golden. To serve, garnish with basil leaves. **Makes 4 servings.**

Per Serving (approx):
Calories 474
Carbohydrate 3 gm

Protein 62 gm
Sodium 169 mg

Fat 24 gm
Cholesterol 172 mg

Pesto Rice Stuffed Chicken

1/2 teaspoon salt
1/4 teaspoon pepper
6 chicken breast halves
1 cup fresh basil leaves
2 garlic cloves, chopped
1/2 cup walnut pieces

1 cup cooked rice
3/4 cup grated Parmesan cheese
2 tablespoons sour cream
2 tablespoons olive oil
1 tablespoon hot sauce
1 tablespoon butter, melted

Preheat oven to 350 degrees. Sprinkle the chicken with salt and pepper. Loosen skin on each chicken breast to form a pocket. In a food processor, combine basil, garlic, and walnuts; process.

In a bowl, combine Parmesan cheese, rice, sour cream, olive oil, hot sauce, and the basil pesto. Place 1/3 cup of this mixture under the skin of each breast half.* Place chicken on foil-lined 9 x 13 glass baking dish. Brush with melted butter and bake about 1 hour until chicken is done. **Makes 6 servings.**

*If skin becomes detached, press it over filling and fasten with toothpicks.

Per Serving (approx):
Calories 427
Carbohydrate 13 gm

Protein 36 gm
Sodium 518 mg

Fat 26 gm
Cholesterol 96 mg

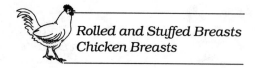

Summer Italian Stuffed Chicken

This unique recipe uses an unusual cooking technique to achieve a beautiful presentation.

4 skinless, boneless chicken
  breast halves
3/4 cup prepared oil and vinegar
  dressing, divided
1 small head radicchio, torn
  into bite-size pieces
1 small bunch watercress, cut
  into bite-size pieces

1/4 cup basil leaves
2 plum tomatoes, thinly sliced
1 tablespoon water
1 egg
2/3 cup Italian seasoned
  bread crumbs
1/2 cup grated Parmesan cheese
4 tablespoons olive oil
Tomato rosettes, for garnish

Between two sheets of wax paper, gently pound chicken to 1/4-inch thickness; place in a large baking pan. Add 1/2 cup of dressing and turn to coat. Cover and refrigerate 30 minutes.

In a bowl, combine radicchio and watercress; add remaining 1/4 cup dressing and toss to mix. Arrange the mixture on a platter; refrigerate.

Remove chicken from dressing; drain. Discard the marinade. Cut each chicken piece in half crosswise. Place equal portion of basil and tomatoes on each half piece; top with remaining half piece. With textured side of meat mallet, pound edges of the chicken together to seal. In a dish, beat water and egg. On wax paper, mix the bread crumbs and cheese.

Dip chicken, one piece at a time, in egg mixture and then in bread crumbs and cheese. In a frying pan, heat oil. Add chicken and cook about 10 minutes until brown.

Arrange chicken on radicchio. Garnish with tomato rosettes.

Makes 4 servings.

Per Serving (approx):
Calories 733
Carbohydrate 22 gm

Protein 40 gm
Sodium 934 mg

Fat 54 gm
Cholesterol 144 mg

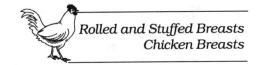

Tricolor Chicken Roulade

Roulade is the French term for a thin slice of meat, rolled around a filling and secured with string or toothpicks. In Italy, it is a Braciola.

4 tablespoons butter or margarine,
   divided
1 cup chopped onions
1/2 pound mushrooms, chopped
1/3 cup Marsala, divided
2 tablespoons lemon juice
2 pounds Swiss chard,
   steamed and chopped
Salt and pepper to taste

2 eggs, lightly beaten
1/2 cup grated Parmesan cheese
3 pounds skinless, boneless
   chicken breasts
1/4 pound thinly sliced ham
1/4 cup vegetable oil
1 cup chicken broth
1 cup whipping cream

In a skillet, melt 2 tablespoons of the butter. Add onion, mushrooms, 1 tablespoon of the Marsala, and lemon juice. Sauté 5 minutes until liquid evaporates. Remove from the heat and add chard, salt, and pepper; toss with remaining 2 tablespoons butter. Stir in eggs and cheese.

Place the breast pieces overlapping each other so that you have 2 rectangles. Pound these to 1/4-inch thickness. Place the ham slices on the chicken and spread with the chard mixture. Starting from the narrow end, roll up chicken jellyroll-style, folding in edges. Secure with kitchen string. (These may be made up to 1 day in advance.)

Preheat oven to 350 degrees. In a Dutch oven heat oil. Add roulades and fry about 10 minutes until brown. Add chicken broth and remaining Marsala; cover and bake 30 to 40 minutes until firm. Remove roulades and keep warm. Bring pan juices to boil. Stir in cream and cook until sauce thickens. Serve on the side with sliced roulades.

Makes 12 servings.

Per Serving (approx):
Calories 370
Carbohydrate 6 gm

Protein 35 gm
Sodium 586 mg

Fat 22 gm
Cholesterol 157 mg

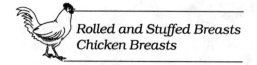
Crab-Stuffed Chicken

Don't let the long list of ingredients and lengthy instructions keep you from making this recipe. It is well worth the effort.

4 skinless, boneless chicken
   breast halves
1/3 cup extra dry vermouth
4 tablespoons butter or margarine
1/4 cup flour
3/4 cup milk
3/4 cup chicken broth
1/4 cup chopped onion
1 can (7 1/2 ounces) crabmeat,
   drained, flaked, and cartilage
   removed

1 can (3 ounces) chopped
   mushrooms, drained
10 saltine crackers, coarsely
   crumbled
2 tablespoons minced parsley
1/2 teaspoon salt
Dash pepper
1 cup (4 ounces) shredded
   Swiss cheese
1/2 teaspoon paprika

Preheat oven to 350 degrees.

Place chicken pieces, one at a time, between 2 pieces of waxed paper. Working from the center out, pound chicken lightly with meat mallet to make cutlets about 1/8 inch thick (8 inches by 5 inches). Brush with vermouth. Set aside.

In a saucepan, melt 3 tablespoons of the butter; blend in flour. Add milk, chicken broth, and vermouth all at once; cook and stir until mixture thickens and bubbles. Set aside. In a skillet, fry onion in the remaining butter until tender but not brown. Stir in crabmeat, mushrooms, cracker crumbs, parsley, salt, and pepper. Stir in 2 tablespoons of the white sauce.

Top each chicken piece with about 1/2 cup of the crab mixture. Fold sides in; roll up. Place seam side down in 7 1/2 x 12 x 2 baking dish. Pour remaining sauce over all. Bake, covered, for 1 hour, or until chicken is tender. Uncover; sprinkle with cheese and paprika. Bake 2 minutes longer until cheese melts. Makes 4 servings.

Per Serving (approx):
Calories 553
Carbohydrate 20 gm

Protein 52 gm
Sodium 1561 mg

Fat 27 gm
Cholesterol 173 mg

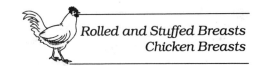

Spinach Cherry Chicken Roll-Ups

1/4 cup dried cherries
1/4 cup dry sherry
4 boneless chicken breast halves
3 tablespoons olive oil
1/4 cup chopped onion
1/2 tablespoon minced garlic
1/2 cup chopped mushrooms
1 package (5 ounces) frozen chopped
   spinach, thawed, drained,
   and squeezed dry

1/4 cup walnuts, toasted and
   cut into small pieces
1 tablespoon minced parsley
1/4 teaspoon dried rosemary
1 lemon, peel only, chopped
1/4 teaspoon salt
1/4 teaspoon pepper
1 tablespoon margarine
Sherry Sauce

Preheat oven to 350 degrees.

In a small bowl, combine sherry and dried cherries; set aside to soften. Place chicken between 2 pieces of wax paper and gently pound to flatten. In a frying pan, heat 2 tablespoons of the oil. Add onion and garlic and sauté about 2 minutes. Add mushrooms and cook about 2 minutes more. Add spinach, walnuts, and cherry mixture and cook until sherry has evaporated, about 3 minutes.

In a small bowl, combine parsley, rosemary, and lemon peel. Rub herb mixture on each chicken breast and sprinkle with salt and pepper. Place breasts skin side down; spoon a portion of spinach-cherry mixture in the center of each breast; roll up, starting on long side, and fasten with a toothpick.

Prepare Sherry Sauce. In another frying pan, heat margarine and remaining oil. Add chicken and cook about 5 minutes or until brown on all sides. Remove to a greased casserole dish. Pour Sherry Sauce over the chicken and bake for about 30 minutes or until a fork pierces chicken easily. Place chicken on a serving dish and spoon Sherry Sauce on top.

Makes 4 servings.

SHERRY SAUCE:
In the same frying pan used to brown chicken, over medium heat, mix 3/4 cup sherry and pan drippings. Boil, reducing the sauce to 1/2 cup. In a small bowl, combine 1/2 teaspoon chicken bouillon granules, 1 teaspoon cornstarch and 1/2 cup hot water and mix until smooth. Add mixture to frying pan and cook, stirring, until thickened.

Per Serving (approx):
Calories 442
Carbohydrate 11 gm

Protein 31 gm
Sodium 308 mg

Fat 27 gm
Cholesterol 79 mg

Chicken Rollovers

8 skinless, boneless chicken
   breast halves
1/8 cup olive oil
Salt and pepper to taste
2 garlic cloves, crushed
3/4 pound spinach, chopped
1/4 teaspoon pepper
1/2 pound feta cheese, crumbled
3 eggs, beaten

1/2 cup milk
1 1/2 cups Italian bread crumbs
3 tablespoons vegetable oil
2 tablespoons butter
3/4 cup sliced mushrooms
1 tablespoon flour
1 cup chicken broth
3/4 cup dry white wine
1/2 lemon, juiced
1 tablespoon capers

Preheat oven to 350 degrees.

Place chicken between two pieces of wax paper and gently pound until almost double in size. Sprinkle salt and pepper to taste. In a frying pan, heat olive oil. Add garlic and cook, stirring, 30 seconds. Add spinach and sauté until barely wilted. Remove mixture from pan, drain, season with salt and pepper to taste, cool, and divide into 8 portions.

On each chicken breast, place a portion of the spinach mixture; sprinkle a portion of cheese evenly over the spinach. Roll up and fasten with toothpicks. In a bowl, mix eggs and milk. Place bread crumbs in separate bowl. Put chicken rolls in the egg mixture and then in bread crumbs, dredging to coat. In a frying pan, heat oil. Add chicken and cook until brown. Remove chicken to a pan with a cover and bake for about 30 minutes until a fork can be inserted easily. To make the sauce, drain and discard most of the oil from the frying pan, leaving brown bits on the bottom of pan; add butter and melt. Add mushrooms and sauté about 2 minutes. Add flour, stirring to blend and thicken. Add chicken broth, wine, lemon juice, and capers. Cook about 4 minutes or until thickened. Place chicken rolls on a serving dish and pour the sauce over the rolls.

Makes 8 servings.

Per Serving (approx):
Calories 478
Carbohydrate 20 gm

Protein 40 gm
Sodium 818 mg

Fat 25 gm
Cholesterol 196 mg

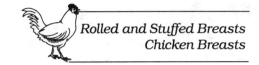
Cheesy Chicken
with Hot Apple Sauce

4 skinless, boneless chicken
   breast halves
3/4 cup shredded cheddar cheese
1/2 teaspoon salt
2 tablespoon minced walnuts
1 tablespoon crushed green
   peppercorns
1 tablespoon vegetable oil
2/3 cup diced tart apples
1/3 cup diced red bell pepper
1 garlic clove, minced

3/4 teaspoon minced ginger
1/4 cup dry sherry
2 tablespoons frozen apple
   juice concentrate, thawed
1/8 teaspoon ground cumin
1/8 teaspoon ground cinnamon
2 tablespoons minced green
   onions
Parsley, for garnish
8 apple wedges, unpeeled, for
   garnish

Make a lengthwise slit in each chicken breast half to form a pocket. Fill each pocket with shredded cheese; close with toothpicks. Gently flatten chicken and sprinkle with salt. In a small bowl, mix walnuts and peppercorns; press mixture into both sides of chicken. In a frying pan, heat oil. Add chicken and cook about 5 minutes on each side until tender. Remove chicken from frying pan, discard toothpicks, and keep it warm.

In the same frying pan, stir-fry the apple, bell pepper, garlic, and ginger for 1 minute. Add sherry, apple juice concentrate, cumin, cinnamon, and onion. Cook, stirring, to reduce liquid by one-half.

Place the chicken on a serving platter and spoon the apple mixture over it. Garnish with parsley and apple wedges.   Makes 4 servings.

Per Serving (approx):
Calories 589
Carbohydrate 67 gm

Protein 36 gm
Sodium 495 mg

Fat 18 gm
Cholesterol 102 mg

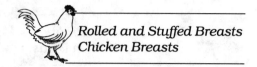

Chicken Breasts with Apricots

2 cups spinach leaves
Salt and white pepper to taste
1/4 teaspoon ground nutmeg
Water
1/2 cup brut champagne
1/2 cup dried apricots
2 teaspoons sugar

1 tablespoon apricot jam
1/2 teaspoon soy sauce
1 tablespoon cornstarch mixed
    with 1 teaspoon cold water
2 skinless, boneless chicken
    breasts, lightly pounded
1 tablespoon butter

Steam spinach with salt and pepper to taste and nutmeg in a little water. Drain well. In a saucepan, bring champagne, apricots, and sugar to a boil. Reduce heat and cook for 5 minutes. Remove apricots from liquid and set aside; add apricot jam and soy sauce. Thicken by adding cornstarch mixture. Bring to a boil and turn heat off.

Lay chicken breasts skin side down and place a thin layer, approximately 1 to 2 leaves thick, of spinach on the chicken breasts. Place cooked apricots on the center of breasts. Roll breasts up and secure middle and ends with toothpicks. Sprinkle lightly with salt and white pepper to taste. In a skillet, heat butter. Add chicken breasts and sauté until golden on all sides (approximately 5 minutes). Turn heat to low, cover and simmer for 8 more minutes.

Pour in the apricot glaze, mixing well. Remove toothpicks and slice chicken breasts 1/2 to 3/4 inch thick. Serve warm or cold.   Makes 2 servings.

Per Serving (approx):
Calories 519
Carbohydrate 3 gm

Protein 62 gm
Sodium 343 mg

Fat 13 gm
Cholesterol 176 mg

> The average American family has chicken for dinner at least once a week.

CORNISH
GAME HENS

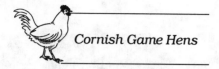

Roasted Cornish Hens

6 Cornish hens
Salt and pepper to taste
Chicken-Flavored Rice Stuffing

6 tablespoons butter, softened
1/2 cup orange marmalade
1/4 cup Gewürztraminer

Preheat oven to 350 degrees. Prepare stuffing.

Rinse game hens and pat dry. Salt and pepper cavity, and stuff with a generous 1/2 cup of stuffing. Secure legs with kitchen string and place hens in a roasting pan. Brush hens with softened butter and roast for 30 minutes.

Melt orange marmalade with the wine and reduce slightly. Raise oven temperature to 400 degrees. Baste hens with marmalade mixture and continue roasting an additional 20 or 30 minutes until juices run clear and hens are browned. Baste occasionally with the marmalade mixture, and if the hens start to darken too much, cover with aluminum foil.

Makes 6 servings.

CHICKEN-FLAVORED RICE STUFFING:
Bring 2 cups chicken broth, 1/2 teaspoon salt, 1 tablespoon butter, 1/4 teaspoon ground cinnamon, 1/4 teaspoon ground cardamom, and 1 teaspoon grated orange rind to a boil. Add 1 cup uncooked long-grain white rice, cover, and simmer 20 minutes. Let sit 5 minutes. Fluff with a fork and stir in 1/2 cup chopped pitted dates and 1/2 cup chopped pecans.

Per Serving (approx):
Calories 1559
Carbohydrate 49 gm

Protein 98 gm
Sodium 1192 mg

Fat 107 gm
Cholesterol 619mg

French Pan-Roasted Hens

3 pounds split Cornish hens
3 tablespoons olive oil, divided
1 tablespoon herbs du
  Provence*

Salt and pepper to taste
3 garlic cloves, divided
1/2 cup white wine or water

Rub hens with 1 tablespoon of the oil and sprinkle with herbs du Provence seasoning and salt and pepper to taste. In a deep skillet, heat remaining 2 tablespoons oil. Add hens and 2 of the garlic cloves. Brown hens lightly on both sides. Discard the fried garlic and add remaining garlic clove. Reduce heat to low. Cover and simmer 30 to 40 minutes until hens are browned and cooked through, turning 2 to 3 times.

Remove hens to a warm serving platter; discard garlic. Add wine to the skillet and cook 1 minute, stirring to incorporate pan juices and bits at the bottom of the pan. Serve hens with pan sauce.

Makes 2 to 4 servings.

*Available in supermarkets, or make your own with equal amounts of ground basil, fennel seed, lavender, marjoram, rosemary, sage, and thyme.

Per Serving (approx):
Calories 779
Carbohydrate 2 gm

Protein 57 gm
Sodium 177 mg

Fat 58 gm
Cholesterol 335 mg

"What is literature compared with cooking? The one is shadow, the other is substance."

E.V. Lucas,
"365 Days and One More"

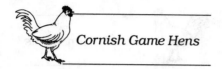

Brandy Orange Barbecued Cornish Hens

The recipe calls for a tablespoon of brandy. Two or three are even better.

2 Cornish hens
1 tablespoon vegetable oil
2 tablespoons lemon juice, divided
1/2 teaspoon ground ginger, divided

Salt and pepper to taste
1/4 cup orange marmalade
1 tablespoon brandy

Prepare a covered grill. Tie drumsticks together with kitchen string. Rub hens with oil and 1 tablespoon of the lemon juice; sprinkle with 1/4 teaspoon ginger and salt and pepper to taste.

In a small bowl, combine marmalade, brandy, remaining lemon juice, and ginger; set aside. Place hens on the grill, breast side up. Grill, covered, 5 to 6 inches from coals 45 to 50 minutes. After 30 minutes, brush hens with brandy-orange sauce. Cook until juices run clear when thigh is pierced, basting 3 to 4 times. Makes 2 to 4 servings.

Per Serving (approx):
Calories 738
Carbohydrate 15 gm

Protein 57 gm
Sodium 239 mg

Fat 50 gm
Cholesterol 335 mg

A hen will turn her eggs as many as five times an hour, rarely less than four.

Tandoori Hens

The marinade provides the flavor of tandoori oven cooking as you grill these hens.

2 Cornish hens
6 tablespoons vegetable oil
4 tablespoons yogurt
3 garlic cloves, crushed
1/2 teaspoon salt
1 teaspoon pepper
1 teaspoon ground cumin

1 teaspoon chili powder
1 teaspoon turmeric
1 teaspoon paprika
1/2 teaspoon cayenne
1/2 teaspoon ground cloves
1/2 teaspoon ground cinnamon

Place hens, breast side down, on a cutting board. Using poultry shears, remove backbone and spread the birds open. Turn them over, press flat, and cut in half along breast bone. Place hens in a baking dish. In a small bowl, combine oil, yogurt, and seasonings. Pour half of the yogurt mixture over hens, turning to coat well. Cover and refrigerate 1 hour or longer. Set aside remaining yogurt mixture.

Prepare covered grill for cooking. Remove hens from marinade; discard marinade. Grill, covered, 5 to 6 inches from coals 15 to 25 minutes or until juices run clear when thigh is pierced, turning and brushing with reserved yogurt mixture 4 to 5 times during grilling.

Makes 2 to 4 servings.

Per Serving (approx):
Calories 857
Carbohydrate 4 gm

Protein 58 gm
Sodium 463 mg

Fat 68 gm
Cholesterol 337 mg

Cheese-and-Chive-Stuffed Hens

2 Cornish hens
Salt and pepper to taste

1/2 cup whipped
    cream cheese with chives

Preheat oven to 375 degrees. Season hens inside and out with salt and pepper to taste. To stuff under the skin, place hen on its back. Using your forefinger, carefully break the skin membrane at the vent opening on each side of breast. Work finger over both sides of the breast under skin. Spoon half the cream cheese under skin of each hen, smoothing it evenly over the breast. Tie legs together and fold back wings. Place hens in a roasting pan. Roast 1 hour until hens are tender and juices run clear when the thighs are pierced with a fork. Serve hot or cold.

Makes 2 to 4 servings.

Per Serving (approx):
Calories 647
Carbohydrate 0 gm

Protein 57 gm
Sodium 164 mg

Fat 47 gm
Cholesterol 335 mg

Baked Cornish Game Hens

4 Cornish hens
1 teaspoon ground cumin
Salt and pepper to taste
2 to 3 tablespoons olive oil

4 garlic cloves
6 sprigs rosemary
1 cup zinfandel

Preheat oven to 350 degrees. Sprinkle hens with cumin and salt and pepper to taste. In an 8-quart Dutch oven, heat oil. Add hens and garlic, and brown over moderate heat for approximately 10 minutes. When birds are nicely brown, add rosemary. Cover the pot and place in oven for 45 minutes to 1 hour until birds are done. Remove hens and keep warm; discard rosemary. Skim fat from pan juices. Mash garlic cloves into juices and deglaze with wine. Increase heat and reduce liquid to about 2/3 of original volume. To serve, spoon sauce over hens. Serve with polenta or buttered noodles.

Makes 4 servings.

Per Serving (approx):
Calories 1195
Carbohydrate 2 gm

Protein 95 gm
Sodium 276 mg

Fat 85 gm
Cholesterol 557 mg

Rock Cornish Game Hens Rosé

1/4 cup currants or raisins
1 1/3 cups rice
1 1/2 cups water, divided
1 3/4 cups rosé, divided
1/2 teaspoon salt
Few grains pepper
1/8 teaspoon ground nutmeg
1/8 teaspoon ground allspice
1 teaspoon sugar
2/3 cup butter or margarine, divided

1/4 cup slivered blanched almonds
4 Cornish hens
2 tablespoons lemon juice, divided
1/2 cup currant jelly
3 whole cloves
Dash cayenne
Cornstarch (optional)

Preheat oven to 450 degrees.

In a small saucepan, cover currants with water; bring to a boil, turn off the heat, and let stand 5 minutes, then drain. Discard water. In another saucepan, combine rice and 1 cup water and mix to moisten. Bring quickly to a boil, fluffing the rice with a fork once or twice. Add 3/4 cup wine, salt, pepper, nutmeg, allspice, sugar, and currants. Cover and remove from heat. Let stand 10 minutes. Meanwhile, melt 1/4 cup butter, add almonds, and stir over low heat until lightly browned; add to rice mixture.

Stuff hens loosely. Skewer legs to body.

In a small bowl, mix 1/2 cup wine, 1/3 cup butter, and 1 tablespoon of the lemon juice for basting sauce. Place hens in roasting pan and brush with basting sauce. Roast at 450 degrees for 15 minutes. Lower heat to 350 degrees and roast 30 minutes longer, basting once or twice more. If necessary, place under broiler for a few minutes to finish browning.

To make gravy, combine 1 tablespoon butter, currant jelly, 1 tablespoon of the lemon juice, cloves, cayenne, and 1/2 cup water. Simmer 5 minutes; strain. Add the remaining 1/2 cup wine and pan juices from hens. Thicken slightly with cornstarch in a bit of water, if desired.

Makes 4 servings.

Per Serving (approx):
Calories 1754
Carbohydrate 56 gm

Protein 99 gm
Sodium 931 mg

Fat 117 gm
Cholesterol 650 mg

Cornish Hens à l'Orange

You're probably familiar with Duck à l'Orange. This is the same approach applied to Cornish hens, using a microwave oven..

2 Cornish hens
1 tablespoon light margarine
  (stick form)
1/2 cup sugarless orange
  marmalade

1/4 cup orange juice
1 tablespoon reduced-sodium
  soy sauce
1 tablespoon cornstarch

Split hens in half, removing backbone if desired. On microwave-safe roasting rack, place hens in a circular pattern, skin side down with meatier portions to outside.

In a 2-cup glass measure, microwave margarine on high (100% power) 25 to 30 seconds until melted; stir in marmalade, orange juice, and soy sauce. Spoon half the sauce mixture over hens and reserve remainder. Cover hens with wax paper; microwave on medium-high (70% power) 20 to 30 minutes until thickest part of flesh can be easily pierced with a fork. Halfway through cooking, turn hens bone side down, and baste with pan juices; re-cover and complete cooking. Cover with foil and let stand 10 minutes.

Remove grease from pan juices. Stir cornstarch into reserved orange mixture and add pan juices. Microwave on high 1 to 1 1/2 minutes until thickened, stirring twice.

Remove skin from hens and serve, passing warm sauce separately.

Makes 4 servings.

Per Serving (approx):
Calories 669
Carbohydrate 32 gm

Protein 48 gm
Sodium 354 mg

Fat 39 gm
Cholesterol 279 mg

Holiday Hens with Deviled Crab Dressing

4 teaspoons butter or margarine
2 teaspoons lemon juice
1 teaspoon Worcestershire
  sauce
6 Cornish hens
Salt and pepper to taste

6 sprigs rosemary (optional),
  for garnish
3 tablespoons flour
1 can (14 ounces) chicken broth
1/2 cup dry sherry
Deviled Crab Dressing

Preheat oven to 350 degrees. In a skillet, melt butter. Stir in lemon juice and Worcestershire sauce. Brush hens with butter mixture, sprinkle with salt and pepper to taste, and tie legs together with kitchen string.

Place hens in a roasting pan. Roast 1 to 1 1/4 hours until skin is crisp and golden brown and juices run clear, with no hint of pink when thigh is pierced. Remove hens to a warm serving platter and discard string. Garnish with rosemary, if desired. When hens have been placed in the oven, prepare the Deviled Crab Dressing which will be baked in the oven during the last 30 minutes of the cooking time for the hens.

To prepare sauce, stir flour into pan drippings. Stir constantly over medium-low heat for 4 to 5 minutes until flour is brown. Gradually whisk in chicken broth and sherry; cook 3 to 4 minutes longer, stirring often, until gravy is smooth and thickened. Strain gravy into sauce dish and serve with hens.   Makes 8 to 12 servings.

DEVILED CRAB DRESSING:
In a deep skillet, melt 6 tablespoons butter. Add 1 cup thinly sliced green onions and 2/3 cup thinly sliced celery; sauté 1 minute. Stir in 1/2 pound fresh crab meat; sauté briefly. Stir in 3 tablespoons minced parsley, 2 tablespoons lemon juice, 2 tablespoons Worcestershire sauce, 1/2 teaspoon ground mustard, 1/4 teaspoon hot pepper sauce, and 1/2 pound herb-seasoned bread stuffing. Stir in enough half-and-half (about 3/4 to 1 cup) to moisten mixture; toss lightly. Place dressing in lightly buttered baking dish; dot with butter. Loosely cover with foil; bake in oven with hens for 30 minutes.

Per Serving (approx):
Calories 688	*Protein 55 gm*	*Fat 44 gm*
Carbohydrate 18 gm	*Sodium 836 mg*	*Cholesterol 302 mg*

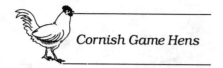

Glazed Cornish Game Hens

Serve this with spiced crabapples for a very festive presentation.

3 Cornish hens, split in half
Salt and pepper to taste
1/4 cup butter, melted
3/4 cup rosé

Rosé Sauce
Watercress or parsley,
    for garnish
1 jar spiced crabapples,
    for garnish

Preheat oven to 450 degrees.

Season hens with salt and pepper to taste. In roasting pan arrange hens cut side down on rack. Baste generously with melted butter. Roast uncovered, basting occasionally with wine, until almost done (about 30 to 40 minutes).

Baste hens with Rosé Sauce. Continue to roast and baste with sauce until fork tender, well-glazed, and nicely brown. Remove to serving platter or individual plates. Garnish with watercress or fresh parsley sprigs and whole crabapples.   Makes 6 servings.

ROSÉ SAUCE:
In a small saucepan, combine 1 tablespoon sugar and 2 teaspoons cornstarch. Stir in 1/2 cup spiced crabapple juice* and 1 cup rosé. Cook, stirring constantly, until sauce thickens and becomes clear.

*From jar of spiced whole crabapples.

Per Serving (approx):
Calories 677
Carbohydrate 299gm

Protein 48 gm
Sodium 267 mg

Fat 46 gm
Cholesterol 299 mg

Can't find any string to tie the feet together? You have some in the medicine cabinet: dental floss!

Cornish Game Hens

Game Hens with Croissant Stuffing

1 large egg, beaten
12 stale croissants, pulled apart
1 cup yellow raisins
3/4 cup sliced almonds
1 onion, diced
5 ribs celery, diced
2 apples, cored and diced
1 tablespoon poultry seasoning
1/2 tablespoon ground cinnamon

1 to 2 cups chicken broth
Salt and pepper to taste
1 cube unsalted butter, melted
6 Cornish hens
2 cups chardonnay
Peppermint leaves, for garnish
1 orange, segmented, for garnish

Preheat oven to 350 degrees.

Combine egg, croissants, raisins, almonds, onions, celery, apple, poultry seasoning, and cinnamon in a bowl. Add broth a little at a time until the mixture takes on a sticky dressing-like consistency. Salt and pepper to taste.

Rub hens with butter and stuff with croissant mixture. Set hens in a baking pan and pour wine over. Add water to the bottom of the pan, as needed.

Bake uncovered for 1 hour, basting every 15 minutes. Garnish with peppermint leaves and orange slices.   Makes 6 servings.

Per Serving (approx):
Calories 1743   *Protein 112 gm*   *Fat 94 gm*
Carbohydrate 99 gm   *Sodium 1492 mg*   *Cholesterol 602 mg*

Cornish Game Hens

Cornish Hens Supreme

Salt and pepper to taste
4 Cornish hens
4 teaspoons minced onion
3 tablespoons butter, melted
1 cup chicken broth

1 jar (2 1/2 ounces) button
  mushrooms
Cornstarch
2 to 3 tablespoons dry sherry
Kumquats, for garnish
Parsley, for garnish

Preheat oven to 350 degrees.

Salt and pepper the hens inside and out to taste. In a shallow baking dish, arrange hens breast side up and sprinkle with onion. Bake for 45 minutes. Baste hens 4 times during baking with mixture of 2 tablespoons of the butter and broth. Brown mushrooms lightly in 1 tablespoon butter.

Remove hens from baking dish. Pour off drippings; measure. Return hens to baking dish. Add 1 teaspoon cornstarch to mushrooms for each cup drippings; mix thoroughly. Add drippings; cook and stir until clear. Stir in sherry; pour over hens. Bake for 10 minutes longer; garnish with kumquats and parsley.   Makes 4 servings.

Per Serving (approx):
Calories 1188   *Protein 95 gm*   *Fat 86 gm*
Carbohydrate 5 gm   *Sodium 727 mg*   *Cholesterol 580 mg*

Cornish Game Hens

Pineapple-Glazed Cornish Hens

4 Cornish hens
1/4 cup dry white wine
Salt and pepper to taste
Wild Rice Stuffing
1/4 cup melted butter, divided
2 cans (8 1/2 ounces each) pineapple
    slices, drained; 1/2 cup syrup
    reserved (divided)

1/2 cup chicken broth
2 tablespoons sugar
1/4 teaspoon ground ginger
1 teaspoon cornstarch

Preheat oven to 350 degrees.

Season inside of hens with wine and salt and pepper to taste; fill loosely
with Wild Rice Stuffing. Skewer openings together. Brush hens with butter; place breast side up in baking pan. Mix 1/4 cup pineapple syrup
with broth; pour over hens. Bake for about 1 hour, basting every 14
minutes with remaining butter and pan drippings.

Increase oven heat to 400 degrees. Top each hen with 1 pineapple slice.
Mix sugar, ginger, and cornstarch; add remaining pineapple syrup; spoon
over hens. Place remaining pineapple slices in pan. Bake, basting occasionally, for 15 minutes or until glazed.   Makes 4 servings.

WILD RICE STUFFING:
Soak 1 cup wild rice in enough water to cover for 1 hour; drain. Spread
on paper towels to dry. Sauté in 1/4 cup butter until golden; add 1 1/2
cups chicken broth and 1 teaspoon salt. Simmer, tightly covered, for
about 25 minutes until tender. Add 6 green onions, chopped, 1 cup
chopped celery, 1/2 cup chopped toasted almonds, 1 can (8 ounces)
sliced mushrooms, 1/2 teaspoon dried marjoram, and 1/8 teaspoon
ground nutmeg. After hens are stuffed, spoon extra stuffing into covered
casserole and bake with hens.

Per Serving (approx):
Calories 1600   *Protein 107 gm*   *Fat 100 gm*
Carbohydrate 65 gm   *Sodium 1372 mg*   *Cholesterol 588 mg*

325

Rock Cornish Hens in Sour Cream

2 Cornish hens
1/2 cup flour
3 tablespoons butter
3/4 cup sliced onions
1 teaspoon salt
1 teaspoon paprika

3/4 teaspoon dried basil
1/2 teaspoon pepper
1 can (3 ounces) sliced
   mushrooms
1 1/2 cups sour cream
Parsley, for garnish (optional)

Coat hens with flour. Sauté in butter for 10 to 15 minutes or until golden brown. Add onions; cook, stirring, for 5 minutes. Combine salt, paprika, basil, pepper, and mushrooms; pour over hens. Bring to a boil; reduce heat. Simmer, covered, for 30 to 45 minutes. Remove hens to platter; keep warm. Add sour cream to onion mixture gradually, stirring constantly. Heat; pour over hens. Garnish with parsley, if desired.

Makes 2 servings.

Per Serving (approx):
Calories 1780
Carbohydrate 40 gm

Protein 105 gm
Sodium 1689 mg

Fat 133 gm
Cholesterol 673 mg

Zinfandel Rock Cornish Hens

1 stalk celery, chopped
1/4 green bell pepper, chopped
1/4 onion, chopped
6 tablespoons butter
1 cup cooked rice

Salt and pepper to taste
1/2 teaspoon poultry seasoning
2 Cornish hens
1/4 cup zinfandel

Preheat oven to 350 degrees. Sauté celery, bell pepper, and onion in 2 tablespoons of the butter; stir in rice and seasonings. Stuff hens with the rice mixture; place in a baking pan. Combine wine and remaining butter; baste hens. Bake for 30 minutes; baste with zinfandel mixture. Bake 30 minutes longer.

Makes 2 servings.

Per Serving (approx):
Calories 1639
Carbohydrate 50 gm

Protein 101 gm
Sodium 1312 mg

Fat 113 gm
Cholesterol 650 mg

BARBEQUE, GRILL, & BROIL

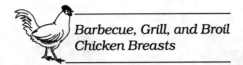

Grilled Caribbean Chicken Breasts

This recipe is pure Jamaican, particularly if you marinate the chicken breasts
overnight.

1/4 cup orange juice
1 teaspoon grated orange peel
1 tablespoon olive oil
1 tablespoon lime juice
1 teaspoon grated ginger
1 clove garlic, minced

1/4 teaspoon hot pepper sauce
1/2 teaspoon dried oregano
4 skinless, boneless chicken
   breast halves
Salt and pepper to taste

In a large bowl, combine orange juice, peel, oil, lime juice, ginger, garlic, hot pepper sauce, and oregano. Add chicken, turning to coat. Cover and marinate in refrigerator 3 hours or overnight.

Sprinkle chicken with salt and pepper to taste. Place on a prepared grill, about 6 inches from heat. Grill, turning, about 10 minutes until a fork pierces the chicken easily.   Makes 4 servings.

Per Serving (approx):
Calories 193
Carbohydrate 2 gm

Protein 29 gm
Sodium 361 mg

Fat 7 gm
Cholesterol 80 mg

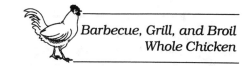
Rotisserie Chicken with Fresh Tarragon

It seems that everyone is cooking chicken on rotisseries these days, from convenience stores to the most elegant charcuteries. Here's a recipe for you on your barbecue or electric or gas range.

1 large chicken, about 4 pounds
4 sprigs tarragon, divided
Salt and pepper to taste

3 tablespoons olive oil
2 tablespoons unsalted butter
1 clove garlic, crushed

Loosen skin of chicken by running fingers between skin and breast meat. Insert 1 sprig of tarragon between the skin and meat on each breast half. Sprinkle chicken with salt and pepper to taste. Truss chicken and tie legs together. In a small frying pan, heat olive oil and butter; mince the remaining tarragon leaves and add to pan. Cook over low heat until mixture sizzles; remove from heat.

Thread chicken on a rotisserie spit and brush on oil-herb mixture. Cook about 1 1/2 hours until drumsticks move easily in their sockets and juices from the chicken run clear. Baste several times while cooking. When done, a meat thermometer inserted into the thigh will register 180 degrees. Remove chicken from the rotisserie and place on a rack to stand for 10 minutes before carving. Place on a platter; remove and discard strings.   Makes 4 servings.

Per Serving (approx):
Calories 604
Carbohydrate 1 gm

Protein 53 gm
Sodium 738 mg

Fat 43 gm
Cholesterol 225 mg

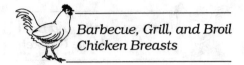

*Barbecue, Grill, and Broil
Chicken Breasts*

Chicken Dijon

2 1/4 pounds skinless breasts, split
1 tablespoon olive oil
1/4 cup reduced fat mayonnaise
1 1/2 to 2 tablespoons Dijon mustard
1 tablespoon lemon juice

1 tablespoon snipped chives or thinly sliced green onions
2 teaspoons chopped tarragon or 1/2 teaspoon dried tarragon
1/2 teaspoon pepper

Prepare outdoor grill for cooking or preheat broiler. Coat chicken with olive oil. In a small bowl, combine mayonnaise, mustard, lemon juice, chives, tarragon, and pepper; set aside.

Remove the chicken from the marinade. Grill or broil the chicken 6 to 8 inches from heat source 15 to 25 minutes until cooked through, turning occasionally. During the last 10 minutes of cooking time, turn and baste frequently with the mustard marinade.   Makes 4 servings.

Per Serving (approx):
Calories 399   *Protein 64 gm*   *Fat 14 gm*
Carbohydrate 3 gm   *Sodium 368 mg*   *Cholesterol 177 mg*

"Shall we never learn the worthlessness of other people's views of food? There is no authoritative body of comment on food. Like all the deeper personal problems of life, you must face it alone."
Frank Moore Colby,
The Colby Essays, Vol 2

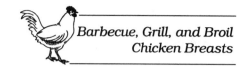
Mexicali Chicken

This originated in Mexicali, a city on the Mexican side of the border town. On the U.S. side, the city is Calexico.

2 to 3 pounds whole chicken breasts	1 teaspoon salt
2/3 cup lime juice	1/2 teaspoon pepper
2/3 cup white vinegar	3 green chiles, chopped
2 teaspoons ground cumin	1/2 cup ketchup
2 teaspoons chili powder	Hot pepper sauce to taste

Place chicken in a large bowl. In a small bowl, combine lime juice, vinegar, cumin, chili powder, salt, and pepper. Pour marinade over breast, reserving 1/2 cup. Cover the chicken and refrigerate 1 hour or longer, turning occasionally.

Prepare a covered grill for cooking. When the coals are hot, arrange at either end of a drip pan. Fill drip pan halfway with water. Remove the chicken from the marinade and discard the marinade. Place the breasts, skin-side down, on the grill over the drip pan. Grill, covered, 45 to 50 minutes, turning occasionally.

Meanwhile, in a small saucepan, combine reserved 1/2 cup marinade, green chiles, ketchup, and hot pepper sauce to taste. Simmer until slightly thickened. Remove from the heat. Brush this sauce over the chicken during the last 10 minutes of cooking time.

Makes 4 to 6 servings.

Per Serving (approx):
Calories 374   *Protein 39 gm*   *Fat 19 gm*
Carbohydrate 11 gm   *Sodium 818 mg*   *Cholesterol 152 mg*

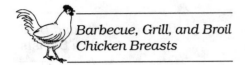
Chicken Diablo

2 tablespoons lemon juice
1 tablespoon olive oil
2 garlic cloves, crushed
1/2 to 3/4 teaspoon red pepper
  flakes

1/2 to 3/4 teaspoon cayenne
Salt (optional)
1 1/4 pounds skinless,
  boneless chicken breast
1 lemon, sliced, for garnish

In a bowl, combine lemon juice, oil, garlic, red pepper flakes, cayenne, and salt, if using. Add chicken to marinade, turning to coat both sides. Cover and marinate in refrigerator 1 hour or longer. Preheat broiler. Drain chicken, reserving marinade. Broil 6 to 8 inches from heat source for 6 to 8 minutes on each side, until cooked through. Meanwhile, in a small saucepan, boil marinade; turn chicken 2 or 3 times during cooking and brush with marinade. To serve, garnish with lemon slices.

Makes 4 servings.

Per Serving (approx):
Calories 226	*Protein 36 gm*	*Fat 8 gm*
Carbohydrate 3 gm	*Sodium 86 mg*	*Cholesterol 97 mg*

Sesame Skewered Chicken

1 1/2 pounds skinless,
  boneless chicken breasts
1 green onion, chopped
1 garlic clove, minced
1/3 cup soy sauce
1 tablespoon toasted sesame seeds

2 teaspoons red wine vinegar
1 teaspoon toasted sesame oil
1/2 teaspoon ground ginger
1/8 teaspoon cayenne
1/2 pineapple, peeled, cored
  cut into 1-inch pieces

Cut chicken into chunks. In zip-lock bag, combine all remaining ingredients, except pineapple. Add chicken to bag. Marinate 30 minutes. Thread chicken on skewers alternating with pineapple chunks. Grill 15 to 20 minutes over medium coals, turning occasionally.

Makes 4 to 6 servings.

Per Serving (approx):
Calories 253	*Protein 30 gm*	*Fat 6 gm*
Carbohydrate 21 gm	*Sodium 984 mg*	*Cholesterol 77 mg*

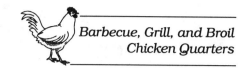

Maple Mustard Chicken Quarters

4 chicken quarters
1/2 teaspoon salt
1/2 teaspoon paprika
1/2 teaspoon pepper
1/4 cup yellow mustard

2 tablespoons spicy brown
mustard
1/3 cup maple syrup
1/4 cup peach preserves
2 teaspoons lemon juice
1 clove garlic, minced

Preheat broiler to 500 degrees. Sprinkle the chicken with salt, paprika, and pepper. In a 9 x 13 baking pan, arrange the chicken skin side up. Combine yellow mustard, spicy brown mustard, maple syrup, peach preserves, lemon juice, and garlic. Broil chicken for 15 minutes. Turn chicken and pour maple-mustard sauce over each chicken quarter. Reduce oven temperature to 350 degrees and bake about 30 minutes. Change oven back to 500 degrees and broil 5 minutes more.   Makes 4 servings.

Per Serving (approx):
Calories 656
Carbohydrate 33 gm

Protein 60 gm
Sodium 778 mg

Fat 32 gm
Cholesterol 207 mg

Lime-Tarragon Chicken

3 1/2 pounds chicken breast or
leg quarters
1 cup lime juice
1/2 cup vegetable oil
1 cup chopped onions

1/2 cup chopped tarragon
or 4 tablespoons dried
tarragon
Salt and pepper to taste

Place chicken in a bowl. In a small bowl, combine lime juice and remaining ingredients; set aside 1/4 cup lime mixture. Pour remaining mixture over chicken; loosen skin and spoon some marinade under skin. Cover and refrigerate 1 hour or longer.

Prepare grill for cooking. Drain chicken and discard the marinade. Grill the chicken, uncovered, 5 to 6 inches over medium-hot coals 30 to 40 minutes or until cooked through, turning and basting frequently with the reserved lime mixture.   Makes 4 servings.

Per Serving (approx):
Calories 890
Carbohydrate 9 gm

Protein 96 gm
Sodium 228 mg

Fat 52 gm
Cholesterol 267 mg

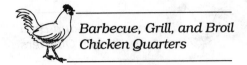

Hot and Spicy Grilled Chicken

1 package (1 1/2 ounces)
   taco seasoning
3 tablespoons light brown sugar
2 cups tomato juice

1 cup chicken broth
4 tablespoons vinegar
4 chicken quarters

In a small saucepan, combine taco seasoning and sugar. Stir in tomato juice and chicken broth. Boil and stir about 8 minutes. Stir in vinegar and cook about 2 minutes more. Pour sauce over chicken and let stand about 10 minutes. Place chicken on a prepared grill, skin side up, about 8 inches from heat. Grill, turning and basting with sauce every 10 minutes, for about 1 hour or until a fork pierces the chicken easily.

Makes 4 servings.

Per Serving (approx):
Calories 600
Carbohydrate 14 gm

Protein 61 gm
Sodium 1817 mg

Fat 31 gm
Cholesterol 207 mg

Grilled Sesame Chicken

1/2 cup low-salt soy sauce
1/4 cup water
1/2 cup vegetable or olive oil
1/4 cup chopped onion
2 tablespoons sesame seeds
1 tablespoon sugar

1 teaspoon ground ginger
2 cloves garlic, minced
1/8 teaspoon cayenne
4 chicken quarters or 6
   breasts

In a bowl, combine soy sauce, water, oil, onion, sesame seeds, sugar, ginger, garlic, and cayenne. Add chicken, cover tightly and refrigerate at least 12 hours, turning occasionally.

Remove the chicken from the marinade and reserve liquid. Grill chicken until done, basting with marinade every 15 minutes.

Makes 4 to 6 servings.

Per Serving (approx):
Calories 590
Carbohydrate 6 gm

Protein 59 gm
Sodium 774 mg

Fat 37 gm
Cholesterol 159 mg

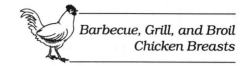

Grilled Chicken Sienna

Arugula, an aromatic salad green with a peppery mustard flavor, is very common in Italy, particularly in the Sienna region, where this recipe was created. Most supermarkets have it these days in the produce section.

2 tablespoons lemon juice
1 tablespoon olive oil
1 teaspoon dried Italian herb
   seasoning
1 1/4 pounds skinless, boneless
   chicken breast and thighs

Salt and pepper to taste
1 cup seeded, finely diced
   tomato
3 cups arugula leaves, well
   washed

In a bowl, combine lemon juice, olive oil, and seasonings. Add chicken; cover and marinate in the refrigerator 1 to 2 hours. Add salt and pepper to taste and sugar to tomatoes; set aside.

Prepare the outdoor grill or preheat broiler. Drain chicken, reserving marinade. Grill or broil the chicken 6 to 8 inches from heat source 15 to 25 minutes, until cooked through. Meanwhile, in a small saucepan, bring the marinade to a boil; turn chicken 2 to 3 times during cooking and brush with boiled marinade. Slice chicken and arrange on a bed of arugula; top with the seasoned tomatoes.   Makes 6 servings.

Per Serving (approx):
Calories 160
Carbohydrate 4 gm
    Protein 24 gm
    Sodium 63 mg
    Fat 5 gm
    Cholesterol 64 mg

> There are a lot of people who must have the table laid in the usual fashion or they will not enjoy the dinner."
> Christopher Morley, Inward Ho

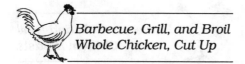

Santa Fe Grilled Chicken

This is an easy recipe for Southwestern flavored chicken.

1/2 cup lime juice, divided
2 tablespoons vegetable oil, divided
1 whole chicken, cut up
Salt and pepper to taste
1 cup diced peaches, fresh or frozen
1/4 cup minced red onion

1 jalapeño, seeded and
  minced
2 garlic cloves, minced
1 teaspoon ground cumin
Chili powder to taste

In a bowl, combine 7 tablespoons of the lime juice and 1 1/2 table-spoons oil. Add the chicken and salt and pepper to taste. Cover and marinate in the refrigerator for 2 to 4 hours. Meanwhile, prepare the salsa. In a small bowl, combine remaining 1 tablespoon lime juice and 1/2 tablespoon oil, peaches, onion, jalapeño, garlic, and cumin.

Prepare the outdoor grill or preheat the broiler. Remove the chicken from the marinade and discard the marinade. Sprinkle the chicken with chili powder and place on the cooking surface of the grill over medium-hot coals or on the broiler pan. Grill or broil 6 to 8 inches from heat source, allowing 20 to 30 minutes for breasts and 30 to 40 minutes for thighs and drumsticks, turning occasionally.

Serve grilled chicken with salsa.   Makes 4 to 5 servings.

Per Serving (approx):
Calories 550
Carbohydrate 8 gm

Protein 56 gm
Sodium 164 mg

Fat 33 gm
Cholesterol 219 mg

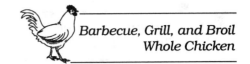
Chicken with Plums and Coriander

2 whole chickens, halved
Butter or margarine, melted
Salt and pepper to taste
1 1/2 cups fresh plums (4 to 6
  plums depending on size)

1 clove garlic, crushed
2 tablespoons chopped
  cilantro
1/8 to 1/4 teaspoon red
  pepper sauce

Brush the chickens with butter or margarine. Season with salt and pepper to taste. Arrange skin side down on grill or broiler rack.

Seed and chop the plums and put into a saucepan. Add garlic, cilantro, and red pepper sauce. Boil the sauce about 20 minutes, stirring carefully. This usually takes 30 to 45 minutes.

While the sauce is cooking, broil or grill the chickens. During the last 15 minutes, baste the chickens with plum sauce. When the chicken is done, boil the sauce briefly before putting it into a bowl alongside the chicken.

Makes 4 servings.

Per Serving (approx):
Calories 1033
Carbohydrate 9 gm

Protein 106 gm
Sodium 428 mg

Fat 64 gm
Cholesterol 451 mg

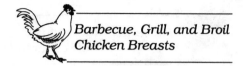

Barbecue, Grill, and Broil
Chicken Breasts

Grilled Chicken Breasts
with Spicy Salsa

You can make this on your stove or on your barbecue, but barbecuing is better.

4 tablespoons lime juice	6 chicken breast halves
1/4 cup olive oil	Spicy Salsa
1/2 teaspoon chili powder	1 avocado, sliced into wedges
1/4 teaspoon pepper	1 tablespoon minced cilantro

In a bowl, combine lime juice, olive oil, chili powder, and pepper. Add the chicken, turning to coat. Cover and marinate in the refrigerator at least 1 hour. Place the chicken on prepared grill,* skin side down, at least 8 inches from heat. Grill about 8 minutes, turn chicken and grill about 8 minutes more until the juices run clear. Remove the chicken to a serving platter. Spoon Spicy Salsa over each piece and garnish with avocado wedges. Sprinkle with cilantro.   Makes 6 servings.

SPICY SALSA:
In a bowl, combine 3 minced red or yellow tomatoes (seeded and chopped), 1/4 cup minced red onion, 1 tablespoon lime juice, 1 clove garlic (minced), 2 teaspoons seeded and minced jalapeño, 2 tablespoons minced cilantro, and 1/4 teaspoon ground cumin. Let sit at room temperature about 1 hour.

*Chicken can be broiled instead of grilled. Place on a broiler pan, skin side down; broil about 10 minutes, turn and broil about 10 minutes more or until fork tender.

Per Serving (approx):
Calories 356		
Carbohydrate 8 gm	*Protein 30 gm*	*Fat 23 gm*
	Sodium 78 mg	*Cholesterol 79 mg*

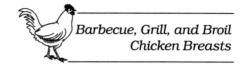

Sweet and Sour Chicken Breasts

This is a delicious, easy addition to your barbecue "specialties."

1 pound skinless, boneless chicken breast	4 tablespoons vegetable oil
1 cup diced onions	3 tablespoons grated ginger
1/4 cup light soy sauce	3/4 cup brown sugar
	2 tablespoons cornstarch

With a mallet, flatten both breast halves between sheets of wax paper; place in a bowl.

In a small bowl, combine onions, soy sauce, oil, and ginger; set aside 1 cup for basting. Pour remaining marinade over chicken; cover and refrigerate 1 hour or longer, turning occasionally.

Prepare lightly greased grill for cooking. Drain chicken and discard marinade. Grill breasts, uncovered, 5 to 6 inches over medium-hot coals for 6 to 10 minutes on each side or until cooked through, turning occasionally.

Meanwhile, in a small saucepan over medium heat, combine reserved marinade with sugar and cornstarch. Simmer 5 to 6 minutes or until thickened. Baste chicken with sauce during last 10 minutes of cooking time.   Makes 3 to 4 servings.

Per Serving (approx):
Calories 403

Protein 31 gm	*Fat 17 gm*	
Carbohydrate 32 gm	*Sodium 554 mg*	*Cholesterol 77 mg*

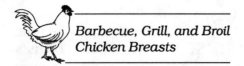

Italian Chicken Kabobs

If you can't find jicama in your market for this recipe, leave it out.

1 1/4 pounds boneless chicken
   breasts, cut in chunks
1/2 cup Italian salad dressing
1/4 cup chopped basil

1 onion
1 red bell pepper
1 zucchini
1 small jicama, peeled

In a large bowl, combine the chicken with Italian dressing. Cut vegetables into large pieces; place in dressing. Cover and marinate 1 to 2 hours.

Prepare grill for cooking. Thread chicken chunks on metal skewers, alternating with marinated vegetables, until all ingredients are used. Grill kabobs over medium-hot coals for 10 to 15 minutes, until chicken is cooked through, turning occasionally.   Makes 4 servings.

Per Serving (approx):
Calories 471	*Protein 37 gm*	*Fat 24 gm*
Carbohydrate 27 gm	*Sodium 320 mg*	*Cholesterol 95 mg*

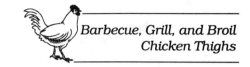

Sunshine Chicken Thighs

Using frozen orange juice concentrate instead of fresh juice gives a far more intense orange flavor. You need it for barbecuing.

1 1/4 pounds skinless chicken
  thighs
1/4 cup frozen orange juice
  concentrate, thawed
1 1/2 tablespoons honey
1 tablespoon vegetable oil

1 tablespoon lemon juice
1/2 teaspoon paprika
1/4 teaspoon turmeric
1/8 teaspoon red pepper flakes
Few drops hot pepper sauce
1 garlic clove, minced

Make 3 to 4 vertical slashes in each thigh. In a bowl, combine the orange juice with remaining ingredients. Add chicken and turn to coat with marinade, rubbing seasonings into slashes. Cover and refrigerate 1 hour or overnight.

Prepare grill for cooking. Grill chicken 5 to 6 inches from heat source for 20 to 30 minutes, until cooked through, turning 2 to 3 times during cooking.   Makes 4 servings.

Per Serving (approx):
Calories 297
Carbohydrate 12 gm

Protein 28 gm
Sodium 95 mg

Fat 15 gm
Cholesterol 101 mg

"When going to an eating house, go to
one that is filled with customers."
Old Chinese Proverb

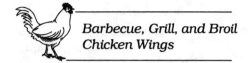

Szechuan Wings

Great finger food for a party, these wings taste even better if you pierce each one with a fork before you put the chicken in the marinade.

6 tablespoons light soy sauce	1 1/2 tablespoons sugar
6 tablespoons chili sauce	1 1/2 tablespoons red pepper
6 tablespoons white vinegar	flakes
2 tablespoons minced ginger	1/2 teaspoon salt
2 tablespoons vegetable oil	1 3/4 pounds chicken wings

In a small bowl, combine all the ingredients for the marinade; set aside 1/4 cup. Pour the marinade over the chicken; cover and refrigerate 1 hour or longer.

Prepare a lightly greased grill for cooking. Remove the chicken to the grill and discard the marinade. Grill chicken, uncovered, 5 to 6 inches over medium-hot coals 25 to 30 minutes or until wings are cooked through, turning and basting frequently with reserved soy sauce mixture.   Makes 3 to 4 servings.

Per Serving (approx):
Calories 535
Carbohydrate 10 gm

Protein 42 gm
Sodium 1144 mg

Fat 36 gm
Cholesterol 125 mg

"At a dinner party one should eat wisely but not too well, and talk well but not too wisely."

W. Somerset Maugham,
A Writer's Notebook

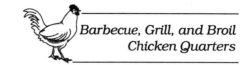
Hot and Spicy Pick of the Chick

If you're sure you like hot and spicy chicken, go ahead and make this recipe.
As the saying goes in Latin America, "It has authority!"

1 jar (5 ounces) roasted peppers, drained

1 can (4 ounces) mild green chiles, drained

2 tablespoons brown sugar

2 tablespoons vegetable oil

2 tablespoons lime juice

1 1/2 teaspoons hot pepper sauce

1 teaspoon ground cumin

1 teaspoon salt

2 to 3 sprigs cilantro

3 chicken breast halves, 3 drumsticks, and 3 thighs

Prepare a lightly greased grill for cooking. In a food processor or blender, combine all ingredients except chicken. Puree until smooth. Set aside 1/2 cup sauce.

Grill chicken, uncovered, 5 to 6 inches over medium-hot coals for about 30 minutes or until cooked through, turning and basting with sauce 3 to 4 times during grilling. Serve reserved 1/2 cup sauce as a condiment with grilled chicken. Makes 6 servings.

Per Serving (approx):
Calories 308	*Protein 32 gm*	*Fat 18 gm*
Carbohydrate 5 gm	*Sodium 530 mg*	*Cholesterol 101 mg*

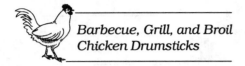

Spicy Lemon Drumsticks

While these can be made in a conventional oven, they taste best when cooked on a barbecue.

1 1/2 pounds chicken drumsticks
1/2 cup lemon juice
1/4 cup minced cilantro
1/4 to 1/2 teaspoon red pepper
   flakes

1 garlic clove, minced
1 tablespoon vegetable oil
Salt and pepper to taste

Cut three to four vertical slashes in fleshy part of the drumsticks. In a bowl, combine lemon juice, cilantro, hot pepper flakes, garlic, oil, and salt and pepper to taste. Add drumsticks, turning to coat. Cover and marinate in the refrigerator at least 3 hours or overnight.

Prepare outdoor grill or preheat broiler. Drain drumsticks from marinade. In a small saucepan, bring marinade to boil; set aside. Over medium-hot coals, place drumsticks on the grill or on the rack of a broiler pan 6 to 8 inches from heat source. Grill or broil 20 to 25 minutes until chicken is cooked through, turning occasionally and basting with boiled marinade. Makes 2 to 3 servings.

Per Serving (approx):
Calories 442
Carbohydrate 4 gm

Protein 45 gm
Sodium 150 mg

Fat 28 gm
Cholesterol 157 mg

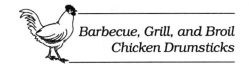

Lemon-Herb Drumsticks

This marinade is much more effective if you can use it overnight, instead of just for an hour or two.

1 1/4 pounds skinless chicken
    drumsticks
1/4 cup olive oil
1 1/2 tablespoons chopped marjoram
    or 1 1/4 teaspoons dried marjoram

1 green onion, minced
1 tablespoon lemon juice
1 teaspoon lemon pepper

With a knife, cut 3 to 4 vertical slashes in each drumstick. In a bowl, combine remaining ingredients. Add the chicken; turn to coat and rub seasonings into slashes. Cover and refrigerate at least 1 hour or overnight.

Prepare grill for cooking. Remove drumsticks from the marinade. Discard the marinade. Grill over medium-hot coals 15 to 20 minutes, until cooked through, turning occasionally.   Makes 3 to 4 servings.

Per Serving (approx):
Calories 318
Carbohydrate 1 gm

Protein 30 gm
Sodium 308 mg

Fat 22 gm
Cholesterol 99 mg

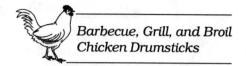

Provençale Herb Drumsticks

The "herbs de Provence," basil, thyme, oregano, and bay, are used in marinades in the South of France where grilling is often done over grapevine cuttings.

1 1/2 pounds chicken drumsticks	1 tablespoon chopped oregano
1/2 cup red wine	or 1 teaspoon dried oregano
2/3 cup water	2 bay leaves
2 tablespoons wine vinegar	2 tablespoons tomato paste
3 garlic cloves, minced	4 teaspoons anchovy paste
1 tablespoon chopped basil	(optional)
or 1 teaspoon dried basil	1/2 teaspoon salt
1 tablespoon chopped thyme	1/2 teaspoon pepper
or 1 teaspoon dried thyme	2 tablespoons olive oil

With a fork, pierce the drumsticks to help the seasonings penetrate the chicken. In a bowl, combine remaining ingredients except the oil; whisk in the oil. Reserve half of herb mixture in a small bowl. Add chicken to herb mixture, turning to coat; cover and refrigerate 1 hour or longer.

Prepare a lightly greased grill for cooking. Grill drumsticks, uncovered, 5 to 6 inches over medium-hot coals for about 20 minutes or until cooked through, turning and basting frequently with reserved herb mixture.

Makes 2 to 3 servings.

Per Serving (approx):
Calories 542
Carbohydrate 5 gm

Protein 47 gm
Sodium 578 mg

Fat 34 gm
Cholesterol 157 mg

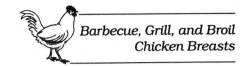

Fire Eaters' Chicken

The name of this recipe came from the fact that it is popular in many firehouses.

3 tablespoons lemon juice
1 tablespoon olive oil
2 garlic cloves, minced
2 teaspoons paprika

1 teaspoon cayenne
3/4 teaspoon salt
1 1/4 pounds skinless, boneless
  chicken breasts
Lemon wedges, for garnish

In a small bowl, combine ingredients for the marinade except the lemon wedges. Pour the marinade over the chicken, turning to coat. Cover and refrigerate 1 hour or longer.

Prepare a lightly greased grill for cooking. Drain the chicken; discard the marinade. Grill chicken breasts, uncovered, 5 to 6 inches over white-hot coals for 6 to 8 minutes on each side, or until cooked through. To serve, garnish with lemon wedges. Makes 4 servings.

Per Serving (approx):
Calories 224
Carbohydrate 5 gm

Protein 36 gm
Sodium 521 mg

Fat 8 gm
Cholesterol 97 mg

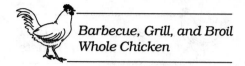
Corn-Smoked Roaster

Save those corn cobs! You'll need them for smoking this chicken on your barbecue.

1 whole chicken (a capon)   Salt and pepper to taste
3 tablespoons vegetable oil   4 corn cobs, kernels removed

Remove and discard giblets from chicken. Rinse bird and pat dry with paper towels. Rub skin and cavity with oil and season with salt and pepper to taste.

If using a gas grill, follow manufacturer's directions. If using covered charcoal grill, open all vents and prepare coals at least 30 minutes before cooking. When coals are medium hot, place a 1 1/2- to 2-inch-deep drip pan at center in bottom of grill and fill halfway with water. Arrange 25 to 30 hot coals at either end of pan. Place corn cobs on the coals.

Place the roaster on the grill over the drip pan, breast side up. Cover grill and smoke bird about 2 1/2 hours. Begin checking after 1 1/2 hours; roaster is done when juices run clear with no hint of pink when thigh is pierced. (Note: Smoking may turn chicken meat pink.)

Makes 6 to 8 servings.

Per Serving (approx):
Calories 268   *Protein 26 gm*   *Fat 18 gm*
Carbohydrate 0 gm   *Sodium 78 mg*   *Cholesterol 105 mg*

Napoleon, whose hunger for glory was matched only by his hunger for chicken, gave standing orders that, during his campaigns, a roasted chicken be ready for him at every hour of the day and night. Because the cook never knew when Napoleon wanted to eat, he roasted one every twenty mintues.

MICROWAVE COOKING

Microwave-Barbecue Drumsticks

1/2 cup smoke-flavored
    barbecue sauce
1 1/2 teaspoons brown sugar
1/2 teaspoon pepper
1/4 teaspoon garlic salt
1/4 teaspoon onion powder

1/2 teaspoon dry mustard
1/2 teaspoon Worcestershire
    sauce
1 1/2 pounds skinless chicken
    drumsticks

In a small microwave-safe bowl, combine all ingredients except drumsticks. Brush drumsticks with some of seasoned sauce mixture; reserve remainder.

On a microwave-safe dish, arrange drumsticks with meatiest portions to outside. Cover with wax paper; microwave on medium high 17 to 18 minutes, turning over and brushing with additional sauce halfway through cooking time.

Remove from microwave; cover with aluminum foil and let stand 10 minutes until drumsticks are cooked through and tender. To serve, microwave remaining sauce on high 1 minute; spoon over drumsticks.

Makes 2 to 4 servings

Per Serving (approx):
Calories 241
Carbohydrate 5 gm

Protein 37 gm
Sodium 712 mg

Fat 8 gm
Cholesterol 119 mg

"If there were no such thing as eating, we would have to invent it to spare man from despairing."

Dr. Wilhelm Stekhell,
The Depths of the Soul

Microwave Curry

1 onion, thinly sliced
1 garlic clove, minced
1 tablespoon butter or margarine
1 can (6 ounces) tomato paste
1 cup hot water
1 tart cooking apple, cored and
  diced
2 tablespoons flour
1 tablespoon curry powder

1 teaspoon chicken bouillon
  granules
1 1/2 teaspoons grated
  ginger or 1/2 teaspoon
  ground ginger
1 1/4 pounds boneless chicken
  thighs, cut into 1-inch chunks
Assorted condiments

In a 3-quart microwave-safe dish, combine onion, garlic, and butter. Cover and microwave on high 4 minutes, stirring twice. Stir in tomato paste, hot water, and apple. Add remaining ingredients; stir to blend.

Cover and microwave on medium high 20 minutes, stirring three times. Let stand, covered, 10 minutes until chicken is cooked through and tender.

Serve with rice pilaf or plain rice and condiments such as coconut, raisins, crystallized ginger, peanuts, chutney, and yogurt.

Makes 4 servings.

Per Serving (approx):
Calories 371
Carbohydrate 24 gm

Protein 29 gm
Sodium 363 mg

Fat 17 gm
Cholesterol 91 mg

Microwave Barbecue Chicken and Spaghetti Squash

If you like long spaghettilike strands to wind around a fork, cut the squash crosswise.

1 spaghetti squash (about 1 pound)
3 plum tomatoes, chopped
1/2 cup thinly sliced zucchini
1/2 cup sliced mushrooms
2 green onions, thinly sliced
1 garlic clove, minced
1 teaspoon water

1/4 teaspoon Italian herb
   seasoning
2 cups cooked, cut up
   chicken
1 tablespoon grated Parmesan
   cheese

With a knife, pierce rind of squash deeply several times for steam to escape. Microwave on a paper towel on high (100% power) for 6 to 7 minutes, turning squash over after 3 minutes. Let stand wrapped in aluminum foil while preparing vegetable sauce.

In a 1 1/2-quart microwave-safe casserole, combine tomatoes, zucchini, mushrooms, green onions, garlic, water, and herb seasoning. Cover and microwave on high for 5 minutes, stirring after 3 minutes. Let stand, covered, while heating chicken in microwave.

To serve, cut spaghetti squash crosswise in half; scoop out seeds and fibers. Using a fork, twist out long strands of squash. Top with vegetable sauce and Parmesan cheese. Serve with cut-up chicken.

Makes 4 servings.

Per Serving (approx):
Calories 615
Carbohydrate 23 gm

Protein 61 gm
Sodium 276 mg

Fat 31 gm
Cholesterol 230 mg

Glazed Microwave Chicken

Nine minutes in the microwave is all it takes to produce these succulent, lemony chicken breasts.

4 skinless chicken breast halves	1/3 cup spicy brown mustard
1 teaspoon paprika	1 teaspoon onion granules
8 thin slices lemon	1/2 teaspoon lemon juice
1/3 cup honey	1/2 teaspoon curry powder

Sprinkle the chicken breast halves with paprika. Place 2 lemon slices on each piece of chicken and arrange it with the meaty area toward the outside and ribs toward center. Cover loosely with wax paper and microwave on high for about 10 minutes, turning the dish after 5 minutes.

In a small microwave-safe bowl, combine honey, mustard, onion, lemon juice, and curry powder. When chicken is done, remove to microwave-safe serving dish (transfer only chicken, not liquid) and let sit while sauce is cooking. Microwave honey-mustard sauce on high for about 2 minutes.

Spoon sauce over the chicken and return to microwave; cook on medium about 2 minutes or until glaze is hot and a fork pierces the chicken easily.   Makes 4 servings.

Per Serving (approx):
Calories 311   *Protein 31 gm*   *Fat 5 gm*
Carbohydrate 36 gm   *Sodium 333 mg*   *Cholesterol 77 mg*

Sesame Microwave Chicken

Including marinating time, 23 minutes is all you need to make this fast and easy recipe.

4 tablespoons soy sauce
2 tablespoons lemon juice
1 tablespoon olive oil
1 clove garlic, minced
4 skinless, boneless chicken breast
  halves, cut in strips
1 tablespoon butter-flavored
  margarine

1/2 cup minced onion
1 tablespoon cornstarch
1 teaspoon grated ginger
1/2 cup chicken broth
1/4 cup toasted sesame seeds

In a microwave-safe measuring cup, mix together soy sauce, lemon juice, olive oil, and garlic. Microwave on high until boiling, about 2 minutes. Place chicken strips in a bowl and pour hot sauce over all; let sit about 10 minutes. Arrange chicken strips on a microwave rack in a baking dish, pouring sauce over strips. Microwave on medium about 2 1/2 minutes; turn dish and microwave on medium about 2 1/2 minutes more or until strips are opaque and fork can be inserted with ease.

While chicken is cooking, place margarine in a frying pan and melt. Add onion and sauté until translucent, about 5 minutes. Stir in cornstarch and ginger. When chicken has cooked in microwave, drain off all liquid in the pan (about 1/2 cup) and add warm broth to make 1 cup.

Place chicken in microwave-safe serving dish. Slowly add broth mixture to onion mixture in frying pan; bring to boil over high heat and cook, stirring, about 2 minutes. Pour hot sauce over chicken and microwave on high about 2 minutes. Stir in toasted sesame seeds. Serve over rice or with oriental noodles.   Makes 4 servings.

Per Serving (approx):
Calories 300
Carbohydrate 7 gm

Protein 33 gm
Sodium 1319 mg

Fat 15 gm
Cholesterol 80 mg

Layered Microwave Meatloaf

3/4 pound mushrooms
1 1/4 pounds ground chicken
2 bread slices, torn into small pieces
1/4 cup ketchup
1 egg, slightly beaten

1/2 teaspoon salt
1/8 teaspoon pepper
4 green onions, chopped
1 can (8 ounces) tomato sauce
1 teaspoon Worcestershire sauce

Set aside 10 whole mushrooms; mince the remaining mushrooms. In a bowl, combine the chopped mushrooms, chicken, bread, ketchup, egg, salt, and pepper.

In center of a 9-inch microwave-safe pie plate, invert a 6-ounce custard cup. Pack half of meat mixture in pie plate, forming circle around cup. Cut 5 whole mushrooms lengthwise in half; place on top of meat mixture. Spoon chopped green onions over the mushrooms and meat; top with remaining meat mixture. Pat meatloaf and press edges firmly to seal; cover with wax paper. Microwave on high (100% power) 5 minutes; reduce power to medium (50% power) and microwave 20 minutes longer. Let stand, covered, 5 minutes.

Slice remaining mushrooms and place in a 2-cup glass measure. Stir in tomato sauce and Worcestershire sauce. Microwave on high 3 minutes, stirring once. Serve the meatloaf covered with the sauce.

Makes 4 to 6 servings.

Per Serving (approx):
Calories 186
Carbohydrate 13 gm

Protein 14 gm
Sodium 662 mg

Fat 9 gm
Cholesterol 95 mg

Light Chicken Cordon Bleu

Yes, you can prepare this elegant dish in a microwave.

1/4 cup seasoned dry bread crumbs
1 tablespoon grated Parmesan cheese
1 teaspoon chopped parsley
1/2 teaspoon paprika
1 egg white

1 1/4 pounds skinless, boneless,
  chicken breasts
6 ounces reduced-fat Swiss
  cheese slices
6 ounces turkey ham slices

In a bowl, combine bread crumbs, cheese, parsley, and paprika. In another bowl, beat egg white lightly; set aside. On each chicken breast slice, place 1 slice of cheese and 2 overlapped slices of ham; roll up, jellyroll style, and secure with toothpick. Dip each roll in egg white and then bread crumb mixture, coating completely.

In a microwave-safe dish, arrange chicken rolls, seam side down, in a circular pattern. Cover with wax paper; microwave on medium high (70% power) 5 minutes. Rearrange chicken rolls; cover with a double thickness of paper towels. Microwave on medium high 8 minutes. Let stand, uncovered, 5 to 10 minutes before serving.   Makes 6 servings.

Per Serving (approx):
Calories 268   *Protein 41 gm*   *Fat 10 gm*
Carbohydrate 4 gm   *Sodium 469 mg*   *Cholesterol 102 mg*

"The cost takes away from the taste."
Old French Proverb

Micro-Meatball Rigatoni

1 1/4 pounds ground chicken
3/4 cup minced onions
1/2 cup seasoned dry bread
  crumbs
1/3 cup grated Parmesan cheese,
  divided

1 can (6 ounces) tomato paste,
  divided
1 teaspoon dried Italian
  seasoning
1 jar (30 ounces) chunky
  vegetable spaghetti sauce
1/2 pound small rigatoni,
  cooked and drained

In a bowl, combine chicken, onions, bread crumbs, 1/4 cup of the grated Parmesan, 3 tablespoons of the tomato paste, and Italian seasoning; mix well. Shape mixture into 12 meatballs. On a 10-inch microwave-safe pie plate, arrange meatballs in a circle; cover with wax paper. Microwave on high (100% power) 6 minutes. Rearrange and turn meatballs. Recover and microwave on high 4 to 6 minutes longer.

Meanwhile, in a bowl, combine spaghetti sauce and remaining tomato paste; add cooked meatballs. Discard juices from pie plate. Combine the rigatoni, meatballs, and sauce. Cover with wax paper. Microwave on high 5 minutes or until sauce is bubbly. Sprinkle with remaining cheese; cover and let stand 5 minutes before serving.   Makes 4 to 6 servings.

Per Serving (approx):
Calories 418
Carbohydrate 54 gm

Protein 21 gm
Sodium 954 mg

Fat 13 gm
Cholesterol 61 mg

Microwave Chicken Thighs

Microwave Chicken Burgundy

Beef Bourguignon is one of France's most traditional dishes. It comes from the Burgundy region, and like other country dishes has many variations. This version makes two thoroughly modern substitutions: chicken for health, microwaving for speed.

3 bacon slices, diced
1 onion, thinly sliced
3 tablespoons flour
12 small white onions, peeled
1/2 teaspoon dried thyme
3/4 cup Burgundy or other dry
    red wine

1/4 cup hot water
1 bay leaf
1 pounds skinless chicken
    thighs
1 cup sliced mushrooms

Place bacon in a 3-quart microwave-safe dish; cover with a paper towel. Microwave on high 3 to 4 minutes until crisp, stirring twice. Stir in onion, flour, white onions, thyme, wine, water, and bay leaf.

Place thighs, smooth side down, on top of mixture; cover with plastic wrap. Microwave on high 5 minutes. Reduce power to medium-high; microwave 30 minutes, turning thighs over halfway through cooking time and adding mushrooms during last 5 minutes.

Let stand, covered, 10 minutes. Remove bay leaf.

Makes 2 to 3 servings.

Per Serving (approx):
| *Calories 570* | *Protein 36 gm* | *Fat 21 gm* |
| *Carbohydrate 49 gm* | *Sodium 236 mg* | *Cholesterol 105 mg* |

SANDWICHES, BURGERS, & PIZZAS

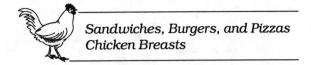
Santa Fe Chicken Hero

Serving this sandwich is a great way to entertain. It's easy to make and fun to eat.

1 pound skinless, boneless
    chicken breast
1 tablespoon vegetable oil
Salt and pepper to taste
Cayenne to taste
Chili powder to taste
5 to 6 thin slices Monterey jack
    cheese with chiles

5 to 6 slices French or Italian
    bread
2 tablespoons melted butter
    or margarine
5 to 6 leaves Romaine lettuce
1 tomato, thinly sliced
1 avocado, sliced and tossed
    with lemon juice
1/2 cup prepared salsa

Prepare grill for cooking. Rub chicken lightly with oil and season to taste with salt, pepper, cayenne, and chili powder. Grill, uncovered, 5 to 6 inches over medium-hot coals about 1 minute on each side. Top chicken with slices of cheese; grill 1 minute longer or until cheese is melted.

Brush bread with melted butter; grill alongside chicken 1 to 2 minutes on each side until golden brown. To serve, place a lettuce leaf on each toasted bread slice. Evenly divide chicken, slices of tomato and avocado on top. Serve sandwiches open-faced with salsa.

Makes 5 to 6 servings.

Per Serving (approx):
Calories 297   *Protein 23 gm*   *Fat 15 gm*
Carbohydrate 19 gm   *Sodium 368 mg*   *Cholesterol 63 mg*

"Eating without conversation is only stoking."

Marceline Cox,
Ladies' Home Journal

Mediterranean Chicken Hero

4 skinless, boneless chicken
  breast halves
3 tablespoons olive oil
1 teaspoon soy sauce
1/4 teaspoon dried basil
1/4 teaspoon dried marjoram
1/4 teaspoon dried rosemary
1 loaf unsliced French bread
1/4 cup reduced-calorie margarine,
  softened

1 large garlic clove, minced
1 green bell pepper, sliced thin
1 red bell pepper, sliced thin
1 yellow bell pepper, sliced thin
1/4 cup black olives, cut from
  pits
1 green onion, sliced thin
Yogurt Sauce
3 tablespoons sliced almonds,
  for garnish

Preheat broiler. Place the chicken between 2 pieces of wax paper and gently pound to 1/4-inch thickness. In a bowl, mix olive oil and soy sauce. Add chicken, turning to coat. Place chicken on broiler pan; sprinkle with basil, marjoram, and rosemary. With chicken about 6 inches from heat, broil, turning, about 12 minutes until chicken is light brown and a fork be inserted easily. Remove chicken from the oven; set aside and keep warm.

Cut bread in half lengthwise. Hollow bottom half of loaf, leaving at least 1 1/2 inches crust. Mix margarine and garlic; spread on the inside of the bread. Place on the broiler pan and broil until brown; remove from the oven. Arrange chicken, bell peppers, olives, and green onion on bread. Spoon half of Yogurt Sauce over all. Garnish with sliced almonds. Cut in 6 parts. Serve remaining Yogurt Sauce in separate bowl.

Makes 6 servings.

YOGURT SAUCE:
In a bowl, mix together 1 cup low-fat yogurt, 2 tablespoons coarsely ground Dijon mustard, and 4 teaspoons honey.

Per Serving (approx):
Calories 253	*Protein 23 gm*	*Fat 12 gm*
Carbohydrate 14 gm	*Sodium 336 mg*	*Cholesterol 56 mg*

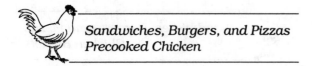

Chicken Sandwich Deluxe

1 skinless, boneless chicken, cooked,
   cut into small chunks
3/4 teaspoon seasoned salt
1/8 teaspoon pepper
1 tablespoon lemon juice

1/2 cup sour cream with chives
1/4 teaspoon tarragon
8 whole-grain sandwich rolls
8 lettuce leaves
1/2 cup sliced black olives

In a bowl, sprinkle chicken with seasoned salt, pepper, and lemon juice and let it sit for 5 minutes.

In another bowl, mix sour cream and tarragon; add seasoned chicken chunks and toss gently to mix. Cover and refrigerate until serving time.

To serve, make sandwiches by placing on the bottom halves of the rolls, in order, lettuce, chicken mixture, olive slices, and top of roll. Cut the rolls in half. Makes 8 sandwiches.

Per Serving (approx):
Calories 322	*Protein 29 gm*	*Fat 18 gm*
Carbohydrate 12 gm	*Sodium 660 mg*	*Cholesterol 111 mg*

"Very different, however, is the case of pate de fois gras, sandwiches, oysters, and meringues. I cannot eat too many of these. I make it, therefore, my rule to consume very limited quantities of plain food in order to leave as much room as possible for delicacies."

E.V. Knox
Gorgeous Times

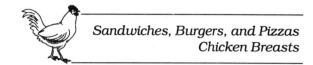
Sun-Dried Tomato Pesto Chicken Sandwiches

4 skinless, boneless chicken
  breast halves
Salt and pepper to taste
8 large slices crusty Italian bread,
  lightly toasted
5 ounces mild goat cheese,
  at room temperature

1 medium bunch arugula,
  washed, dried, and torn into
  small pieces
1 red onion, thinly sliced
Basil leaves, for garnish
Cherry tomatoes, for garnish
Sun-Dried Tomato Pesto

Preheat broiler.

Place the chicken on a broiler pan and sprinkle with salt and pepper to taste. With the rack about 6 inches from heat, broil the chicken about 6 minutes on each side or until brown. Remove chicken from oven and let rest 5 minutes; slice into thin strips and keep warm.

Spread 4 slices of the bread with goat cheese; add arugula and evenly layer chicken slices and red onion on top. Top with Sun-Dried Tomato Pesto and remaining 4 slices bread. Garnish with basil and cherry tomatoes.   Makes 4 servings.

SUN-DRIED TOMATO PESTO:
In a food processor or blender, combine 1/2 teaspoon dried thyme, 2 garlic cloves, 1/4 cup toasted pine nuts, 1/2 cup blanched sun-dried tomatoes, 1/4 cup grated Parmesan cheese, 2 tablespoons tomato paste, and 3/4 cup olive oil. Process with on-and-off control until mixture is almost pureed. Set aside.

Per Serving (approx):
Calories 1154   *Protein 79 gm*   *Fat 75 gm*
Carbohydrate 40 gm   *Sodium 1277 mg*   *Cholesterol 204 mg*

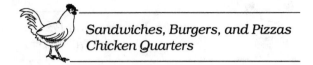
Do-Ahead Barbecue Chicken Sandwiches

Here's an easy way to entertain: all the work is done long before your guests arrive.

1 quart apple cider vinegar
3 cups low-sodium chicken
   broth
3 teaspoons onion salt
1 1/2 teaspoons pepper

2 bay leaves
12 chicken quarters
24 sandwich buns
1 cup Dijon mustard

In a saucepan, combine vinegar, chicken broth, onion salt, pepper, and bay leaves. Bring to a boil. Arrange chicken in a bowl and pour hot vinegar mixture over. Cover and marinate in the refrigerator at least 2 hours.

Place the chicken on a preheated grill, skin side up, about 8 inches from heat. Place 2 cups of marinade in a small saucepan and bring to a boil on grill or stovetop. Grill chicken, turning and basting with this marinade every 10 to 15 minutes, about 1 hour or until fork can be inserted in chicken with ease. Remove chicken from the grill and let cool about 10 minutes.

Remove chicken from bone, discarding bones and skin. Place meat from 4 quarters at a time in food processor* and chop with off-on motion 3 or 4 times until chicken is coarsely chopped. Repeat with remaining chicken (should be about 9 cups). Boil remaining marinade to reduce to 1 1/4 cups; pour over minced chicken.

Serve on buns spread with mustard. Garnish with dill pickle slice, if desired.   Makes 24 sandwiches.

*Chop with knife if processor is not available.

Per Serving (approx):
Calories 276   *Protein 19 gm*   *Fat 8 gm*
Carbohydrate 30 gm   *Sodium 842 mg*   *Cholesterol 63 mg*

Chicken and Cheese Sandwich

1 1/2 pounds chicken breast fillets
2 teaspoons vegetable oil
1/2 cup chopped onion
1 clove garlic, minced
1 cup grated cheddar cheese
3 tablespoons milk

2 tablespoons flour
1/2 teaspoon chili powder
1 can (4 ounces) diced green chiles
4 sour dough rolls, cut in half
4 tomato slices

In a skillet, heat oil, add chicken, onion, and garlic and cook until chicken is no longer pink inside. Remove chicken, keep warm. Stir in cheese, milk, flour, chili powder, and chiles into the skillet. Simmer on low until cheese melts, stirring constantly. Do not boil. Place one fillet in each roll; top with cheese sauce and tomato slice.   Makes 4 servings.

Per Serving (approx):
Calories 484
Carbohydrate 25 gm

Protein 55 gm
Sodium 504 mg

Fat 18 gm
Cholesterol 147 mg

Hot Chicken Salad in Pita

2 tablespoons vegetable oil
2 skinless, boneless chicken
  breasts, cut in thin 2-inch strips
1 onion, sliced
1 cup sliced celery
1 cup chopped green bell pepper
1/2 cup sliced mushrooms

1/2 teaspoon salt
1/8 teaspoon pepper
3 tablespoons mayonnaise
2 tablespoons spicy brown mustard
8 Romaine lettuce leaves
4 large pita breads, cut in half

In a frying pan, heat oil. Add chicken and stir-fry about 2 minutes or until lightly browned. Add onion, celery, bell pepper, mushrooms, salt, and pepper. Cook about 5 minutes. Add mayonnaise and mustard, stirring constantly for about 1 minute, or until heated.

To serve, line pita bread halves with lettuce leaves and stuff with chicken mixture.   Makes 4 servings.

Per Serving (approx):
Calories 435
Carbohydrate 29 gm

Protein 35 gm
Sodium 764 mg

Fat 20 gm
Cholesterol 84 mg

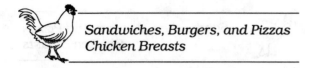

Pita Chicken Sandwiches

Yogurt replaces mayonnaise in this elegant but simple recipe for picnic fare.

2 tablespoons olive oil
1 1/4 pounds skinless, boneless
    chicken breast
1 medium onion, sliced thin
1 teaspoon salt
1/2 teaspoon pepper

1 tablespoon wine vinegar
1 1/2 teaspoons chopped chives
1/2 cup nonfat yogurt
1/2 shredded cucumber
4 pita breads (8-inch size)

In a frying pan, heat olive oil. Add chicken and cook about 6 minutes.
Turn chicken, add onion and cook about 6 minutes more or until onion
is translucent and chicken is tender. Remove from heat. Cut chicken
into thin slices and place in bowl. Add sautéed onion; sprinkle with salt
and pepper, mixing carefully. Add vinegar and chives; mix well.

In a small bowl, combine yogurt and cucumber. On each pita bread,
spread 2 tablespoons yogurt-cucumber sauce. Then place 1/4 of the
chicken mixture on pita bread; fold bread in half, wrap in plastic wrap
and chill in refrigerator at least 2 hours.

For picnic, place in ice chest until serving time. Cut each sandwich in
half to serve.   Makes 4 servings of 2 wedges each.

Per Serving (approx):
Calories 395   *Protein 42 gm*   *Fat 13 gm*
Carbohydrate 29 gm   *Sodium 905 mg*   *Cholesterol 97 mg*

> Thanks to the fast-food industry,
> chicken is one of the most popular sand-
> wiches in America today.

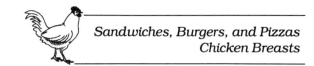

Chicken and Swiss Extraordinaire

A classic recipe for more than 20 years, this can easily be increased to feed a crowd.

3 skinless, boneless chicken
   breast halves
1/2 cup flour
1/4 cup vegetable oil
1 tablespoon butter
1/2 pound mushrooms, sliced

2/3 cup white wine
1 teaspoon salt
1/4 teaspoon pepper
6 thick slices French bread
6 slices Swiss cheese

Dredge the chicken in flour one piece at a time. In a frying pan, heat oil. Add chicken and cook, turning, about 10 minutes or until brown on all sides. Reduce heat; cover and simmer about 10 minutes or until a fork pierces the chicken easily.

Remove the chicken from the pan. Add butter to the pan; add mushrooms and sauté over low heat about 3 minutes. Push mushrooms to the side; add wine and stir to loosen browned bits. Add salt and pepper. Return chicken to frying pan and simmer, uncovered, about 10 minutes until sauce is slightly thickened.

On a baking sheet, arrange slices of bread. Top each slice with a slice of cheese. Place in 200-degree oven until cheese melts. Remove to a serving platter. Place a piece of chicken on top of each slice of bread. Spoon mushrooms and sauce over chicken. Makes 6 servings.

Per Serving (approx):
Calories 388
Carbohydrate 24 gm

Protein 34 gm
Sodium 628 mg

Fat 16 gm
Cholesterol 87 mg

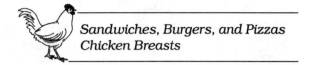

Orange and Onion Chicken Sandwich

We weren't too sure about this recipe until we tried it. It's great—try it.

1/2 teaspoon grated orange peel
1/2 teaspoon pepper
1/2 teaspoon cinnamon
4 skinless, boneless chicken
   breast halves
1 large white onion, cut in 1/4-inch
   slices

1/2 cup broth, warmed
2 navel oranges, peeled and
   sliced into rounds
4 club rolls with sesame seeds,
   warmed
4 tablespoons creamy mild
   mustard

Combine orange peel, pepper, and cinnamon; dredge the chicken breasts in this mixture. Spray a frying pan with vegetable spray and heat. Add the seasoned chicken breasts and place onion slices on top of each; cook about 2 minutes.

Move onion into frying pan and turn breasts; cook about 4 minutes more. Add broth to frying pan but do not pour over chicken. Place orange slices on chicken and continue to cook until broth is almost evaporated and a fork pierces the chicken easily (about 4 minutes). Onion should be tender and slightly crisp.

To assemble sandwiches, spread each roll with 1 tablespoon mustard. Place chicken breast half on each roll; top with onion and then orange slices. Cover with roll top.   Makes 4 servings.

Per Serving (approx):
Calories 366
Carbohydrate 36 gm

Protein 39 gm
Sodium 426 mg

Fat 7 gm
Cholesterol 94 mg

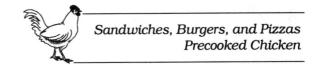

Baked Cream Sandwiches

3 cups very thick White Sauce
2 cups cooked chicken breast,
    cut in small pieces
1 can cream of mushroom soup
1 tablespoon minced onion or small
    green onion tips, minced
2 tablespoons minced parsley
2 tablespoons chopped pimiento

2 tablespoons white wine
12 thick slices white bread
4 eggs, beaten
4 tablespoons milk
1 1/2 cups crushed potato chips
1/4 cup slivered almonds
6 dashes paprika

Combine sauce, chicken, soup, onion, parsley, pimiento, and wine. Chill it.

Cut crusts from bread. Spread 6 slices with 1/2-inch-thick chicken mixture. Place 6 slices of bread on top. Individually wrap in freezer wrap and freeze overnight or longer.

When ready to serve, preheat oven to 325 degrees. Blend together 4 beaten eggs and 4 tablespoons cream or milk. Dip sandwiches in egg mix. Roll in crushed potato chips to cover completely. Top with slivered almonds and a dash of paprika. Place sandwiches on a well-greased baking sheet. Bake for approximately 45 minutes. Cover with foil as necessary to make sure they do not brown before they are thoroughly done.

Makes 6 servings.

WHITE SAUCE:
In a saucepan, melt 6 tablespoons butter over low heat. Add 14 tablespoons flour and stir until well blended. Very slowly, add 3 cups milk,* stirring constantly. Once milk is incorporated, increase heat to medium. Stirring constantly, cook sauce until thickened.

*Part chicken broth can be used for the white sauce.

Per Serving (approx):
Calories 663
Carbohydrate 59 gm

Protein 31 gm
Sodium 987 mg

Fat 33 gm
Cholesterol 228 mg

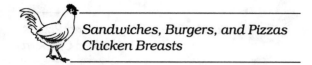

Chicken Strips in Croissants

1/2 cup prepared nonfat red
   wine vinegar salad dressing
1/4 cup low-sodium soy sauce
1 clove garlic, minced

4 skinless, boneless chicken
   breast halves, cut in strips
4 large croissants, split and
   warmed
1 cup alfalfa sprouts

In a small saucepan, combine salad dressing, soy sauce, and garlic; bring to a boil over high temperature. Add chicken and let sit 10 minutes. Remove chicken and boil sauce about 4 minutes.

Heat a frying pan; spray with vegetable spray. Add chicken strips; cook 2 minutes without stirring. Turn chicken and cook 4 minutes more, stirring occasionally.

To assemble sandwiches, divide the chicken among the croissants; spoon 1 tablespoon sauce over the chicken in each croissant and top with 1/4 cup alfalfa sprouts.   Makes 4 servings.

Per Serving (approx):
Calories 255
Carbohydrate 18 gm

Protein 34 gm
Sodium 1482 mg

Fat 5 gm
Cholesterol 83 mg

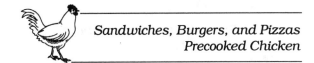
Croque Mademoiselle

The name translates as "crunchy young woman," which has absolutely nothing to do with this favorite sandwich of French children and adults.

4 to 8 slices cooked chicken
8 slices whole wheat bread
4 slices Swiss cheese
2 tablespoons butter or
   margarine, softened

1 egg, beaten
1/4 cup milk
1 teaspoon prepared mustard
Salt and pepper to taste

Divide chicken among four slices of bread. Top with cheese and second slice of bread. Spread outside of sandwich with butter. In a small bowl, whisk together egg, milk, mustard, salt, and pepper.

Dip sandwiches in egg batter, coating both sides. Spray large, nonstick skillet with vegetable spray. Place over medium heat. Add sandwiches to skillet. Cook 1 to 2 minutes until sandwich is nicely browned and cheese has melted, turning once. Serve hot.   **Makes 4 servings.**

Per Serving (approx):
Calories 364
Carbohydrate 30 gm

Protein 31 gm
Sodium 445 mg

Fat 13 gm
Cholesterol 136 mg

"Be content to remember that those who can make omelettes properly can do nothing else."

Hilaire Belloc,
"A Conversation with a Cat"

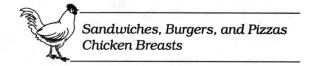

Chicken and Vegetables on Toast Points

Colorful and delicious, this dish can be prepared up to the broil stage and held until you are ready to serve.

1 tablespoon butter-flavored margarine
1 1/2 pounds skinless, boneless chicken breasts, cut into 1-inch pieces
1/2 teaspoon salt
1/4 teaspoon pepper
1 1/2 cups sour cream
1 teaspoon soy sauce
1 teaspoon paprika

2 tablespoons white wine
1 package (5 ounces) frozen peas, pearl onions, and mushrooms, cooked according to package directions
4 tablespoons grated Parmesan cheese
6 slices bread, toasted and cut into 4 triangles

Preheat broiler.

In a frying pan, melt margarine. Add chicken; cook about 4 minutes. Turn all pieces and cook until light brown, about 4 minutes more. Sprinkle with salt and pepper. Stir in sour cream, soy sauce, and paprika; reduce temperature to low and cook until heated through, about 4 minutes. Stir in white wine and cook 1 minute more. Add hot cooked peas, pearl onions, and mushrooms.

Pour all into a greased 1 1/2-quart shallow baking dish. Sprinkle with Parmesan cheese and broil until light brown, about 4 minutes. Serve on toast points.   Makes 6 servings.

Per Serving (approx):
Calories 400
Carbohydrate 20 gm

Protein 35 gm
Sodium 596 mg

Fat 20 gm
Cholesterol 104 mg

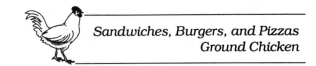

Santa Barbara Burgers

This is a very California hamburger. It originated in Santa Barbara, probably because olives and avocados are grown there.

1 pound ground chicken, formed
  into 4 burgers
1 tablespoon lemon pepper, divided
1 1/2 tablespoons canola or
  olive oil
1/4 cup low-fat mayonnaise
1 green onion, thinly sliced
2 large, black California olives, cut
  from pits and chopped

1 1/2 teaspoons lemon juice
8 slices sourdough bread,
  toasted
1/4 cup salad sprouts (such as
  spicy radish, dill or alfalfa
  sprouts)
1 small avocado, thinly sliced

Sprinkle burgers with 1 1/2 teaspoons lemon pepper seasoning. Oil a skillet and heat. Add burgers; cook 1 minute on each side until browned. Reduce heat to medium low; continue cooking 1 to 2 minutes on each side or until burgers are cooked through and spring back to touch.

In a small bowl, combine mayonnaise, green onion, olives, remaining lemon pepper, and lemon juice. To serve, layer bread slices with sprouts, avocado slices, and burgers. Top with mayonnaise sauce and serve immediately.   Makes 4 servings.

Per Serving (approx):
Calories 444
Carbohydrate 31 gm

Protein 20 gm
Sodium 1068 mg

Fat 27 gm
Cholesterol 74 mg

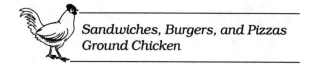
Stuffed Cheeseburgers

1 1/4 pounds ground chicken
2 tablespoons prepared steak sauce
1 teaspoon salt
1/4 teaspoon pepper
1 cup shredded cheddar cheese

4 hamburger buns, toasted
1 red onion, thinly sliced
1 tomato, thinly sliced
Condiments

Prepare grill. In a bowl, combine ground chicken, steak sauce, salt, and pepper. Divide mixture into 8 portions; form into 8 thin burgers. Mound 2 tablespoons cheese on each of 4 burgers and top with a second burger. Pinch edges shut to seal cheese inside meat. Place at center of grill. Grill, uncovered, 5 to 6 inches over medium-hot coals for 5 minutes. Turn burgers, move to cooler edge of grill, and top with remaining cheese. Grill 10 minutes longer or until burgers are cooked through and spring back when touched. Serve on hamburger buns, garnished with onion, tomato, and ketchup.   Makes 4 servings.

Per Serving (approx):
Calories 397
Carbohydrate 30 gm

Protein 24 gm
Sodium 1219 mg

Fat 20 gm
Cholesterol 103 mg

Chinese Plum Burgers

1 1/4 pounds ground chicken
2 to 3 tablespoons prepared
  Chinese plum sauce*
3 green onions, chopped
1 tablespoon minced ginger

1 1/2 teaspoons Chinese chile
  paste with garlic*
1/2 teaspoon salt
4 or 5 hamburger rolls, split,
  lightly toasted

Prepare grill or preheat broiler. In a bowl, combine all the ingredients except the rolls. Form into 4 or 5 burgers. Grill or broil 4 to 6 minutes on each side until the burgers are cooked through and spring back to the touch. Serve burgers warm on toasted rolls.   Makes 4 or 5 servings.

*Sold in many supermarkets in the ethnic or Asian food section.

Per Serving (approx):
Calories 256
Carbohydrate 24 gm

Protein 16 gm
Sodium 523 mg

Fat 11 gm
Cholesterol 73 mg

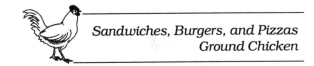

Swiss Burgers

You guessed it. Swiss cheese. Prefer Cheddar? Change the cheese, and the name.

1 1/4 pounds ground chicken	Salt and pepper to taste
1/2 cup thinly sliced green onions	4 to 5 slices Swiss cheese
1 teaspoon Worcestershire sauce	Dijon mustard
1/4 pound mushrooms, thinly sliced	4 to 5 Kaiser rolls
2 teaspoons olive oil	6 to 8 tablespoons sour cream

Prepare outdoor grill or preheat broiler. Combine ground chicken, green onions, and Worcestershire sauce. Shape mixture into 4 or 5 patties.

To grill: when coals are medium-hot, place burgers on hottest area of grill. Cook 1 to 2 minutes on each side to brown. Move burgers to outside of grill and cook 4 to 6 minutes longer on each side until thoroughly cooked and burgers spring back to the touch.

To broil: Place burgers on rack in broiling pan 4 inches from heat source. Broil 4 to 6 minutes on each side until burgers are thoroughly cooked and spring back to the touch.

While burgers are cooking, toss mushrooms with oil and sprinkle lightly with salt and pepper to taste. Place mushrooms on sheet of heavy-duty aluminum foil. Grill or broil along with burgers during last 1 to 2 minutes of cooking time.

When burgers are cooked through, place a slice of Swiss cheese on top and cook 1 minute longer or just enough to melt cheese. To serve, spread mustard on rolls, place one burger and a portion of the mushrooms on each of four roll halves. Top each with a generous dollop of sour cream and remaining roll half.   Makes 4 or 5 servings.

Per Serving (approx):
Calories 318

Protein 18 gm

Fat 17 gm

Carbohydrate 24 gm

Sodium 519 mg

Cholesterol 81 mg

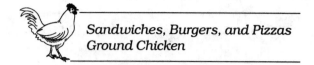
Latin American Burgers

A unique crunchiness, coupled with a real zest makes this hamburger worthy to be served as a main course.

1/2 cup yellow cornmeal	2 tablespoons olive oil
1 1/2 teaspoons chili powder, divided	3 green onions, sliced
1/2 teaspoon cayenne, divided	1 can (17 ounces) corn with
1/4 teaspoon salt	peppers, undrained
1 pound ground chicken, formed	1 can (4 ounces) diced mild
into 4 burgers	green chiles, undrained

Preheat oven to 375 degrees.

Combine cornmeal, 1 teaspoon chili powder, 1/4 teaspoon cayenne, and salt. Coat burgers with cornmeal mixture.

Oil a skillet and heat. Add burgers; cook about 2 minutes on each side, or until golden brown. Remove to a baking sheet and bake about 15 minutes.

Meanwhile, add the green onions to the same skillet; cook 1 to 2 minutes, or until soft. Add corn, chiles, remaining chili powder, and the remaining cayenne. Cook 1 to 2 minutes longer until vegetables are heated through.

To serve, spoon corn mixture over burgers.   Makes 4 servings.

Per Serving (approx):
Calories 307   *Protein 16 gm*   *Fat 17 gm*
Carbohydrate 22 gm   *Sodium 685 mg*   *Cholesterol 71 mg*

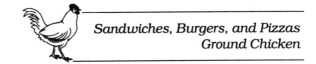
Southwestern Chicken Patties

For a very easy, fast meal, this is it!

1 pound ground chicken
1/3 cup dry bread crumbs
1/2 teaspoon chili powder

1 can (4 ounces) chopped mild
  chiles, drained
1/4 teaspoon salt (optional)
Avocado Sauce

Preheat broiler.

In a bowl, mix chicken, bread crumbs, chili powder, chiles, and salt. Shape chicken into 4 patties. Place chicken on a rack sprayed with vegetable spray in broiler pan. Broil, about 3 inches from heat, for 4 to 5 minutes on each side, or until chicken is done. Serve with Avocado Sauce.

Makes 4 servings.

AVOCADO SAUCE:
In a blender, combine 1/3 cup nonfat yogurt, 1 tablespoon reduced calorie sour cream, 1 teaspoon lemon juice, 1/8 teaspoon garlic powder, 1/8 teaspoon chili powder, and 1/2 avocado. Cover and blend on high speed until smooth, scraping sides of blender container occasionally.

Per Serving (approx):
Calories 229
Carbohydrate 11 gm

Protein 16 gm
Sodium 225 mg

Fat 13 gm
Cholesterol 72 mg

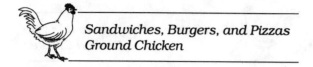
Pita Burgers

We've not only taken the pitas of Turkey for this recipe, we've also appropriated the spices.

1 1/4 pounds ground chicken
2 garlic cloves, minced
2 teaspoons paprika
1 teaspoon ground cumin
1 teaspoon ground allspice
1 teaspoon salt

1/4 teaspoon cayenne
6 pita breads, opened and
   lightly grilled
Yogurt Sauce
3 plum tomatoes, thinly sliced
1 small cucumber, thinly sliced

Prepare grill for cooking. In a bowl, combine ground chicken, garlic, and seasonings. Form mixture into 6 burgers. Grill, uncovered, 5 to 6 inches over medium-hot coals for 4 to 5 minutes on each side, or until burgers are cooked through and spring back when touched.

Serve burgers in pita pockets topped with yogurt sauce, tomatoes, and cucumbers.   **Makes 6 servings.**

YOGURT SAUCE:
In a small bowl, combine 1 cup yogurt, 1 tablespoon minced parsley, 2 teaspoons minced cilantro, and 1 1/2 teaspoons minced mint or 1/2 teaspoon dried mint. Season with salt and pepper to taste.

Per Serving (approx):
Calories 253
Carbohydrate 26 gm

Protein 17 gm
Sodium 683 mg

Fat 9 gm
Cholesterol 64 mg

Reuben Burgers

1 pound ground chicken, formed
   into 4 burgers
2 teaspoons caraway seed, divided
1/2 teaspoon pepper
1 can (4 ounces) sauerkraut
   (preferably reduced-sodium),
   drained

4 slices Muenster cheese
2 tablespoons prepared
   Russian dressing
8 slices rye or onion rye bread,
   lightly toasted

Preheat broiler.

Spray the broiler pan with vegetable spray. Press 1/2 teaspoon caraway seed into top of each burger; sprinkle with pepper. Broil burgers 4 to 5 inches from heat source 2 1/2 to 3 minutes on each side, or until they are thoroughly cooked and spring back to the touch.

Top burgers with sauerkraut and cheese; broil about 1 minute longer, or until cheese melts. To serve, spread Russian dressing on rye toast; place burgers on top.   **Makes 4 servings.**

Per Serving (approx):
Calories 340
Carbohydrate 36 gm

Protein 19 gm
Sodium 686 mg

Fat 13 gm
Cholesterol 74 mg

Russians love them enough to make Russia the largest importer of U.S. chicken products in the world—more than $1.2 billion dollars worth during 1995.

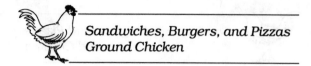

Tarragon-Mustard Burgers

1 1/4 pounds ground chicken
2 tablespoons tomato paste
1 1/2 teaspoons minced tarragon
   or 1/2 teaspoon dried tarragon
Salt and pepper to taste

4 to 5 tomato slices
2 to 3 English muffins, split,
   lightly toasted
Tarragon-Mustard Sauce
Sprigs of tarragon, for garnish
   (optional)

Preheat broiler or prepare grill.

In a bowl, combine chicken, tomato paste, tarragon, salt, and pepper. Form into 4 or 5 burgers and broil or grill 4 to 6 minutes on each side, or until burgers are cooked through and spring back to the touch. Place a slice of tomato and a burger on top of an English muffin half. Top with warm Tarragon-Mustard Sauce. Garnish with sprigs of fresh tarragon.

Makes 4 to 5 servings.

TARRAGON-MUSTARD SAUCE:
In top of double boiler over hot water, blend 1 1/2 tablespoons butter or margarine and 1 1/2 tablespoons Dijon mustard. Remove from heat; add 1 tablespoon tarragon vinegar. Stir in 1/4 cup light sour cream and 1 teaspoon minced tarragon or 1/4 teaspoon dried tarragon. Season with salt, pepper, and cayenne to taste.

Per Serving (approx):
Calories 271	*Protein 17 gm*	*Fat 14 gm*
Carbohydrate 19 gm	*Sodium 392 mg*	*Cholesterol 82 mg*

He-Man Burgers

1 1/4 pounds ground chicken
1/2 cup chopped green onions
1/4 to 1/3 cup prepared shrimp
   cocktail sauce
Salt and pepper to taste

4 or 5 pumpernickel or onion
   rolls, split, lightly toasted
1/4 cup prepared horseradish
   sauce or sour cream

Preheat broiler or prepare grill.

In a bowl, combine chicken, green onions, cocktail sauce, and salt and pepper to taste. Form into 4 or 5 burgers and broil or grill 4 to 6 minutes on each side until burgers are cooked through and spring back to the touch.

Spread cut side of rolls with horseradish sauce. Place burgers on lower half of rolls; top with lids. Makes 4 or 5 servings.

Per Serving (approx):
Calories 308
Carbohydrate 37 gm

Protein 19 gm
Sodium 581 mg

Fat 9 gm
Cholesterol 11 mg

More than 5 billion pounds of chicken are sold at fast-food restaurants every year.

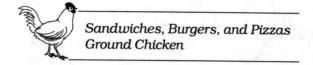

Stuffing Burgers

3 tablespoons butter or margarine,
  divided
1/4 cup chopped celery
1/4 cup chopped onion
3/4 cup seasoned dry stuffing mix
1/3 cup boiling chicken broth
  or water

Salt and pepper to taste
1/4 teaspoon dried sage or
  poultry seasoning
1 1/4 pounds ground chicken
1/4 cup chopped parsley
Cranberry relish (optional)

In a skillet, melt 2 tablespoons butter. Add celery and onion; sauté 5 minutes or until softened. Add stuffing, broth, salt, pepper, and sage; mix well. Let mixture cool completely.

In a large bowl, combine chicken, stuffing mixture, and parsley. Form into 4 or 5 burgers. Add remaining butter to the same skillet and melt it. Add burgers; brown 1 minute on each side. Reduce heat and cook 4 to 5 minutes on each side until burgers are cooked through and spring back to touch. Serve with cranberry relish, if desired.

Makes 4 to 5 servings.

Per Serving (approx):
Calories 214
Carbohydrate 4 gm

Protein 14 gm
Sodium 303 mg

Fat 16 gm
Cholesterol 90 mg

> "When God gives hard bread, He also gives sharp teeth."
> Old German Proverb

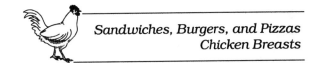

Florentine Chicken Pizza

1 tablespoon olive oil
3 skinless, boneless chicken
   breast halves, cut in 1-inch strips
1 teaspoon Italian seasoning
1/2 teaspoon garlic salt
1/4 cup chopped green onion
3/4 cup frozen chopped spinach,
   thawed and squeezed dry
3/4 cup ricotta cheese

1 tablespoon lemon juice
Salt and pepper to taste
1 16-ounce Italian pizza shell
1 Roma tomato, thinly sliced
1/4 cup pitted quartered olives
2 tablespoons chopped pimiento
1/2 cup grated Parmesan
   cheese
1/4 teaspoon pepper

Preheat oven to 425 degrees.

In a pan, heat oil. Add chicken and cook, stirring, about 4 minutes until a fork pierces the chicken easily. Remove chicken from the pan.

In a small bowl, combine Italian seasoning and garlic salt. Sprinkle 1/2 teaspoon of this mixture over the chicken. In another bowl, combine onion, spinach, ricotta cheese, lemon juice, and salt and pepper to taste. Spread mixture over bread shell, add tomato slices and top with chicken. Sprinkle with olives, pimento, and Parmesan cheese. Bake for about 8 minutes.   Makes 4 servings.

Per Serving (approx):
Calories 621
Carbohydrate 70 gm

Protein 44 gm
Sodium 1106 mg

Fat 18 gm
Cholesterol 94 mg

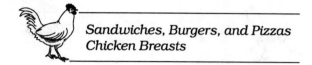

Chicken Pizza

1 package (8 rolls) refrigerated
   crescent rolls
1/4 cup vegetable oil
2 skinless, boneless chicken breast
   halves, cut into 1-inch pieces
1 onion, sliced into rings
1 green bell pepper, cut into
   thin rings

1/2 pound mushrooms, sliced
1/2 cup sliced pitted olives
1 can (10 1/2 ounces) pizza
   sauce with cheese
1 teaspoon garlic salt
1 teaspoon dried oregano
1/4 cup grated Parmesan cheese
2 cups shredded mozzarella
   cheese

Preheat oven to 425 degrees.

Unroll crescent dough into 8 triangles. Press dough into a lightly oiled 12-inch pizza pan, being sure to seal at the perforations.

In a frying pan, heat oil. Add chicken, onion, bell pepper, mushrooms, and olives. Cook, stirring, about 5 minutes. Spread pizza sauce over dough. Spoon chicken mixture evenly over sauce. Sprinkle with garlic salt, oregano, and Parmesan. Top with mozzarella. Bake uncovered for 20 minutes until crust is done.   **Makes 4 servings.**

Per Serving (approx):
Calories 789   *Protein 49 gm*   *Fat 48 gm*
Carbohydrate 40 gm *Sodium 1494 mg*   *Cholesterol 129 mg*

STUFFING

Stuffing

Today the terms stuffings and dressings are interchangeable. Many years ago, these were different dishes. Long ago, stuffing went inside the bird before cooking, and dressing was made in a separate container and served with the bird.

If you are going to fill the cavity of the bird with stuffing, you need a half cup of stuffing for every pound of ready-to-cook chicken. A 3-pound chicken requires 1 1/2 cups of stuffing, and so on.

If you are going to make the dressing in a separate pan, you can make as much or as little as you want.

A word of caution: It's best to refrigerate the stuffing and meat separately and stuff the bird just before cooking. Above all, don't stuff the bird several hours in advance of cooking and leave at room temperature. Keep these ingredients refrigerated until cooking. When you are storing leftovers, remove the stuffing from the chicken and package them separately.

Following are 8 classic stuffing-dressing recipes. Vary your ingredients to fit your needs, or make the amount shown and store the excess in your freezer.

Simple Bread Stuffing

3 tablespoons butter
3/4 cup chopped celery
3 tablespoons chopped parsley
2 tablespoons chopped onion

4 cups fresh bread crumbs
1/2 teaspoon dried sage
1/2 teaspoon salt
Dash pepper

In a frying pan, melt butter. Add celery, parsley, and onion. Cook until tender. Scrape into a large bowl. Add bread crumbs and seasonings. Mix well.   Makes 4 to 5 cups stuffing.

Prune-Apple Stuffing

1/2 cup large pitted prunes
1/2 cup chopped onion
4 tablespoons butter
1 cup peeled, chopped apples
1/2 teaspoon salt

1/4 teaspoon pepper
1/8 cup water
2 eggs, well beaten
1 1/2 cups fresh bread cubes
1/4 cup chopped walnuts
  (optional)

Quarter prunes, cover with water; cook slowly for 45 to 50 minutes until plump. Drain and chop.

In a frying pan, cook onion in butter until soft. Add apples, salt, and pepper; cook until brown. In a large bowl, combine water, eggs, bread cubes, and apple-onion mixture. Add prunes and walnuts, if desired, and mix well.   Makes 3 to 4 cups stuffing.

 *Stuffing*

Apple Stuffing

1/2 cup butter
3 cups diced tart apples
1 cup chopped onion
1 cup chopped celery

1 teaspoon salt
1/4 cup sugar
3 cups fresh bread cubes

In a frying pan, melt butter and mix with apples, celery, and onion. Sprinkle with salt and sugar. Cook for 10 minutes until apples are browned all over. Remove to a large bowl; add bread cubes and mix well.

Makes 6 to 8 cups stuffing.

Onion-Potato Stuffing

1 1/2 cups chopped onion
1 cup minced celery
3/4 cup butter
1 teaspoon salt
1/2 teaspoon pepper
1/4 cup milk

2 cups fresh bread cubes
2 eggs, lightly beaten
5 medium potatoes, peeled,
    cooked, and mashed with
    1/2 cup butter
1/2 cup chopped parsley

In a large frying pan, cook onion and celery in butter until soft. Sprinkle with salt and pepper. In a large bowl, combine bread cubes and milk. Add eggs and onion-celery mixture. Stir in potato mixture and parsley.

Makes about 6 cups stuffing.

Cornbread Sausage Stuffing

1/2 cup chopped onion
1 cup chopped celery
1/4 cup butter
3 cups fresh bread cubes
3 cups crumbled cornbread
1/2 cup hot water

1/2 pound pork sausage links,
    cut into 1/2-inch pieces
1/2 teaspoon salt
1/4 teaspoon pepper
2 eggs, beaten
3/4 cup chopped walnuts or
    pecans (optional)

In a large frying pan, cook celery and onion in butter until soft. In a bowl, combine cornbread and bread cubes. Add water, onion-celery mixture, salt, pepper, eggs, and nuts. Cook sausage in frying pan. Combine thoroughly with bread mixture.   Makes about 6 cups stuffing.

Parsley, Lemon,
and Butter Stuffing

6 tablespoons butter
1 medium onion, chopped
3 cups fresh bread crumbs*
Grated zest of 2 lemons

1 1/2 cups chopped parsley
2 eggs, well beaten
3/4 cup melted butter
Salt and pepper to taste

In a skillet, melt butter. When hot, add onions and sauté until tender and translucent, about 4 minutes.

In a large mixing bowl, combine bread crumbs, lemon zest, parsley, and onions. Stir in the beaten eggs and melted butter, and mix well. Season with salt and pepper to taste.   Makes about 6 cups stuffing.

*Crumble a loaf of fresh bread with your hands. Packaged dry bread crumbs will make a heavy, less tasty stuffing.

Chile-Cornbread Stuffing

4 tablespoons butter
1/2 medium onion, chopped
1 garlic clove, minced
3 cups crumbled cornbread
1 can (4 ounces) peeled green
   chiles, chopped

4 ounces Monterey jack cheese,
   diced
1/2 cup canned whole kernel
   corn
6 tablespoons sour cream
2 eggs, well beaten
Salt and pepper to taste

In a skillet, melt butter. When hot, add onion and garlic. Sauté until tender and translucent, about 4 minutes.

In a mixing bowl, combine onion mixture with cornbread, chiles, cheese, corn, sour cream, and eggs. Mix well. Taste, and season with salt and pepper to taste.   Makes 4 to 6 cups stuffing.

Mushroom Stuffing

4 tablespoons butter
1 small onion, minced
1 celery stalk, minced
2 garlic cloves, minced
1/4 pound mushrooms,
   coarsely chopped

1/4 cup chopped tarragon,
   or 2 to 3 teaspoons
   crushed dried tarragon*
1 1/2 cups fresh bread crumbs
2 eggs, well beaten
Salt and pepper to taste

In a large skillet, melt butter. When hot, add onion, celery, garlic, and mushrooms. Sauté until tender and translucent, about 6 minutes. Stir in tarragon and sauté 1 minute longer.

In a large mixing bowl, combine onion mixture with bread crumbs and eggs. Mix thoroughly. Season with salt and pepper to taste.
                    Makes about 4 cups stuffing.

*Fresh tarragon gives this stuffing a real zest, so use it if it's available.

Index

394

RELATED BOOKS FROM THE CROSSING PRESS

The Global Kitchen
Meat and Vegetarian Recipes from Africa, Asia, and Latin America for Western Kitchens with Country Information and Food Facts
By Troth Wells

The Global Kitchen celebrates the wholesome food cooked over fires, stirred in pots, sprinkled with spices and eaten by the ordinary people in Asia, the Middle East, Africa and Latin America. In this unique cookbook, some of the world's tastiest dishes come to us—from appetizers and snacks to desserts and drinks.
Paper • $16.95 • ISBN 0-89594-753-6

Good Food: The Complete Guide to Eating Well
By Margaret M. Wittenberg

An indispensable guide and nutritional resource, perfect for both the adventurous cook and the inquisitive novice. Wittenberg shows us a realistic and enjoyable approach to eating well, based on the wide variety of great-tasting, easy-to-prepare food.
Paper • $18.95 • ISBN: 0-89594-746-3

Great American Dessert Cookbook
By Andrea Chesman and Fran Raboff

"It takes a second look to capture and appreciate the wonderful recipes contained in this book." —Cookbook Collectors Exchange
Paper • $12.95 • ISBN 0-89594-437-5

The Great Turkey Cookbook: 385 Turkey Recipes for Every Day and Holidays
By Virginia and Robert Hoffman

The Great Turkey Cookbook puts turkey on the table every day with its recipes for favorite foods such as lasagna, tacos, meat loaf, Wiener schnitzel, burgers, quiche, stir-fries, curries, chile con carne, and many others.
Paper • $16.95 • ISBN 0-89594-792-7

The Holidays Cookbook
Menus, Recipes and Wine Selections for Holiday Entertaining
By Virginia and Robert Hoffman

The Holidays Cookbook meets the challenge of preparing holiday dinners with a spectacular collection of menus for Thanksgiving, Christmas, Hanukah, and New Year's. Separate sections feature regional holiday recipes from the South, Midwest, New England, and the Southwest.
Paper • $6.95 • ISBN 0-89594-839-7